THE CASTELVECCHIO FAMILY

WILLIAM R. TYLER

Antigny-le-Château, France
1980 – 1983

Formatted and supplemented by Royall Tyler
New South Wales, Australia
2014

Copyright © 2014 Royall Tyler

All rights reserved.

ISBN 13: 978-1496155375
ISBN 10: 1496155378

The Castelvecchio Family

CONTENTS

Introductory Note by Royall Tyler
Foreword   3
Louis Bonaparte
     and François Louis Gaspard Castelvecchio   11
The Mother   26
The Family Name   30
Florence (1847 – 1855)   31
The de Larderel Connection   34
Paris (1855 – 1860)   36
Nice (1860 – 1867)   43
The Family Finances   62
The Title of Count and the Légion d'Honneur   64
Rennes (1867 – 1869)   65
Louis de Castelvecchio's Death and Burial   68
The Return to Italy   72
The Marriages of Louise and Joséphine   73
The Move to England   75
The Break-up of Joséphine's First Marriage   77
The Gower Strain   81
Santa Anna and Cheltenham   86
George Slythe Street   92
Elise's Last Years (1890 – 1894)   92
Linetta's Notes on Louis de Castle and Elisina   109
The Twentieth Century   112
Antonio Frabasilis   119
Joséphine's Visit to Antigny   124
Correspondence Concerning Joséphine   129
Louis de Castle's Letter about His Mother   145
Joséphine's Death, and René Puaux   152

Appendices

Louis Bonaparte's Last Illness	169
Report on Louis Bonaparte's Death	173
Draft Letter to Napoléon III	178
Jean Baptiste Fortuné de Fournier	186
Legal Separation of Joséphine and Palamidessi	190
George Slythe Street	192
Obituary Notices on Joséphine	195
Elisina Tyler	205
Linetta Richardson	214

Appendices Added by RT

Letter from Joséphine to Linetta Richardson, January 14, 1925	220
Letter from Marguerita P. Williams to Linetta Richardson, May 27, 1932	233
Louis de Castle and His Voyage to Calcutta	239
E.H.M. Gower	262
Leon Gower	264
Register of Family Members in Père Lachaise Cemetery, Paris	267

Genealogical Charts

Genealogical Chart A	268
Genealogical Chart B	279

Illustrations

William R. Tyler, ca. 1926	4
François Louis de Castelvecchio	31
Elise de Castelvecchio	42
François Louis' signature on a letter	43
Joséphine de Castelvecchio, 1860	42
Joséphine at about 19	75
Elisina, Linetta, Louis as children	77
Linetta ("A.P.") & Elisina	85
Louis de Castle	86
Antonio Frabasilis	119
Josephine's grave monument	165
Linetta Richardson at 60	214
Louis among mine workers in South Africa	239
The *Falls of Clyde* in Honolulu Harbor	241
The beginning of Louis' first letter	241

Introductory Note

In 1983 my father, William R. Tyler, wrote out by hand on A4 paper an account of his mother's family, with margins as narrow as possible in order to save on the cost of photocopying. I do not know how many bound copies he made or where they went; I only know that he gave me one. He had then done all he reasonably could to make his work available to those likely to be interested. However, one can now do more. I came recently to feel that I should try.

I scanned the book and e-mailed it to a few people. One was my cousin Linetta de Castle, with whom it has been a constant pleasure to work on this project. Linetta also supplied most of the material (letters and photographs) that I have added to my father's work.

The scanned manuscript files are uncomfortable to read, and my father's work incorporates many documents in French, which not everyone knows. Therefore Linetta approached her sister Monica, in Johannesburg, who kindly typed out the English. Meanwhile Linetta herself, in Athens, had the French typed, and I, in rural New South Wales, translated it. I then fitted the elements together and formatted them for print.

I do not know what has become of the documents that my father consulted and often copied at length. Perhaps they will reappear one day.

The Castelvecchio line begins with François Louis Castelvecchio, an illegitimate son of Louis Bonaparte, himself a younger brother of Napoleon I. (In 1860 François Louis' half brother, Napoleon III, awarded him the title of Count; hence the *de* often inserted into the family name.) Napoleon I had great hopes for Louis and appointed him in 1806 King of Holland. Louis surprised him by seeking stubbornly to uphold the interests of his new country over those of France (i.e. his brother). Needless to say, he failed. He was no more a match for Napoleon than anyone else. Chateaubriand, no friend of the Emperor, wrote in his *Mémoires d'outre-tombe:*

> To fall back from Bonaparte and the Empire into what followed is to fall from reality into the void, from a mountaintop into the abyss...Of whom, of what is one to speak after such a man?...I blush to think that I must now drone on about a horde of infinitesimal beings, myself among them—dubious, nocturnal creatures that we were in a world the great sun of which was gone. [My translation]

Napoleon lost patience. In 1810 Louis abdicated and fled Holland under cover of darkness. Thereafter he lived in bitter although not uncomfortable retirement.

Louis's experience of life can hardly have discouraged his undoubted foibles and eccentricities. Even his marriage (1802) to Hortense de Beauharnais, forced upon him for pure convenience by Napoleon and his Empress Joséphine, Hortense's mother, was a disaster. However, his efforts on behalf of Holland were remembered there long and favorably. Until his death he remained devoted to the country and its people.

Many documents and letters by or about Louis survive in archives. So, it seems, do his poetry, plays, and a novel. The only book-length biography of him is D. Labarre de Raillicourt, *Louis Bonaparte*, Paris: J. Peyronnet, 1963. A sympathetic overview of his years in Holland ("La destinée tragique du 'bon roi' Louis") concludes Annie Jourdan, ed., *Louis Bonaparte: Roi de Hollande*, Paris: Nouveau Monde éditions, 2010.

Royall Tyler

THE CASTELVECCHIO FAMILY

The Castelvecchio Family

Foreword

I was raised in ignorance of my mother's family history. Except for a few fragments of information I remained ignorant until I retired. I do not recall ever having asked my mother — or my father, for that matter — anything about their families; and neither of them attempted to arouse my interest. Never having known any of my grandparents, and not having been brought up with brothers or sisters, I never knew family life. Since I was born and raised in France which was not the native country of either of my parents, this was perhaps to some extent inevitable. From my earliest age I was looked after by others than my parents, who lived their own active life. My first recollections of their company involved my appearance in the drawing-room at 21 Quai Bourbon in my best clothes, to be introduced to the guests and to kiss the ladies' hands. In those years such an upbringing was normal for children like myself. It contributed to my assumption that I had appeared out of nowhere: I might as well have been hatched from a solitary egg in a desert.

The first member of the family other than my parents of whom I became conscious was Linetta (Auntie Pitzy), my mother's younger sister. She had lived in England since 1896, when she was 15, and it wasn't until I was sent to school there in 1919 that I came to know her. She greatly endeared herself to me by sending me regularly on my birthday a splendid Dundee cake from a very superior store in Birmingham by name of Kunzle.

My half-sister Gioia, then Grant Richards, I met for the first time in 1921 or 1922 at the country house of a friend of my parents, Violet Carruthers, Moon Green, Wittersham, near Rye in Kent. I took to Gioia at once, I recall, although slightly awed by her because she seemed to me too grown-up to be my sister. I remember thinking her very pretty in a pink dress with flounces — quite unlike anything my mother wore.

During my Harrow years (1924-1929) a brother of Gioia, Charles Grant Richards came to Antigny one summer. My mother made much of his visit, but I never came to know him well.

I happened to be alone with my mother at Antigny in early September, 1929, when she learned of the death of her brother, Louis. Never having met him and barely knowing his name, I was struck, even disconcerted, by the intensity of her grief. The following summer, his son Gerard came to stay at Antigny, and this gave me much pleasure.

The last member of the family I met was Geoffrey Grant Richards, in London in 1937 or 1938. We were then living there at 50 Argyll Road. We both liked him very much and wished we had known him earlier.

One of my Grant Richards half-brothers, Gerard (after whom Gerard le Castle was named) I never saw. He was killed in 1916, while at school at Eton, in an accident at Poldhu Cove, in Cornwall, near the house, Caerleon, my mother owned, not far from The Lizard).

In 1933 I went for the first time to the United States in search of a job in New London, in order to be able to marry Betsy. Before leaving Europe I was told by Gioia that my maternal grandmother had died there within the last year. Never having even heard of her before, I was unmoved by the news, and remained uninterested in her until almost 50 years later.

My father only rarely referred to his childhood in Massachusetts and hardly ever mentioned his parents. His father, William Royall Tyler, who was Principal of the Adams Academy in Quincy where my father was born, died in 1897. One

FOREWORD

I was raised in ignorance of my mother's family history. Except for a few fragments of information I remained ignorant until I retired. I do not recall ever having asked my mother—or my father, for that matter—anything about their families; and neither of them attempted to arouse my interest. Never having known any of my grandparents, and not having been brought up with brothers or sisters, I never knew family life. Since I was born and raised in France, which was not the native country of either of my parents, this was perhaps to some extent inevitable. From my earliest age I was looked after by others than my parents, who lived their own active life. My first recollections of their company involved my appearance in the drawing-room at 21 Quai Bourbon in my best clothes, to be introduced to the guests and to kiss the ladies' hands. In those years such an upbringing was normal for children like myself. It contributed to my assumption that I had appeared out of nowhere: I might as well have been hatched from a solitary egg in a desert.

The first member of the family other than my parents of whom I became conscious was Linetta (Auntie Pitzy), my mother's younger sister. She had lived in England since 1896, when she was 15, and it wasn't until I was sent to school there in 1919 that I came to know her. She greatly endeared herself to me by sending me regularly on my birthday a splendid Dundee cake from a very superior store in Birmingham by name of Kunzle.

My half-sister Gioia, then Grant Richards, I met for the first time in 1921 or 1922 at the country house of a friend of my parents, Violet Carruthers, Moon Green, Wittersham, near Rye in Kent. I took to Gioia at once, I recall, although slightly awed by her because she seemed to me too grown up to be my sister. I remember thinking her very pretty in a pink dress with flounces—quite unlike anything my mother wore.

During my Harrow years (1924–29) a brother of Gioia, Charles Grant Richards came to Antigny one summer. My mother made much of his visit, but I never came to know him well.

I happened to be alone with my mother at Antigny in early September, 1929, when she learned of the death of her brother, Louis. Never having met him and barely knowing his name, I was struck, even disconcerted, by the intensity of her grief. The following summer, his son Gerard came to stay at Antigny, and this gave me much pleasure.

William R. Tyler in the 1920s

The last member of the family I met was Geoffrey Grant Richards, in London in 1937 or 1938. We were then living there at 50 Argyll Road. We both liked him very much and wished we had known him earlier.

One of my Grant Richards half-brothers, Gerard (after whom Gerard de Castle was named) I never saw. He was killed in 1916, while at school at Eton, in an accident at Poldhu Cove, in Cornwall, near the house, Caerleon, my mother owned, not far from the Lizard.

In 1933 I went for the first time to the United States in search of a job in New York, in order to be able to marry Betsy. Before leaving Europe I was told by Gioia that my maternal grandmother had died there within the last year. Never having even heard of her before, I was unmoved by the news, and remained uninterested in her until almost 50 years later.

My father only rarely referred to his childhood in Massachusetts and hardly ever mentioned his parents. His father, William Royall Tyler, who was Principal of the Adams Academy in Quincy where my father was born, died in 1897. One year later, his mother took him to England and put him to school at Harrow. He never returned to live in the United States.

My mother gloried—I don't think the word is too strong—in the family ties with the Bonapartes, while my father detested—I think this, too, is the right word—Napoleon and all his works, especially his abolition of the Holy Roman Empire. My mother assembled a considerable collection of books on the Bonapartes at Antigny. I don't remember my father ever looking at it or mentioning it. Since—in addition to this divergence in their historical interests and sympathies—my mother's first marriage was obviously not a topic of family conversation, both sides of my family remained to me largely *terra incognita*. However, I do not remember having been conscious of this at the time. It was only after I had resigned from government service, in 1969, that I felt any curiosity about my mother's family. My half-sister,

Gioia, having died in that year, and Auntie Pitzy being in England, it was some time before I was able to start gathering information on the subject. After we settled down at Antigny in July 1977, I made more rapid progress thanks both to the material I found there and to most valuable help from Uncle Bob and Tommy Owtram. In the winter of 1980–81 I worked on a preliminary draft of the history of the family, consisting chiefly of selected documents in chronological order, and of (incomplete) genealogical tables. I finished it by the spring of 1981, but the text was poorly organized, my information was spotty, and thus the result was inadequate.

I think I have by now assembled about as much information as I can hope for. It is a great pity that neither my mother nor her sister ever wrote an account of their youth, especially their memories of their grandmother, Elise. On the other hand, I have found a great deal of information in letters, and in notes of Auntie Pitzy which Uncle Bob kindly passed on to me, as well as in documents at Gragnano collected by Gioia. I was able to take plentiful notes from these during our stay there in March 1983, thanks to the help of Tommy and Gillian.

Among the missing information is the true story of Joséphine's affair with an Englishman called Gower. For a long time I confused him with his brother, Abel Anthony James, who died at Livorno on January 15, 1899, at the age of 62. Thanks to the copy of the death certificate, which Monsieur Valynseele obtained for me, I discovered the initials of his brother (E.H.M.) but not his full name. I have no evidence that Joséphine and E.M.H. Gower were ever married, but she bore him a son. The little we know about this son and his wife is set forth in the text below.

By far the most interesting unsolved problem is the identity of Louis de Castelvecchio's mother. Thanks to Gillian de Zulueta, who spotted the name of the Roman Contessa Carolina Negroni, nata Duchessa Caffarelli, in Louis Bonaparte's will as a financial beneficiary, we have in her a plausible candidate for that role. What evidence we have points in that direction – or, at least, is compatible with the attribution; but it seems unlikely that we shall ever obtain proof.

I have proposed an explanation of the choice by Louis Bonaparte and, presumably by Louis de Castelvecchio's mother, of the name Castelvecchio. However this is, and is likely to remain mere conjecture.

I am indebted to the distinguished French genealogist monsieur Joseph Valynseele for his generous assistance and for much useful information. He has told me that there had been "pas mal d'affabulation" as regards the titles of Suzanne Sophie Longuet de Breuil, her lover, Marcel de Bruges de Camps, and her husband, Pasteur d'Etreillis. He has been unable to find any genealogical evidence justifying their use. It seems that after the Restauration, many families indulged their social ambitions by assuming titles of nobility. This practice was apparently tolerated—or at least not sternly discouraged—so that in the course of years the titles acquired recognition by usage.

I am most grateful to my cousin, the Marchesa Fiammetta Gondi, for her interest, assistance and encouragement in my efforts, as well as for the information she has provided, particularly on the de Larderel family.

I am also much indebted to my friend Vincent Laloy, who has spent much time and gone to great trouble digging up for me information which I could not otherwise have hoped to acquire; as well as to my old friend George Picard who has been helpful in many ways—particularly in relation to Italian matters, and in obtaining for me through his contacts in Italy the so-called "Decree" of the Lucca "Tribunale" on the suit brought by Joséphine for separation from her husband, in 1886.

Within the family I owe much to Uncle Bob, Tommy, Gillian, and Gerard (Bill) de Castle for their help and their patience in responding to my innumerable and—I am sure—

often tiresome requests for information.

The salient facts about the Castelvecchio family are soon told: the first member, François Louis Gaspard Castelvecchio was born in 1826, and the last to die who was born with the name was Linetta de Castelvecchio Richardson, in 1975.

The fourteen years between 1855, when Louis and Elise moved from Florence to Paris (in response to the urging of Napoleon III) and Louis' death in 1869 constitute the peak of the family's fortunes. The ties of the young couple to the imperial Court at the Tuileries ensured them an enviable social position in Paris, and facilitated Louis' career. In 1860 he was ennobled by the Emperor, being created Count (which included the right to use the particle *de*).

His early death seems, at first sight, catastrophic for the family, but in light of the events which followed shortly after—the Franco-Prussian war and the abdication and flight to England of the Emperor—it may be seen as a mercy. At least Elise was spared the misery of the experience of her husband's eclipse in addition to the ruin of the family's prospects.

Their eldest daughter, Marceline, died little over one year later than her father, during the Franco-Prussian war; and not long afterwards Elise left France for Tuscany with her two surviving daughters, Louise and Joséphine. The two girls married there rapidly, Louise in 1872 and Joséphine in 1874, and from then on the family chronicle is enlivened by the repercussions of Joséphine's turbulent existence. She and her eldest daughter, Elisina continued to use the title Comtesse de Castelvecchio in addition to their married names. So far as I can tell, neither Louise, who had married a German Businessman settled in Florence, nor Louis, Josephine's son (who changed his name to "de Castle" while still in the United States, before emigrating to South Africa) ever used the title. Linetta Richardson, who made her home in England, used it only sparingly. In fact, the imperial decree conferring it explicitly restricts its transference to Louis de Castelvecchio's *male* heirs in direct descent by primogeniture.

Having no national base, and owning no property other than a summer residence in Pescia, the family gradually scattered and more or less disintegrated.

At one time or another members of it settled down in Italy, England, France, the United States of America and South Africa. It even seems in keeping with its unconventional history that a descendant of Louis Bonaparte, King of Holland, should have been appointed American Ambassador at The Hague one hundred and fifty-five years after the abdication there of his ancestor.

I have tried to tell the story of the family, as I have been able to reconstruct it, objectively and "sans parti pris". In this I have been guided by a passage quoted by Vincent Laloy in writing his family's history: "A genealogy naturally bores those whom it does not concern…It ceases to be tedious if each individual who figures in it is treated as a whole person, situated in his or her proper world and period."

> *"Une généalogie ennuie naturellement ceux qu'elle ne concerne pas... elle cesse d'être fastidieuse si chacun des individus qui la composent est réintégré dans sa personne, situé dans son milieu, replacé dans son époque."*

Finally, a note on certain diminutives which appear in the text. Linetta wrote to her niece Gioia in 1958: "There was a time when your mother was, in England, called by intimate friends and me, Zizi and often just Zi. And it was she who first called me Pitzy. This came about because during my first 3 months in England we were boarding together in Cheltenham (where she was teaching for her last term at Cheltenham Ladies' College), and having always felt rather grandmotherly towards those I love, I used to tuck her up in bed, and the Italian form of endearment corresponding to 'darling', i.e: 'piccinina' was always on my lips. From 'picci' she made Pitzy in English. As for 'Lil'…..that is the entirely fancy name by which my mother referred to me (never *called me*) to her friends when talking English." Linetta (to whom I usually refer in the text as A.P.) adds: "Accapit was *your* baby version of 'Auntie Pitzy'. That's why the stress falls at the end"…….

> W.R.T.
> Antigny-le-Château
> 1983

P.S. To quote the coda of a medieval scribe: *Hoc feci totum, pro Deo da mihi potum!* [I've finished the whole thing! For God's sake give me a drink!]

Louis Bonaparte (1778 – 1846)

At his abdication as King of Holland at the age of 32, Louis assumed the title of Comte de Saint-Leu from a large estate near Paris which he had acquired in 1804. He is buried there in a chapel (which his son Napoleon III built for this purpose in 1851) together with his two other sons, Napoléon-Charles, Prince Royal of Holland (1802– 07) and Napoléon-Louis, Grand Duke of Berg and Cleves (1804–31).

His body had been brought back to Saint-Leu in 1847 in accordance with his wishes, with the permission of Louis-Philippe. The body of his father Charles Bonaparte has also been brought there from Montpellier where he had died. In 1951 it was translated to Ajaccio.

After 1814, Louis Bonaparte spent the rest of his life in Italy—first in Rome with "Madame Mère" and later in Florence where he established himself permanently in 1829, in the palace Gianfigliazzi at No. 4 Lungarno Corsini (next to the British Consulate). He used to spend the summer months at Livorno where he died in 1846.

On April 26, 1826 Francois Louis Gaspard Castelvecchio was baptized in Rome, "natum hac eadem die ex incertis et fictis parentibus Marco Antonino Castelvecchio et Johanna Felice Rolandi". The Act of Baptism is signed by the Parish priest of the church "S. Mariae in Porticu in Campitello Urbis". The text does not state that the baptism took place in the church. Indeed this would have been most unlikely, given the circumstances of his birth and the fact that it occurred on the same day. It was then usual in Italy for priests to go to the home of the child as soon after birth as possible, lest the child should die without the sacrament of baptism.

We know that Louis Bonaparte was the father for reasons that will later become apparent. However the identity of the mother is not known and may never be proved, although there is a plausible candidate for this role, whose name was first suggested, as I have already noted, by Gillian de Zulueta. Before considering what evidence can be marshalled in support of this possibility, let us take a look at François Louis Gaspard's upbringing and his relations with Louis Bonaparte.

In her notes, A.P. states that François was brought up as a baby in his father's palace in Florence until sent at a very early age to the Istituto Cicognini in nearby Prato. She visited Prato in 1925, and the Director of the Istituto showed her some large marble tablets on which were carved the names of former pupils. Each tablet covered a period of about six years. On the tablet started in 1830 was the name Castelvecchio "only 3rd or 4th from the top", from which A.P. deduced that he must have been very young indeed to have been sent there as a boarder. A close friend of the Castelvecchios when they were living in Paris, Countess Emilia Hierschel de Minerbi, told A.P. that François claimed he had done all he could to find out who his mother was, but in vain. As will be seen further on, François was told by his father about his "origine". One can assume that he was under oath to keep it a secret, and his comments to Countess Hierschel de Minerbi should be understood accordingly. Elisina once told A.P. "it was supposed that the mother was a Barberini or a Colonna" but there is no evidence for this. Josephine had a story that François remembered a "lovely lady" coming to see him in Florence when he was a child "and embracing him passionately before he was sent away to school". He would then have been about four and a half years old. There is no record at Prato of the date of his departure, but we know that in 1840 he entered the highly regarded Pension Sillig in Switzerland, near Vevey. The first letter we have which his father wrote to him there is dated October 31 of that year. It is most fortunate many letters to him from his father have survived. I thought it worthwhile to give extensive extracts from them, particularly those which shed light on Louis Bonaparte's personality and on his conception and of the kind of education François should receive to prepare him for the future. Hard and unfeeling though they often seem, they convey—taken as a whole—a sense of his deep feelings for François, and of his strong moral obligations toward him.

Florence, October 31, 1840
"I received your letter from Livorno, and I thank you for it; however, I had hoped that you would write to me in French. You know how important I feel that to be, and with me you need have no fear of making mistakes, since I am familiar with the education that you have received."

> *J'ai reçu votre lettre de Livourne & je vous en remercie ; j'espérais cependant que vous m'écririez en français, puisque vous savez combien j'y tiens et que vous ne devez pas craindre de faire des fautes avec moi puisque je connais le degré de votre instruction.*

Pisa, December 16, 1840
"I received your letter of the tenth and am answering it in person. Why do you tell me that you have forgotten something? It seems to me that it is entirely up to you to forget nothing at all: take notes.

First, why do you begin your letter with the word "Excellence," since I have told you always to refer to me as "Monsieur le Comte"—understood that "Comte" [Count] is not a title that I claim personally, since I reject any that does not describe a man's actual office. I simply adopted the title "Comte de Saint Leu" thirty years ago in order to distinguish myself from others, and I countenance the use of "Monsieur le Comte" only because it amounts, for me, almost to personal name... Farewell, Monsieur François.

    Work hard, make great efforts.

    That is the investment least likely to fail.

I hope that you have not forgotten the book from which these lines are drawn."

(An interline, in ink: La Fontaine)

J'ai reçu votre lettre du 10 et j'y répondre [sic] moi-même. Pourquoi me dites-vous que vous avez oublié quelquechose? Il me semble qu'il ne tient qu'à vous de ne rien oublier : prenez des notes.

D'abord, pourquoi votre lettre commence-t-elle par le mot Excellence *quand je vous ai dit de me nommer toujours Monsieur le Comte, en retenant bien que ce mot de Comte n'est pas un titre pour moi, qui n'en admet [sic] d'autres que ceux des emplois que l'on exerce. J'ai adopté depuis trente ans le nom de Comte de Saint Leu pour m'individualiser, et c'est comme faisant partie de mon nom que j'admets que l'on me nomme Monsieur le Comte...   Adieu, Monsieur François.*

'Travaillez, prenez de la peine, C'est le fond qui manque le moins.'
J'espère que vous n'avez pas oublié le livre d'où ces vers sont tirés.

From Pietro Orsini, Louis' secretary, January 13, 1841
"He asks me to tell you that your handwriting tends to be English in style, something that he does not like at all, for the reason that this style is the most likely of all to deteriorate, and that it is insufficiently precise and clear. You will therefore accord him the pleasure of adopting genuinely French handwriting: clear, precise, and without ornamentation. He wishes to know what is the point of these 4 or 5 long lines that follow your signature. By all means add a flourish to your signature, since it is the custom to do so, but no more than one short, neat line.

Monsieur le Comte is keenly interested in you, but only as long as you merit his interest; otherwise, no. You are no longer child enough to fail to consider your own interests, of which the most important of all is to take advantage of the chance given you to gain the knowledge you need in order to acquire the means to support yourself. This is a thoroughly urgent task for one as old as you already are. If you were to lose Monsieur le Comte, what would you do?"

> *Il me charge de vous dire que votre écriture prenne [sic] de l'anglaise qu'il n'aime point du tout par [sic] la raison qu'elle est la plus susceptible de toutes à se gâter et qu'elle n'est ni assez exacte ni assez distincte. Vous lui ferez donc plaisir d'adopter une écriture véritablement française, bien distincte, sans broderie et exacte. Il vous demande à quoi servent ces 4 ou 5 longs traits après votre signature en manière de paraphe. Mettez donc une paraphe à votre signature puisque c'est l'usage, mais par un petit trait bien arrêté .*
>
> *Monsieur le Comte vous porte beaucoup d'intérêt, mais à condition que vous le mériterez; si non, non. Vous n'êtes plus si enfant pour ne pas songer à vos intérêts, et le plus spécial est celui de profiter de l'occasion qui vous est offerte d'acquérir les connaissances qui vous sont nécessaires pour vous donner les moyens de pourvoir à votre existence. Cela est même très pressé pour vous qui êtes assez âgé: si M. le Comte venez [sic] à vous manquer, qu'est-ce que vous feriez?*

The letter goes on to urge him to become a "past master" in the French language, to perfect his calligraphy, to master mathematics and to be a good Latin scholar, "le fondement de toute instruction" [the basis of any decent education]. He must also practice fencing, swimming and riding in his leisure hours. Then, and only then, will he be permitted to turn to dancing and music. The letter ends: "Monsieur le Comte asks me to tell you that your welfare will concern him as long as he lives, but you must not forget that you are poor and an orphan. M. le Comte expects to see evidence of progress in every letter that you write him."

> *M. le Comte me charge de vous dire que tant qu'il vivra il ne cessera de vous porter de l'intérêt, mais il ne faut pas que vous oubliez que vous êtes pauvre et orphelin. M. le Comte s'attend à voir de nouveaux progrès à chaque lettre que vous lui écrivez.*

Then, a final touch: "P.S.: M. le Comte requests that you delete the particle "de" from your surname."

> *M. le Comte vous prie de supprimer la particule 'de' à votre nom de famille.*

April 1, 1841

"M. le Comte has received the latest letter from Monsieur Sillig, in which M. Sillig reports on your occupations and your progress. M. le Comte praises you and will continue to praise whatever progress you make; however, he finds your progress insufficiently rapid, and he urges you to redouble your zeal and your activity. He reminds you that you are no longer as young as you think and that you have no time to lose. M. le Comte's aim, as you know, is that you should be able to take responsibility for yourself as soon as possible and take up whatever profession you choose, so that you can provide for yourself.

Whatever M. le Comte may have done for you, and whatever his hopes for you in the future, he cannot ignore the fact that you were made to lose a great deal of time at Prato and that you must therefore work very hard in order to regain that lost time.

M. le Comte wishes you to make every effort to write French perfectly. He doubts that Vevey offers any perfect school of calligraphy, but your writing is good enough that you should be able to perfect it yourself with the help of good models, of which there are many; you need only cultivate the will to do so.

M. le Comte urges you above all to apply your mind to what you do and to concentrate wholly on the occupation of each moment; for the best way to accomplish nothing—in other words, to succeed in nothing—is to be distracted and to be thinking of several things at the same time.

M. le Comte has been unwell this winter, which has been very hard here; but he is less unwell now and wishes me emphatically to tell you so. (Signed: Pietro Orsini)

> *Monsieur le Comte a reçu la dernière lettre de Mr Sillig par laquelle il lui a rendu compte de vos occupations et de vos progrès; il vous loue et vous louera toujours des progrès que vous ferez, mais il ne trouve pas qu'ils soyent assez marquans [sic] et il vous engage à redoubler le zèle*

> *et l'activité. Il vous fait réfléchir que vous n'êtes plus aussi jeune que vous le pensez et que vous n'avez pas le temps à perdre. Le but de M. le Comte, vous le savez, serait que vous fussiez le plutôt [sic] possible en état de vous conduire vous-même, d'embrasser un état à votre choix, afin de pourvoir vous-même à votre existence.*
>
> *Quels qu'aient été les soins et le désir de M. le Comte à votre égard, il ne peut se dissimuler qu'on vous a fait perdre beaucoup de temps à Prato et que par conséquent il vous faut donner beaucoup de peine pour regagner le temps perdu.*
>
> *M. le Compte vous prie de mettre vos soins à écrire parfaitement le français. Il ne croit pas qu'il y ait à Vevey une école parfaite de calligraphie, mais votre écriture est assez bonne pour que vous puissiez la perfectionner par vous meme à l'aide de bons modèles qui ne manquent pas; il suffit de le vouloir bien fermement.*
>
> *…M. le Comte… vous engage surtout à vous recueillir dans vos occupations et à être tout entier à celle du moment; car le vrai moyen de ne rien faire, c'est à dire de ne réussir en rien, c'est d'être distrait et de penser à plusieurs choses à la fois.*
>
> *M. le Comte a été souffrant cet hiver qui a été très mauvais dans le pays; il est moins mal maintenant et me charge de vous le faire savoir expressément. (Signed: Pietro Orsini)*

The faithful Orsini has to write François another letter, dated *June 22, 1841,* which reflects Louis' displeasure, and starts as follows: "…M. le Comte received your most recent letter with pleasure; he is not yet writing to you in person because he is not yet satisfied with your progress…"

> *Monsieur le Comte a reçu avec plaisir votre dernière lettre; il ne vous écris [sic] pas encore directement parce qu'il lui reste à desirer sur vos progrès.*

There follows a reiteration of the substance of the previous letter, on the need for François to make up for the time lost at Prato, to master the French language, arithmetic, fencing, and above all to write "a perfect French hand without any trace of ornamentation because M. le Comte detests English handwriting, which you imitate."

> *Une parfaite écriture française sans aucune broderie parce que M. le Comte déteste l' écriture anglaise qui est celle que vous imitez.*

To this letter, Pietro Orsini pens a note which expresses his sympathy for Francois' situation: "My dear M. Cecchino, the Emperor used to say, 'The bullet destined to kill me has not yet been cast.' I myself would say that the man destined to satisfy Louis, his brother, is not yet born and never will be."

> *Mon cher M. Cecchino—La balle qui doit me tuer n'est pas encore fondue, disait l' Empereur. Je dirai moi que l'homme qui doit contenter son frère Louis n'est pas né et ne naitra jamais.*

And so it goes on, letter after letter! In one he urges François to work night and day, unceasingly. In another he begs him to look after his health: "It is a treasure too little valued in youth."

> *… c'est un trésor qu'on n'apprécie pas assez dans la jeunesse…*

At the same time, a note of concern about his own health is sounded, together with an occasional message of affection, all the more conspicuous because hitherto absent.

On *February 21, 1843*, he informs François: "Now that you are grown up and no longer a child, I have considered your interests, since I am your only protector, and am old and ill. Therefore I wish you to know that Monsieur le Notaire Francesco del Greco, of this city of Florence, has in his hands a document that I have entrusted to him, one that concerns you, and thanks to which everything that you need has been provided for…" (Signed L. de St Leu)

> *… comme vous voilà grand maintenant et que vous n'êtes plus un enfant, j'ai pensé à ce qui vous concerne, puisque je suis votre seul protecteur, et que je suis vieux et malade. En consequence je vous préviens que M. le Notaire Francesco del Greco de cette ville de Florence a dans ses mains un écrit que je lui ai confié, qui vous concerne, et au moyen duquel il est pourvu à tout ce qui vous est nécessaire…*

March 17, 1843
Louis is angry with François because of two things "that have made displeased me greatly and that I will mention now so that they should not recur…"

> *qui m'ont fait beaucoup de peine et qui je vais vous rappeler pour que cela n'arrive plus…*

First, he has discovered that François' letters to him were corrected and improved by M. Sillig. This must stop. Second, François has not replied concerning the text which Louis had sent him—nor had he told Louis where the text is kept, who looks after it, and whether he has obeyed Louis' instruction not to let anyone else know about it. "This secret must be a point of honor for you, if you really have the wit and character that I see in you. Avoid taking the slightest step without my permission. The step that might seem to be the very simplest to you could in reality be quite different and lead to consequences for you…" However, Louis has a third grievance: "I have been sorry to learn that in Florence you were in correspondence in with Monsieur de Filippi. You have forgotten one of the first things I enjoined upon you: never to correspond with anyone whatsoever without my express permission. This order I now repeat to you, with the warning that disobedience would lose you my good will and my concern for you. Good-bye… "

> *Ce secret doit être un point d'honneur pour vous, si vous avez réellement l'esprit et le caractère que je vous attribue. Gardez-vous de faire la moindre démarche sans ma permission; celle qui vous paraîtrait la plus simple, peut être toute autre réellement et avoir des suites pour vous…*
>
> *J'ai appris avec peine que vous étiez en correspondence à Florence avec M. de Filippi; vous avez oublié l'une des premières choses que je vous recommandai, savoir: de ne correspondre avec qui que ce l'est [sic], sous quelque prétexte que ce puisse être sans ma permission spéciale, et c'est un ordre que je vous renouvelle ici sous peine de perdre*

> *mon amitié et mon intérêt; c'est à vous d'y songer, Adieu…*

and as a postscript: "Identify precisely for me all persons to whom you have written hitherto, and likewise all those who have written to you."

> *Faites-moi connaître précisément toutes les personnes auxquelles vous avez écrit jusqu'à présent et de même celles qui vous ont écrit….*

June 12, 1843
"Dear M. Castelvecchio, you will receive this letter from the hands of Madame Augier, who looked after you at times during your infancy, when she was a governess in my household. However I doubt that you will remember her because you were then too small and also because she then went by her maiden name of Roulet. As a matter of fact, I will mention to you that, although married in Florence, she is Swiss—from Vevey, I believe. She is a widow now and lives with her only son, named Joseph. He is extremely young , and she hopes to place him in the same boarding school as yourself. Tell M. Sillig that I recommend him, if my recommendation can be of any value, as it was for Madame Augier herself with respect to her choice of a school for her son."

> *Mon cher Mr Castelvecchio, cette lettre vous sera remise par Mad. Augier, qui vous a donné quelques soins dans votre enfance, quand elle était gouvernante chez moi. Mais je ne crois pas que vous puissiez vous la rappeler parce que vous étiez alors trop enfant et qu'elle portait son nom de famille, celui de Roulet. Au reste, je vous dirai que quoique mariée à Florence, elle est Suisse, je crois même de Vevay [sic]. Elle est veuve maintenant; elle mène avec elle son fils unique, qui se nomme Joseph, qui est extrêmement jeune et qu'elle compte mettre dans la même pension que vous. Dites à M. Sillig que je le lui recommande, si ma recommandation peut être de quelque poids auprès de lui, comme elle l'a été pour Mad. Augier dans le choix d'un pensionnat pour son fils.*

This letter bears out A.P.'s statement about his infancy.

It is understandable that Francois, on the basis of the above, should have corresponded with Mad. Augier. However, the result was the following rocket from his irascible and touchy father.

November 7, 1843 (from Orsini)
"I am answering your letter of 28 October on behalf of M. le Comte. He has instructed me to tell you that he absolutely forbids you to correspond with Madame Augier, however deserving she may be, because it is not in the proper order of things that you should do so. He urges you to contain your feelings of friendship and trust toward persons whom you hardly know. To his mind, trust and friendship must grow with time and frequency of contact, and come naturally, not spring up suddenly. Guard yourself, therefore, against impulses that contravene M. le Comte's wishes and instructions. It is not that Madame Augier is not a thoroughly good and worthy person, but you know that M. le Comte dislikes that others should share your relationship and your feelings toward himself."

> *Je réponds pour Mr le Comte à votre lettre du 28 octobre. Il me charge de vous dire qu'il vous défend absolument de correspondre avec Mad. Augier, quel que soit le mérite de cette dame, parce que cela n'est pas dans l'ordre. Il vous prie de vous contenir dans vos élans d'amitié et de confiance pour des personnes que vous ne connaissez que depuis fort peu de temps. Il pense que la confiance et l'amitié doivent naître avec le temps et l'habitude et venir naturellement et non subitement. Tenez-vous donc en garde contre les velléités qui vous prennent en contradiction avec les sentiments et les instructions de Mr le Comte. Ce n'est pas que Mad. Augier ne soit une personne très estimable et très bonne, mais vous savez que Mr le Comte n'aime pas que d'autres partagent vos relations et vos sentiments envers lui.*

In other words, Louis is jealous of anyone with whom François might have friendly relations! The good Pietro Orsini is himself affected by Louis' attitude to the point that he encloses with his letter, a tiny scrap of paper with the words "Taken down, as you can easily see, from M. le Comte's dictation."

Ecrite, comme vous vous apercevez aisément sous la dictée de S. M.

July 2, 1844

The last letter Louis wrote to Francois at the Pension Sillig dates from July 2, 1844. My dear Castelvecchio, you must not torment yourself unnecessarily, because it is essential to save one's strength for real sorrows instead of indulging in imaginary ones. Nothing I can think of should suggest to you that my feelings toward you have changed. They remain the same as before, and there is no reason for you to doubt it. Unbeknownst to you, I have just given you further proof of that. I have written to M. Sillig to have you come and spend a short break with me, under the supervision of one of your teachers, M. Dardel. I hope that you will spend this autumn here, and you must not doubt the pleasure it will be for me to see you again, particularly if you do not disappoint me: in other words, if I find you more advanced in your studies than expected, and especially if you return to me better versed in your religion and in your language—which, as I have often reminded you, is French. Prepare yourself, therefore, to insure that I am pleased with you when you get here, for that is the true way to merit my esteem and affection for you, and also to serve me.

Therefore set your mind at rest and see to it that you appear to me in a good light.

Adieu, my dear pupil, I bless you and kiss you." (signed L. de St Leu)

Mon cher Castelvecchio, il ne faut pas se tourmenter mal à propos parce qu'il faut garder ses forces pour les peines réelles, et ainsi ne point s'en faire d'imaginaires. Je ne vois rien qui puisse vous faire penser que j'ai changé des sentiments envers vous; mes sentiments sont toujours les mêmes, et vous n'avez aucune raison pour en doubter. Je viens de vous en donner une nouvelle preuve à votre insu. J'ai écrit à

> *Mr Sillig de vous faire venir auprès de moi et passer un petit congé, sous la direction et la conduite de Mr Dardel l'un de vos Précepteurs. J'espère que vous serez ici pour cet automne et vous ne devez pas douter du plaisir que j'aurai de vous revoir, surtout si mon attente n'est pas trompée. C'est à dire si je vous trouve plus avancé dans vos études que je ne m'y attend, [sic] et surtout si vous me revenez bien instruit dans votre Religion et votre langue qui, comme je vous l'ai dit souvent est la française. Mettez-vous donc en état que je sois content de vous à votre arrivée, c'est le vrai moyen de mériter toute mon estime et par là mon attachement, et de m'être utile.*
>
> *Soyez donc sans inquiétude et occupez-vous, comme je vous l'ai dit, de vous mettre en état de bien paraître à mes yeux.*
>
> *Adieu, mon cher pupille, je vous bénis et vous embrasse."*

This letter is unique in the series in starting with "Mon cher Castelvecchio", and in the degree of affection of affection it expresses, particularly in the last sentence.

It is possible that François may have destroyed some. At any rate, it seems that he must have written one which shook Louis and prompted him to write this unprecedented reply. Even so, Louis reasserts the conditions for his affection of François, almost as a reflex action. It is possible that Louis destroyed, or left orders to destroy François' letters to him. He was a very sick man, and had just two years more to live.

When one thinks of the conditions under which François was brought up, and lived until he was 18, cut off from normal childhood and subjected to the iron will and pressures of his father, his loyalty to him and his complete discretion about him reflect highly on the strength and the quality of his character.

It is easy to find fault with Louis Bonaparte. He laid himself open to criticism and to reprobation. In his book on the Bonapartes in Florence, Andréa Corsini describes Louis in the eighteen-thirties as *pedante, instabile, di umor tetro*…Louis' niece, Mathilde, daughter of his brother Jerome, said he was volatile, excessively suspicious of others, inquisitive and miserly. His doctor wrote that Louis "suffered from an illness that prevented normal use of his legs and arms, allowing him to walk only slowly and poorly, and giving him only difficult use of his hands."

> *era tormentato da una malattia che gl'impediva il normale uso delle gambe e delle braccia permetendogli soltanto il camminare poco e male, e di valersi con difficoltà delle mani.*

His moodiness, Corsini states, made people avoid him. Always malevolent and suspicious of others, he only mentioned the past in order to speak evil of his wife. He calls Louis *minuzioso, avaro, caparbio.*

His biographer, Labarre de Raillicourt, writes that from an early age Louis had been eccentric, and that he followed the prescriptions of quacks and charlatans. He was already plagued with rheumatism at the age of 24, and took the advice of one of them to soak in baths of tripe and to wear shirts of sufferers from the mange! One remedy he is said to have tried consisted in drinking "le marc de raisin de Joigny."

In 1816, when not yet 40, he appeared, according to the Governor of Pisa, to be *attacato da una paralisi che rende assai vacillante la sua salute.* Notwithstanding this, Louis managed to have affairs with assiduity and success. Labarre de Raillicourt writes that he adores secret adventures, loves moving about incognito, which makes his love life very difficult to penetrate." Elsewhere he again refers to "the secret amours favored by this taciturn king, who never reveals them to the world or even to his closest intimates."

Whatever one's opinion of Louis Bonaparte may be, and of his conception of how François should be educated, his loyalty to him and the measures he took to protect his interests for the future are wholly admirable. We have seen that in his letter of Feb 21, 1843, Louis mentions "un écrit" [a document] which he has entrusted to a notary in Florence, whereby François is to be provided with all that he will need. This "ecrit" is related to a Deed of Gift executed in Florence by Louis on Feb 8, 1843, in favour of François: "giovane e orfano" [young and orphan] The gift is irrevocable, and provides that after Louis' death *("e non altruinente")* 100,000 Swiss Francs are to be paid to François in cash immediately *per cause l'animo suo movimenti.* Other provisions are made in case Louis dies before François comes of age. Louis would like François then to reside in France, specifically in the Commune de St. Leu *ove una volta aveva e teneva il donante stesso alcune proprieta.*

It seems that François lived with his father from the autumn of 1844 until the latter's death on July 25, 1846, at the Locanda San Marco at Livorno, where Louis spent the summers.

The only record we have of François Castelvecchio's activities in Florence while his father was alive consists of the seven water-color copies he made of the Bonaparte family portraits in the drawing-room of his father's palace. These are in the order of their dates:

Caroline (signed F. Castelvecchio)	August 25, 1845
Louis (signed Castelvecchio)	August 31, 1845
Napoleon (signed F. Castelvecchio)	Nov. 13, 1845
"Madame Mere" (as above)	March 4, 1846
Lucien (as above)	May 1, 1846
Pauline (as above)	1846 (day, month illegible)
Joseph (as above)	Sept.15, 1846

The only signature with no initial is that on his father's portrait. One can assume that François felt his father would have preferred it this way. There is one obvious omission among these family portraits, that of Louis Napoleon, later the Emperor Napoleon III. Because of Caroline's insistence on Hortense's promiscuous conduct, Louis long believed that he was not Louis Napoleon's father. However, after subsequently learning that Caroline's accusations against Hortense had been motivated by jealousy and a thirst for revenge because Hortense had seduced Caroline's lover, Louis' feelings toward Louis Napoleon changed. "He now rather regrets", writes Labarre de Raillicourt (p.448-9), "having shown his visitors often and so willingly, that, among the gallery of family portraits in his splendid drawing room in Florence, only that of Louis-Napoléon was missing."

Since François had given up his apartment in his father's palace by August 3, 1846 – a week after his death – and had taken his possessions with him, I assume that Pauline's portrait was finished before he left for Livorno with Louis, and that he added some finishing touches on Joseph's portrait after his return to Florence, and signed it then.

François wrote an account of his father's last illness (see Appendix). Within a few hours of Louis' death, H. de la Rochefoucauld, Ministre de France après du Grand Duc de Toscane, wrote a letter to the French Foreign Minister, Francois Guizot, which alludes to François Castelvecchio without mentioning his name, and comments on the political implications of the event (see Appendix).

The Mother

Section XI, the last in Louis Bonaparte's will of December 1, 1845, enumerates "the things that I leave in my will, and the persons to whom I leave them" *(le cose, che io lascio per legato, e le persone alle quali le lascio)*. After a long list of bequests ranging from the Grand Duke and the Grand Duchess of Tuscany to his own close relatives, he confirms the gift to his "Pupillo" Francesco Castelvecchio, "educated by my care at the Pension Sillig at Vevey, Switzerland, of the sum of 100,000 Swiss Francs equal to 150,000 French Francs, which has already been given by me by an Act.... of February 8, 1843".... The immediately following sentence is: "I leave to Contessa Carolina Negroni of Rome, born Duchessa Caffarelli, the sum on five hundred Roman scudi" *(Lascio alla Contessa Carolina Negroni di Roma nata Duchessa Caffarelli la somma di Scudi cinquecento romani)*. After this came the bequests to his domestic staff.

Gillian de Zulueta spotted this bequest in the text of the will published by Andrea Corsini in his book on the Bonapartes in Florence, and the thought occurred to her that Carolina Negroni might have been François' mother. Neither Corsini nor Labarre de Raillicourt mentions this idea.

The names of the two beneficiaries, Francesco Castelvecchio and Carolina Negroni are juxtaposed in the text between Louis' own family and the family retainers. It was already widely known before Louis' death that Francesco Castelvecchio was his natural son. To have Louis' gift to him confirmed as a bequest in the two sentences immediately preceding the sentence in which a sum of money is left to a woman of noble birth is indeed suggestive. However the question arises why Louis went to such pains to conceal the identity of François' mother when he was alive, while at the same time mentioning her as a beneficiary of a sum of money in his will, particularly in such a conspicuous context.

The church of St Mariae in Porticu in Campitello Urbis where the baptism of Francois is registered is the Parish church of the Caffarelli palace, which is only a few hundred yards distant. Of course this doesn't prove anything, but we know François was born in Rome, that he was baptized by the parish priest S. Mariae in Porticu, and that the Caffarelli palace lies within this parish and is not far from the church.

We do not have a Birth Certificate ("Fede di nascita") for François but we know that one existed. In the same folder as the letters from his father, François kept a paper which had been folded and sealed by Louis Bonaparte, and which contained the "écrit" mentioned in his letter of February 21, 1843, described by him in the following terms: "M. le Notaire Francesco del Greco, of this city of Florence, has in his hands a documented with which I entrusted him, which concerns you, and through which everything you need is provided."

Mr le Notaire Francesco del Greco de cette ville de Florence, a dans ses mains un écrit que je lui ai confié, qui vous concerne, et au moyen duquel il est pourvu à tout ce qui est nécessaire...

This ambiguous language is clarified by a note addressed to François on August 5, 1846 (10 days after Louis' death) by one of the two Executors of the Italian portion of his will, "il Signor Avvocato Cavalier Ranieri Lamporecchi," as follows:

Ella mi disse di avere seco la Fede della sua nàscita. Cío essendo, converrebbe, che la portasse alla sessione di questa mattiera per renderla ostensibile al Signor Agrifoglio ed al.

The paper which contained the "écrit" (ie: the birth certificate) has written on it in Louis' own and barely legible hand: "Document concerning Mr François Castelvecchio, which he must preserve carefully, in accordance with the instructions that he has received."

Ecrit concernant Mr François Castelvecchio qu'il devra conserver soigneusement conformément à l'instruction qu'il a reçue.

and Louis' signature. I wonder whether the "Fede di nascita" has survived – perhaps buried somewhere in the musty files of the notary, Francesco del Greco, or of one of the two Executors of Louis' will, Agrifoglio and Lamporecchi? It is more likely that Louis should have left instructions that it be destroyed once it had served its legal purpose. Perhaps it did not even reveal the mother's real name!

Fiammetta Gondi is convinced that Carolina Negroni was the mother. "The fact that she was left by Louis neither a souvenir, nor a jewel....but money!" seems to her conclusive. "I think she was the lady he loved," she writes "and the mother of his son! And we have arrived at the end of the story!!" She kindly obtained an informed estimate for me of what 500 Scudi romani would represent today: "It was in Silver, 5 lire, now about 35,000 L – total 17 500 000 L, a beautiful souvenir but I would prefer *a jewel*!" As of now this sum is roughly $13,500.

A few weeks later (our correspondence having switched to French) she writes of the bequest: "That suffices to *prove* his liaison with this lady, the mother of his son. This is no legend, but history! And everyone knew. I believe that your research is over and that you can now let these lovers sleep—these lovers who had their pleasure and who suffered!!"

> *cela suffit pour prouver sa liaison avec cette dame, mère de son fils... ce n'est pas une légende mais l'Histoire! Et tout le monde était au courant. Je pense que vos recherches sont finies et que vous pouvez laisser dormir ces amants, qui ont joui.. et souffert!!*

While I am not as convinced by this identification as is Fiammetta, I am happy to abide by her suggestion that the matter be allowed to rest. I assume that François knew his mother's name, but did not feel at liberty to tell anyone, or even to imply that he knew it. This would account for his remark to Countess de Minerti that he had tried all his life to find it out, but in vain. My assumption that François knew is based on the following passage in the draft of his letter to Napoleon III: "When King Louis called me back to him, he told me of my origin and of the reasons for his affection."

> *Lorsqu il m'eût rappelé auprès de lui... le Roi Louis m'a fait savoir mon origine et les motifs de son affection...*

The draft is undated, and I don't know whether the letter was ever sent. However the passage quoted above is unambiguous. Since François must have known that Louis was his father (by 1844, when he was recalled from school to live with Louis, he was 18), the only aspect of his "origine" which Louis could have revealed was his mother.

The Family Name

The name Castelvecchio first appears on the Act of Baptism. The parents must have given considerable thought to the choice of a name, long before the child was born. In retrospect I find it curious that I never heard my mother speak about the name, and that I have come across no comments on its origin in any of the family letters, notes and other documents that I have consulted.

One day, I happened to look up Ajaccio in the *Grande Encyclopédie Larousse* to see what it had to say about the place, and found the following: Ajaccio is mentioned for the first time in the letters of Gregory the Great. However, the town has moved since then. At first it apparently occupied the hill known as Castelvecchio. Then, after being destroyed by the Arabs in the tenth century, it seems to have been moved to San Giovanni, 2 km. from its present location. The hill of Castelvecchio has long since been absorbed within the town limits.

It occurred to me that in selecting a family name, Louis and the mother would naturally take several factors into consideration. It should be compatible with the social position of the parents and of their child. At the same time, it should not already be that of a well-known family. A place name not already borne by a prominent family would be suitable, but the place should not belong to a noble family, in order to avoid any implication of being associated with it. The fact that there are many places with the name Castelvecchio in Italy reduced the chance that someone bearing that name would be linked to a particular locality or family.

Castelvecchio meets these requirements, and it does not seem to me far-fetched to suppose that the name might have occurred to Louis because of its ties to his own birthplace.

François Louis de Castelvecchio

Florence (1847 – 1855)

After his father's death, François Louis Gaspard evidently felt free to use his second name, Louis, instead of François as his father had understandably always called him. His third name, Gaspard dropped out of sight. I have no idea why it was given to him in the first place.

On May 6, 1847, Louis (as he will be referred to from now on) and Elise Pasteur d'Etreillis were married in the church of

Santa Maria Maggiore in Florence.

In his biography of Louis Bonaparte, Labarre de Raillicourt writes: "Shortly before his death, he [Louis Bonaparte] chose a fiancée for him [François]: Elise Caroline Pasteur d'Etreillis, also born in 1826."

Assuming that Louis Bonaparte picked out Elise as a wife for Louis Castelvecchio, he must have done so before he left Florence for Livorno in 1846. Why did he choose her in particular? Did he know who she really was? The question arises because Elise, who was born in Paris, was brought up in Florence from her infancy under a name other than her own. Her father, Charles Thomas Pasteur d'Etreillis married Suzanne Sophie Longuet de Breuil. They had two children: a son, Charles Jules Ferdinand Sainte-Aure Pasteur d'Etreillis, and Elise. However we have a conflict of dates: Elise, born the same year as Louis, was a few months older. Her brother died in 1885 aged 65 according to the Acte de Décès. This would mean 1820 as the year of his birth, but the year of their parents' marriage is 1825 (Nov 24).

When Elise was still a very small child, her mother left her husband and her son in Paris and took Elise with her to Florence in order to live with a Frenchman named Marcel de Bruges de Camps who had settled there. Elise told her granddaughters, Elisina and Linetta, that she only learned from her mother on her wedding day that her real name was not de Bruges de Camps but d'Etreillis. Her mother was known in Florence as Madame de Bruges de Camps, and Elise also had been known by that name. The Comte de Saint-Leu as well as François Castelvecchio must have thought that this was Elise's name, as is shown by a letter the latter received from Louis Napoleon before he became Emperor, written in London on January 25, 1847, in which he writes: "I learn with pleasure the news of your coming marriage with Miss de Bruges de Camps."

> *J'apprends avec plaisir la nouvelle de votre prochain mariage avec Mlle de Bruges de Camps.*

He could only have learned of the engagement from François himself.

The Comte de Saint-Leu's selection of a bride for his son is consistent with his highly protective attitude toward him from the day of his birth. He wanted him to have the best possible French education to be obtained outside of France (to which François could not have been sent for political reasons), to provide him with financial independence, and in general to do what he could to give him the best chance in life.

Louis Bonaparte, of whom his mother had once said, "This unfortunate Louis has turned himself into a Dutchman, and he is not French at all any more",

> *Ce pauvre Louis s'est fait hollandais, et il n'est plus français du tout...*

wanted François to be brought up as a Frenchman. This is clear from his letters to him, and even though he gave him an Italian surname, his Christian names were French. He would naturally have looked for someone financially as well as socially suitable, and of French nationality. It is not surprising that his eye should have lit on Elise de Bruges le Camps. It is no disparagement to Elise to note that the number of young ladies in Tuscany meeting these requirements cannot have been unlimited.

The only reference to Marcel de Bruges de Camps I have found in our papers is in an unnamed French language newspaper probably published in Italy in which he is described as a "riche et honorable negociant français" [a rich and honorable French businessman]. A.P. had an idea that a family of this name was prominent in southern France but Monsieur Valynseele has found no trace of it, nor of the title of Count which Marcel used. He had long been settled in Florence, but in view of his intimate ties to Suzanne Sophie it is likely that he had lived for some time in Paris before moving south. He appears to have been devoted to her and to their daughter, Suzette, as well as to

Elise her half-sister. He conferred on her a dowry of 110,00 Francs and a place with garden and dependencies which he owned in Florence at 16 Via dei Benci, in which Suzette retained a life interest. According to René Puaux the latter was born on or about January 1, 1831. He quotes from her Certificate of Baptism at the cathedral of Livorno dated January 4, 1831 in the name of Adelaide Anne Suzanne Caroline, "issu de lui et de Mme Suzanne de Camps." From this it would seem that Suzanne Sophie arrived in Florence to join Marcel with little Elise in the early months of 1830, when she was about 3½ years old.

So far as I know Elise lived with Louis in the Via dei Benci for about 8 years after they were married, until they moved to Paris with Elise's mother a few months after Marcel's death. (Sept 5, 1854) and the birth of their second daughter, Louise, (Sept 18, 1854). Elise's father, Charles Thomas d'Etreillis, was still living in Paris at the time and only died October 10, 1865.

The de Larderel Connection

The family's ties to the de Larderels were established by Suzette de Bruges de Camps, half-sister of Elise. The founder of the financial and social fortunes was François Larderel, a Frenchman from the Dauphiné, who was in the hardware and cutlery business. He crossed the Alps in order to promote and sell his wares in the early nineteenth century. He hit upon the idea of exploiting the mineral deposits, chiefly borax, in Tuscany, and settled in Livorno in 1810. He prospered greatly and founded a mining and refining centre in the region, which was named Larderello. François became Francesco, and such was his success that the Grand Duke of Tuscany conferred on him the title of Count of Montecerboli. His elder son, Federico, died in 1876, while the younger, Adriano, married Suzette (1831–86). Their daughter Elise (1850–1902) married her cousin Florestano de

Larderel (1848 – 1925) a son of Federico.

Adriano predeceased Suzette, who then went to live in Pisa with the Marchese Cesare Mastiani-Sciamanna (1820 – 1906) at his Palazzo Upezzinghi (previously Lanfreducci). From the inscription on the façade it was known as "Alla Giornata", and is now part of the University of Pisa. "Uncle Sciemanna", as he was known in the family, had been the last Chamberlain of the Court of the Grand Duke, Leopold II, until the latter's abdication in 1859, when Tuscany was incorporated into the kingdom of Italy. He was said to have been devoted to Suzette. He married her on her death-bed. My mother writes that he kept, and carefully looked after her clothes and possessions after her death. He later married a Swiss woman, Martha Konrad. My mother and Linetta stayed with him in Pisa for some time after the break-up of their mother's marriage in London in 1884-85, and they both had fond memories of him. We have two photographs of him which suggest that he was indeed lively and amusing.

The name de Larderel is today perpetuated by Count Folco Aloisi de Larderel, who lives in Mexico, and by his sons Francesco, married to a Guicciandini, who lives in Rome, and Corso, married to a French woman, who lives in Paris. Folco is the grandson of Elisa and Florestano de Larderel.

I am greatly indebted to the Marchesa Fiammetta Gondi, Folco's first cousin, for her interest and most generous assistance to me in my quest for reconstructing the Castelvecchio-de Larderel relationship, and for much other interesting information.

While Elise and Louis were living in Florence a friend of theirs, Jean-Baptiste Fortune de Fournier d'Ajaccio, whose name appears in various family documents and letters, painted in 1851 a charming miniature we have of Elise seated and wearing a bright blue dress, with a view of Florence in the background. He also painted nine years later a watercolor of Elise's bedroom in their apartment at 216 rue de Rivoli. According to Louis de Castelvecchio in a letter from which I have quoted below, he was an old friend of the Bonaparte family, and of the Comte de Saint-Leu in particular. He was born in Ajaccio in 1798 and died in Paris on February 17, 1864.

Elise and Louis had two children—both girls—while they were in Florence. The elder one, Marcellina (in French Marceline) also known as Lina, or Linetta, after whom A.P. was named, was born in 1848. As has been already noted, the second daughter, Louise, was born in 1854. Her name was chosen for her by Napoleon III and the Empress Eugénie, who arranged to be "dignement representées" [worthily represented] at her baptism by the French Minister in Florence. Louise's nickname was "Lucciola" meaning firefly, "probably because" explains A.P. in one of her notes, 'her eyes were very dark, but with a special glow".

I don't know how Louis occupied himself during the years he and Elise spent in Florence. One likes to think that "Maman", as he called his mother-in-law, and Marcel de Bruges le Camps helped to make life easy and pleasant for them.

Louis was "reçu a domicile" in France in 1853 and naturalized a French citizen on June 15, 1854. On July 1 he received a financial gift from the Emperor for which he signed a receipt, of which we have a copy. He was made an officer of the Order of Saints Maurice and Lazare. This ancient and prestigious Order was created in 1572 by Pope Gregory XIII, who united the two existing Orders of St. Maurice and St. Lazare under Philippe Emanuel, Duke of Savoy.

Paris (1855 - 1860)

I do not know the exact date of their move to Paris, but it was probably early in 1855. An article, which must have given them some concern, appeared in the press shortly before their arrival. I have neither the name nor the date of the paper. I have already quoted the reference to Marcel de Bruges de Camps.

"We cannot pass from society news to another subject without mentioning the coming arrival of Monsieur de Castelvecchio, an extremely close relative of the emperor. Mr. de Castelvecchio, to whom the will of the late King of Holland granted an inheritance of 200,000 francs [WRT comment: No, 100,000 Swiss francs=150,000 French] enjoys widespread esteem in Tuscany, where he married Mademoiselle Decamps, the daughter of a wealthy and honorable French businessman. After 1846 he pursued an active correspondence with the emperor, who urged him repeatedly to leave Florence and come to Paris. Hitherto Mr. de Castelvecchio, thoroughly modest and without ambition, indeed without any passion except for painting, declined to do so. Now, it appears that his resistance has been overcome and that he will soon appear at court, where naturally he already has his assigned place.

> *Nous ne pouvons laisser les nouvelles du monde sans parler de l'arrivée prochaine de Mr de Castelvecchio, bien proche parent de l'empereur. Mr de Castelvecchio, qui a eu par testament du feu roi de Hollande un legs de 200,000 francs [This is wrong. It was 100,000 Swiss Francs, the equivalent of 150,000 French Francs] jouit en Toscane d'une grande considération. Il y a épousé Mlle Decamps, fille d'un riche et honorable négociant français. Après 1846 il était en correspondance suivie avec l'empereur, qui l'a plus d'une fois engagé à quitter Florence pour Paris. Jusqu'ici Mr de Castevecchio, très modeste, sans ambition, sans passions si ce n'est le goût de la peinture, avait refusé; il parait que sa résistance est vaincue et qu'on le verra bientôt à la Cour, où naturellement sa place est marquée.*

On the other side of the piece of paper onto which this text was copied, is a draft letter to a "Monsieur le Comte" in Louis' handwriting: "I have read in the paper an article that concerns me. I dare to hope that if this article comes to the attention of His Majesty, His Majesty will be good enough to believe that I had nothing to do with it. Should it be otherwise, however, allow me to beg you to assure the emperor of my deep and respectful devotion and to let him know that I had no part in it, and that I knew nothing about it."

> *J'ai lu dans le journal xxx [sic] un article qui me concerne. J'ose espérer que S. M. si cet article arrive jusqu'à elle voudra bien croire que j'y suis étranger. Mais dans le cas où il en serait autrement, permettez-moi de vous prier de vouloir bien, en assurant l'Empereur de mes sentiments de profond et respectueux dévouement, lui faire savoir que je n'y ai pris aucune part, et que je l'ignorais totalement.*

Although not entirely accurate, the article was obviously written by someone well informed on the personal affairs of Louis, probably in early 1855. On February 18, 1856, Louis entered the Ministry of Foreign Affairs as an "attaché surnuméraire" in the political section. On December 30th of that year he was assigned to the Cabinet of the Foreign Minister, Alexandre Walewski, son of Napoleon I and Countess Marie Walewska. He remained there for three years, until January 4, 1860, when Walewski was replaced following a difference with the Emperor over policy toward Italy.

In January 1857, Louis' third daughter, Josephine, was born at 216 rue de Rivoli (corner of the rue d'Alger). In early July of the same year, Elise and he went to Switzerland to visit Schloss Arenenberg, where Queen Hortense (d. 1837) had spent her last years. A letter from his friend Dr. Conneau (the Emperor's physician) gives him instructions on how to get there. It was written on June 26, 1857:

> To reach Arenenberg you must first go to Basel and then, if you must spend the night there, leave by the Baden train line for Schaffhouse. Since the Schaffhouse train does not actually go all the way there, you must reserve seats in the coach. You will spend the night at Schaffhouse, and if you do so at the hotel built before the falls, you will see the Rhine Falls without having to make

any extra effort to do so. The steamboat leaves Schaffhouse early for Constance. However, you will reserve seats on it only as far as Ermatingen, where you will disembark after passing below Arenenberg, which you will see from the lake. At Arenenberg you will find the concierge, Florentin, formerly Queen Hortense's coachman. The man really responsible for Arenenberg, Mr. Ammann, is at Ermatingen. You will give him my letter and you will convey my warmest compliments to him and to the charming Madame Ammann. You will tell her [them?] that we hope to see her [them?] in Paris.

Good-by, my dear Mr. Castelvecchio. My compliments to Madame Castel[vecchio] and to her mother; and kiss the children for me.

Your devoted
Dr. Conneau

Pour aller à Arenenberg, il faut se diriger sur Bâle, et si vous êtes obligé à dormir à Bâle, partir par le chemin de fer Balois pour Schaffhouse. Comme le chemin de fer de Schaffhouse ne conduit pas jusqu'à cette ville, il faut s'assurer des places dans la diligence. Vous dormez à Schaffhouse, mais en logeant à l'Hôtel en face de la Chute, vous voyez la chute du Rhin sans vous donner la peine d'aller la chercher. On part de bonne heure de Schaffhouse pour Constance par le bateau à vapeur. Cependant vous ne prenez vos places que jusqu'à Ermatingen où vous descendez, après avoir passé sous Arenenberg que vous voyez du lac. Vous trouverez à Arenenberg le Concierge qui s'appelle Florentin, ancient cocher de la Reine Hortense. A Ermatingen se trouve Mr. Ammann qui est le vrai Régisseur d'Arenenberg. Vous lui donnerez ma lettre et vous présenterez à lui et à la charmante Mme Ammann nos complimens [sic] les plus empressés et les plus sincères. Vous lui direz que nous espérons la voir à Paris.

Adieu, mon cher Monsieur Castelvecchio, mille choses amiables de notre part à Madame Castel [sic] et à la Mère, et embrassez les

enfans [sic].
Tout à vous, votre très devoué et très sincère
Dr. Conneau

One can assume either that Louis had asked the Emperor whether he had any objection to their going on this visit, or that he himself had suggested it. Louis would certainly never have undertaken it without the Emperor's knowledge and approval.

While they were still in Paris (i.e., before 1861), their fourth child, a son christened Adrien, was born, but he died in infancy, perhaps in 1862. He may have been named after Adriano de Larderel, the husband of Suzette de Bruges de Camps.

Napoleon III would have liked Louis and his family to move to Paris from Florence earlier that they did. Louis' delay was because of his family ties in Florence: Elise's mother and her "husband" Marcel, who had been very loyal to both of them. It cannot have been easy for Louis not to respond with alacrity to such an invitation. However, honorable his motives, it would be understandable if the Emperor felt somewhat impatient. In the draft of a letter composed after he had been working at the quai d'Orsay for some time (perhaps 1859?), Louis explains to the Emperor what had been his reasons for delaying his move to Paris: "…the pain that I would have caused the man who who had been a father to my wife, in depriving him of her, and, on the other hand, the thought that my resources would have been insufficient for life in Paris, decided me to return to Florence. The following year I received the same warm greeting from Your Majesty, and both Your Majesty and Her Majesty the Empress urged us to remain in Paris; and Your Majesty, speaking to my eldest daughter, who at the time was six years old [Marceline, born October 12, 1848] said, 'Do you think you are doing the right thing by your parents, to be taking them back to Florence?' Not wishing to be a burden upon you, I declined again, despite being somewhat shaken in my resolve. I changed my mind completely when, the next year, the death of my father-in-law freed me from that tie that bound me to Florence."

> *le chagrin que j'aurais fait à celui qui avait tenu lieu de père à ma femme, en le privant d'elle, et - d'un autre côté la pensée que ma fortune n'avait pas suffi pour rester à Paris, me déterminèrent de rentrer à Florence. L'année d'après je reçus de V. M. le même accueil affectueux, et V.M. ainsi que S. M. l'Impératrice nous pressèrent de rester à Paris; et V.M. s'adressant à ma fille ainée qui avait alors six ans [Marceline was born Oct. 12, 1848], lui dit : Tu crois donc leur faire du bien, à tes parents, en les ramenant à Florence? Ne voulant pas vous être à charge, je refusai encore quoique ébranlé dans ma résolution. Je changeai d'avis entièrement, lorsque l' année suivante, mon Beau-Père étant mort, je me trouvais dégagé de ce côté des liens qui me retenaient à Florence.*

He goes on to complain to the Emperor about his situation in the Ministry: "I hoped that Your Majesty would not make me dependent upon the good will of a Minister."

> *J'espérais que V.M. ne me ferait pas dépendre du bon vouloir d'un Ministre.*

He feels that the way the Emperor had previously spoken to him had justified him in expecting something better.....

I don't know whether this letter was ever sent off, or whether Louis drafted it only to relieve his frustration. For his sake I hope the latter was the case. On July 9 1861, he wrote to "Monsieur Thélin aux Tuileries", evidently a Court official close to the Emperor: "I deeply regret the Emperor's reply, which seems meant to make me regret my answer to him six years ago! However, I have great confidence, despite being sorry to see certain favors doled out to me in only a *measured* way."

> *Je regrette bien la réponse de l'Empereur : elle a l'air de vouloir me faire repentir ma réponse d'il y a six ans ! - mais je suis plein de confiance quoique je regrette de me voir mesurer certaines faveurs.*

He evidently still feels that the Emperor is not as responsive to his desires as he had hoped. The reference to his own reply of six years ago presumably concerns his reluctance to move to Paris, as the Emperor had pressed him to do, because of family considerations which Marcel de Burges de Camps' death shortly thereafter were to remove.

Elise de Castelvecchio

François Louis' signature in 1860

Joséphine de Castelvecchio
Portrait by Coedès, 1860

Nice (1860 - 1867)

Not long after the replacement of Walewski as Foreign Minister in early January 1860, Louis was appointed "Trésorier Payeur Général des Finances du département des Alpes-Maritimes" at Nice, to which he and his family moved that same year. Possibly this was the result of his plea that the Emperor give him a position with greater authority and independence. It was evidently at this time that the following incident occurred, as reported by Labarre de Raillicourt in his biography of Louis Bonaparte, pp. 466-67, footnote no. 17:

"Castelvecchio astonishingly resembled Napoleon III. In about 1860 Alfred Maury, the librarian of the Tuileries and the future director of the Archives, wrote: "I was in waiting near the emperor's private quarters [*cabinet*] when I saw enter, led by the usher Félix, a man who struck me by his physical resemblance to the man whose presence he was about to enter. His expression and eyes were exactly those of Napoleon III. I asked Félix for his name.

"That," he told me, "is le Comte de Castelvecchio, newly appointed *receveur politique* [should be *receveur des finances*] of the department of the Alpes-Maritimes." And he added with a laugh, "He is the emperor's brother. He is a bastard son of King Louis."

> *Castelvecchio ressemblait étonnament à Napoléon III. Vers 1860 Alfred Maury, bibliothécaire des Tuileries et futur directeur des archives, écrivait : 'Etant de service près du cabinet de l'Empereur, j'y vis entrer conduit par l'huissier Félix, un personnage qui me frappa par la ressemlance plysique qu'il avait précisément avec celui près duquel il était introduit. C'était toute l'expression du regard de Napoléon III. Je demandai son nom à Félix: "c'est me dit-il, M. le Comte de Castelvecchio, nouvellement nommé receveur politique [sic!] du département des Alpes-Maritimes... » Et il ajouta en riant : «c'est le frère de l'Empereur, il est fils naturel du roi Louis ...*

The date must have been after November 7, 1860, when Louis was made Count by imperial decree, being thereby also entitled to the particle *de* before his name.

In a long *letter to Gioia written in 1958*, A.P. writes: "From Aunt Lucciola—and from nobody else—I heard that the reason for his leaving the Foreign Office was a 'scandal' about grandmother and one of their friends, 'mon ami Bosino' of whom I knew nothing else at all, except a carte-de-visite size photograph that there was, like so many others, in a family album."

A.P. also mentions this story in her notes adding that she doesn't believe it. The man allegedly involved was Charles Jules Labarte, brother-in-law of Marcel de Bruges de Camps,[1] whose sister, Joséphine Sophie Gisèle de Bruges-Dumesnil he had married. Louise ("Lucciola") was 5 or 6 in 1860, according to the month of the year. Had there been such a scandal it is unlikely

---

[1] In notes headed "Told me by Aunt Lucciola in August 1924," A.P. connected the scandal with "Mr. Henri Labatte (a relation of the de Bruges de Camps)." (RT)

that François Louis de Castelvecchio would have received the title of Count, and been named to a position of responsibility. As we shall see later, Louise turned against her grandmother from the time of her marriage.

We are fortunate in having among Louis' papers a record of letters written by him from Nice, between March 1861 and May 1862. The record consists partly of full copies of letters and partly of a summary of a letter's substance. During this period Elise became gravely ill, both physically and emotionally, to the point where their very marriage was endangered. In addition it was beset by severe financial problems.

The first of these letters, dated March 3, 1861 to Countess Walewska, recounts the health problems of Elise and the children: "We would be happy at Nice, were it not for the distance that separates us from Paris and the character of the air, which does not at all suit a family. Madame de Castelvecchio is so unwell that I can foresee the time when I might have to let her go to a climate in which the air is less *excitant* [stimulating? excites one less]. She grows paler and thinner day by day, and the children, although so far unaffected by any major illness, are constantly indisposed. Even today, the doctor has just diagnosed that our Baby has a mucous fever [*fièvre muqueuse*]. You cannot imagine how greatly this torments us!"

> *Nous serions heureux à Nice sans la distance qui le sépare de Paris, et surtout sans les qualités de l'air qui ne convient pas du tout à ma famille. Madame de Castelvecchio est si souffrante que je vois venir le moment où je devrais la laisser aller dans un climat où l'air soit moins excitant : elle pâlit et maigrit tous les jours, et les enfants, sans avoir encore eu de grandes maladies, n'ont cesse d'être indisposées.*
> *Aujourd'hui même le médecin vient de déclarer que notre Baby a une fièvre muqueuse. Vous ne sauriez croire combien nous sommes tourmentés de cela !*

However, the real purpose of this letter is not to tell Countess Walewska about the family's health problems, but to get her to intervene with her husband on Louis' behalf in order to obtain for him the Legion of Honor. For this decoration, however, he had to wait for almost another six years.

There is a *letter of March 8, 1861*, addressed to "Mme S. de Camps" at Casa Palamidessi, Lungo Arno, Pisa. This reveals that friendly relations existed between Elise's mother and the Palamedissi family of Pescia many years before Josephine married Francesco Palamidessi. At the time, this letter was written, she was 4 and he was 11 or 12. It is also the only indication I have come across that the Palamidessis owned a house at Pisa, which suggests that they were comfortably off. "Mme S. de Camps" cannot have been Suzette, Elisa's half-sister, because she was Comtesse Adriano de Larderel, and earlier had been Mademoiselle, not Madame de Camps.

The following letters from Louis to Elise and her doctor, Dr. Conneau, who was also a personal friend, give me an idea of the crisis they were going through.

Aug 6, 1861 to Dr. Conneau:
"Details concerning Elise's health—she will not touch food—can never sleep—pain and intermittent paralysis caused by her lying position—It is necessary to lift her up and place her in a sitting position, despite her cries, in order to get her through it—written opinions received from Arnal and Léon Simon—discouragement, sadness—air burns her lungs—wishes not to struggle any longer—she tried out the climate from August 1860 to April 1861—request a medical examination."

> *Détails sur la santé d'Élise—dégoût pour le manger—le sommeil manque complètement—souffrances et paralysie momentanées causées par la position horizontale—il faut la soulever et l'asseoir malgré ses cris pour que cela lui passe—consulations eues par écrit de Arnal et Léon Simon—découragement, tristesse—l'air lui brûle la poitrine—désir de ne pas continuer l'épreuve—elle a essayé le climat depuis le mois d'août 1860 au mois d'avril 1861—demander une consultation.*

Aug 9, 1861, to Dr. Conneau:
"I fear that my letter of the 6th may have alarmed you. Its purpose was to inform you regarding the state of Elise's health and to ask you, our friend, for the opinion that affection may prompt a doctor to give. If Elise must leave here, I will send her to Paris, near you, or to Passy, to the house that we bought there, and I will stay here until it becomes possible for me to be reassigned. Bordeaux has already been mentioned to me, since the incumbent is soon to reach retirement age. Should the emperor be willing to place me there I could see Elise without requesting leave, since a Receveur Général de Bordeaux always has some position at the Bank or at the Crédit Foncier. But what matters above all is Elise's health. Please give me your opinion and accept my assurances of sincere friendship."

> *Je crains que ma lettre du 6 vous ait effrayé. Son but était de vous instruire de l'état de la santé d'Elise et de vous demander à vous, notre ami, l'avis que l'affection peut dicter au médecin. S'il faut qu'Elise quitte ce pays je la placerai à Paris près de vous, ou à Passy à la maison que nous avons achetée, et je resterai ici jusqu'à ce qu'il fut [sic] possible d'être changé. Déjà on m'a parlé de Bordeaux qui deviendra vacant (par limite d'âge). Si l'Empereur voulait me mettre là, comme les Receveurs généraux de Bordeaux sont toujours quelquechose à la Banque ou au Crédit Foncier, je pourrais voir Elise sans demander de congé —mais avant tout c'est la santé d'Elise qui prime. Veuillez me dire votre avis et croyez à ma vive et sincère amitié.*

August 26, 1861, to Dr. Conneau:
Louis starts with a note to himself on how Dr Conneau might have reacted to his previous letter. "I was quite worried because I feared to have upset him. I did not want to arm myself with his opinion in order to put in for a different posting. I only wanted advice from a doctor who is also a friend."

J'ai été très affecté car je craignais de lui avoir fait de la peine. Je ne voulais pas me faire fort de son avis pour réclamer un autre poste. Je désirais seulement avoir le conseil d'un ami médecin.

Then he starts the letter in quotation marks. "Please note that the costs are enormous, that the climate has already forced me to make two difficult and expensive journeys, that my income is small in comparison with what I spend, and that the children are growing—growing up far from anyone concerned with their welfare. But none of this matters (I cannot repeat this too often) in comparison with the most important reason of all: Elise's health. Was I wrong? That is possible, as you agree. For myself, I wish without daring to hope. Last year I feared the expense, the trouble, and the consequences of a journey to Paris. For too long I fought this project that the influence of the climate had brought to mind, but in the end I had to give in. Elise and, especially, the children came back as though they had bathed in the Fountain of Youth!

Was this an illusion? Perhaps it was, and we are now going to repeat the experiment! May God grant it success! I would be only too glad, my dear doctor and friend, to say to you that you did not let yourself be influenced by the desire to see us happy where we are.

In any case, and whatever decision necessity may ultimately force me to take, I cannot thank you enough for having expressed yourself so clearly and openly to me. The doctor, enlightened by the friend, must in the end advise us to wait and see what we can do; and I am sure that time will enlighten us further on this matter!"

Veuillez remarquer que les frais sont énormes, que le climat m'a déjà obligé à deux voyages pénibles et chers, et les rentrées sont petites en proportion des dépenses et que les enfants grandissent, et grandissent loin de ceux qui peuvent leur porter intérêt. Mais tous ces motifs cèdent le pas, je ne saurais trop le répéter, à la raison majeure de la santé d'Elise. Me trompé-je ? Cela est possible et vous êtes de cet avis là. Pour moi je le désire sans oser l'espérer. L'année passée je redoutais les frais, les ennuis, les suites d'un voyage à Paris. J'ai trop longtemps combattu ce projet que l'influence du climat avait faire naître, mais enfin il a fallu s'y décider. Elise et surtout les enfants, sont revenues comme si elles avaient été trempées dans la Fontaine de Jouvence!

Est-ce une illusion ? Je le veux bien, et nous allons recommencer l'expérience. Dieu fasse qu'elle réussisse !! Je serai trop heureux, mon cher Docteur et Ami, de vous dire que vous ne vous êtes pas laisser influencer par le désir de nous voir heureux là où nous sommes.

De toute manière et quelle que soit la décision ultérieure que la nécessité me force à prendre, je ne saurais assez vous remercier de m'avoir parlé si clairemement, si ouvertement.

Le médecin éclairé par l'ami doit au fond conseiller d'attendre et de voir ce que nous pourrons faire; et je suis sûr que le temps nous éclairera mieux sur cette question.

August 18, 1861 to Dr Conneau:
"...Elise no longer wishes to leave, but her condition worsens day by day. I do not know what to do. There is something burning her beneath her heart!..."

Elise ne veut plus partir, mais elle empire tous les jours. Je ne sais que faire. Elle a quelquechose qui la brûle au dessous du coeur!..

On Nov 14, 1861, he writes to Dr. Conneau:
"...Elise's pain grows worse every day, and the new symptoms now appearing force upon us the decision to send her to Paris in order to consult with the most famous physicians and then to look after herself. She has promised to look after herself..."

Les douleurs d'Elise qui augmentent tous les jours et les nouveaux symptômes qui apparaissent nous forcent à prendre la résolution d'envoyer Elise à Paris consulter des célébrités et ensuite de se soigner. Elle a promis de se soigner ...

Elise leaves Nice for Paris (Hotel Windsor, 226 rue de Rivoli) on November 18th and Louis writes to a woman who is obviously a close friend of theirs, Mme Oleermayer, at 162 rue de Rivoli: "This time I fear for everything: for her, for her health, for her absurd courage, for Baby, should a crisis strike her on the way! Why is this happening? Is there a moral to be derived from it? Try to discover this secret, if it exists; try to find out, and please let me know what it is, however painful it may be, because I am determined to save her, if possible. I beg you to keep me abreast of her condition and to send me a telegram if any particular need should arise! Thank you in advance.

P.S. Elise undertook to reimburse you for the expenses that you kindly incurred on our behalf!"

> *Cette fois j'ai peur de tout, d'elle, de sa santé, de son courage absurde, de Baby si un étourdissement la prenait en route !.. Quelle est la cause ? Y-en-a-t'il [sic] une morale ? Ce secret, s'il existe, tâchez de le savoir et veuillez me le communiquer quelque douloureux qu'il puisse être, car je suis résolu à tout pour la sauver, s'il se peut. Je vous prie de bien vouloir me tenir au courant de sa santé et de m'écrire une dépêche télégraphique si un besoin quelconque arrivait ! Merci d'avance.*
>
> *P.S. Elise s'est chargée de vous remettre le montant des dépenses que vous avez bien voulu faire pour nous !*

The part about a possible secret (which, if it exists, he would wish to know about, however painful it might be) is curious. Does he have suspicions about another man?

Louis writes to Elise on November 26 asking for news of her health. He asks her not to press too much for them to leave Nice. On the 27th he writes again: "Thank you for your letter. Why are you so loving from a distance, and why do you seem so unhappy when nearby? I used to entertain certain illusions—I had become accustomed to count on you as upon Providence, and to me our marriage announced the future happiness that God had granted me. Why do you not look after yourself?

Thank you for all the details regarding your health! Always tell me the whole truth! A 400-franc apartment all for yourself—that is a lot. *Must* you stay there? Kiss Baby for me. I prefer your love to your devotion, particularly since the former includes the latter…"

> *Merci de ta lettre. Pourquoi es-tu si affectueuse de loin, et pourquoi as-tu l'air malheureuse de près? Je me faisais des illusions autrefois – je m'étais habitué à compter sur toi comme sur ma Providence, et je regardais notre mariage comme le gage de bonheur futur que Dieu m'avait donné. Pourquoi ne te soignes tu pas ?... Merci des détails de ta santé ! - dis-moi toujours toute la vérité ! Un appartement de 400 Francs pour toi toute seule, c'est beaucoup - est-ce que tu dois rester? Embrasse Baby pour moi - J'aime mieux ton amour que ton dévouement : d'abord le premier comprend le dernier ….*

It is clear that Louis is in great distress not only about Elise's state of health, but about her feelings towards him.

His *letter of December 17* to her reveals the intensity of the crisis:

> "My dear Elise, I open your letter of the 15th, and you tell me that I am reproaching you. No, dear Elise, I do not reproach you at all, I only open my heart to you. To whom might I convey my true feelings for you, if not to yourself? You do not want me to, what I say hurts you. I will say no more. Look after yourself then, that is all I ask of you.
>
> As for myself, I will get on as best I can. However, if the Friend [*Amie*] that you offer me in place of the wife [*compagne*] that I am losing could only grant me a little confidence and latitude… from so far away… there would be no danger… since a danger does exist!
>
> But let us say no more about that. Look after yourself and get better: that must be your only care. Believe only that I never wanted to cause you sorrow; that I was sorrowing myself; and that the excess overflowed. But my miserable failure pains me greatly,

and I protest once more my devotion to you in all things. Forgive me, then, since what I wrote hurt you, and believe that to my last breath I will be your devoted *Friend!*"

Ma chère Elise, j'ouvre ta lettre du 15 et tu me dis que je te fais des reproches. Non, chère Elise, ce ne sont pas des reproches que te fais, mais je t'ouvre mon cœur. A qui dirais-je quels sont mes sentiments pour toi, si ce n'est à toi-même?

Tu ne le veux pas, cela te blesse – Je ne t'en parlerai plus- Soigne-toi donc, c'est tout ce que je te demande.

Moi, je ferai comme je pourrai !.. Si cependant l'Amie que tu m'offres en place de la compagne que je perds m'accordait un peu de confiance et d'expansion… de si loin… il n'y aurait aucun danger… puisque danger [il] y a !

Mais n'en parlons plus, soigne-toi et guéris, ce doit être là ta seule préoccupation. Persuade-toi seulement que je n'ai jamais voulu te faire de la peine, que moi j'en avais et que le trop déborde-mais puisque j' ai si mal réussi, j'en suis fâché et je proteste encore de mon dévouement pour toi en tout et pour tout! Pardonne-moi donc puisque malgré moi je t'ai fait du mal en t'écrivant, et crois que je serai jusqu'à la mort ton tout dévoué Ami !

On December 18 Louis drafts the following letter, through which he afterwards drew an ink-stroke, also writing on the margin: "non envoyée" [not sent].

"My dear *Friend*, I have just received your letter of the 16th… which confirms the one of the 15th! I read there that you will be only my *Friend*! The mother of my children is *my friend*, as much so as anyone else with who I might enjoy some sort of friendly relations. My friend Garroni, for example, now occupies exactly the same level as you in my affections. I like and respect Garroni, God knows, and any chilling of his feeling for me would certainly affect me. What am I to think of what you propose? My heart pains me, I assure you, and I reproach myself a thousand times for not having known how better to win your love!...

But I promised you yesterday to say nothing more on this subject, and I remain silent. Are you yourself, though, quite sure that, when you are better, you will be pleased with what you propose? Perfect though you are, will human nature never manifest itself in you? Would it not be playing with fire to wish to preserve with me—who, after all, have memories that, alone, put fire in my heart—a simple, honest friendship?

As far as your return here is concerned, it is exclusively for your sake that your mother and I agree that you should stay. Should it be necessary for you to come to Nice and to interrupt your treatment in order to prepare to leave, it seems to me that that should only happen only if you were *never* going to live in Nice. [I don't understand what he means.] But do you not think that if you recover soon, as I hope you will, you will be able to return here for the winter months of next year? And, in that case, why incur new expenses? Besides, between now and 15 January we have time to talk all that over, since you tell me in any case that you will not be able to return before then...

...Good-by, and save at least your friendship for me! Do you remember our first years? Does it not seem to you that we breathed in heady fragrances? The air is dry today, youth's illusions drop away, and chill of evening brings solitude, especially in the heart! Good-by! Can you tell me when you will shake my hand like a friend?

Louis

P.S. I re-read your letter of the 16th, and the idea I mentioned, that someone may have spoken ill of me to you, apparently offended you. However, I insist on defending myself by citing something that you said to me a long time ago with reference to Suzette, which could easily suggest such notions. You once said to me, "Is it possible to let a man know that one is jealous! As for me, I would rather die!"

Ma chère Amie, je viens de recevoir ta lettre du 16… qui confirme celle du 15! Il est dit que tu ne seras que mon Amie! La Mère de mes enfants est mon amie, aussi bien qu'une personne quelleconque [sic] avec laquelle je pourrais avoir eu quelques rapports d'amitié. Mon ami Garroni, par exemple, doit donc venir exactement sur la même ligne que toi dans mon affection! J'aime et j'estime Garroni, Dieu le sait, et un refroidissement de sa part me ferait une vive impression- que dois-je penser de la proposition que tu me fais ? – J'ai le cœur serré, je te l'assure et je me fais mille reproches de n'avoir pas su captiver d'avantage ton affection !...

Mais hier je t'ai promis de ne plus rien te dire à ce sujet – et je me tais mais, toi-même, es-tu bien sûre que lorsque tu seras guérie tu séras enchantée de la proposition? Pour parfaite que tu sois, est-ce que la nature humaine ne paraîtra jamais en toi? Est-ce que ce ne sera pas jouer avec le feu si tu veux conserver avec moi - qui après tout ai des souvenirs qui à eux seuls réchauffent mon cœur – une franche amitié?

Quant à ton retour ici, c'est dans ton seul et unique intérêt que nous pensions, Maman et moi, qu'il te conviendrait de rester. S'il est nécessaire que tu viennes à Nice et que tu interrompes ta cure pour faire des arrangements de depart, ce ne serait, il me semble, que dans le cas où tu ne devrais jamais habiter Nice. Mais ne penses-tu pas que si tu guéris bientôt comme je l'espère, tu pourras revenir ici pour les mois d'hiver de l'année prochaine? Et, dans ce cas, pourquoi faire de nouvelles dépenses? Du reste, d'ici au 15 janvier nous avons le temps de causer de cela puisque dans tous les cas tu me dis que tu ne pourras pas revenir avant cette époque-là …

…Au revoir, et conserve-moi au moins ton amitié! - Te souviens-tu de nos premières années? Ne te semble-t'il pas que nous respirions des parfums enivrants? L'air est sec aujourd'hui, les illusions de la

jeunesse tombent, et avec le froid du soir vient la solitude dans le cœur surtout! Au revoir! Peux-tu me dire quand tu me serreras la main en amie?

Louis

PS: Je relis ta lettre du 16 et l'idée que j'ai émise que l'on pouvait t'avoir parlé contre moi a paru t'offenser. Je tiens cependant à me justifier en te citant une phrase que tu m'as dite il y a longtemps en songeant à Suzette et qui pouvait bien dénoter des idées dans ce sens. Ainsi - tu dis une fois « Peut-on montrer à un homme qu'on est jaloux!.. Pour moi je mourrais plutôt! »

Letter of December 20

"My dear Elise, your letter of the 16th struck me dumb. So you are really determined! You will be no more than my *friend*. This word, so sweet on the lips of others, seems to me very cold—almost an insult—a disavowal of the past. Did I then misunderstand my mission, since every man has his own! I reproach myself a thousand times for not having known how to move your heart. But these are useless regrets that can have no effect but hurting you. So I will say no more.

Your mother and I have discussed the subject of the letter that you sent me. For various reasons I do not see your travel, and its consequent cost and fatigue, as necessary. As far as the things that you need are concerned, Mother, Josephine, and I are available to send you whatever you ask for. Moreover, the issue could hardly be a full-scale move. You can take only furnished lodgings until it is decided whether or not you are to come back to live in Nice; that is to say, until next winter. Your two trips therefore seem very close to each other, and they will be followed by the one made by the children and mother! Considering the resulting expenses for me and the fatigue for you, I believe that you would do better to stay—especially since, according to Dr. Conneau, the climate here is not good for you.

As for myself, please understand how much such advice costs me—especially after your letter! …I might hope that talking over the subject in a friendly manner, face to face, might shed light on a situation that I find so painful. But my concern must go first of all to your health, and then to the interests of the children, whom whom I now wish to look after diligently. Please help me to do that! Linette is 13 years old and will soon be 14! Time is passing, and what will we have to give her?"

Ma chère Elise, Ta lettre du 16 m'a pétrifié. C'est donc une détermination bien arrêtée. Tu ne seras que mon amie - ce nom si doux dans de bouches étrangères me parait bien froid, presque une offense - un désaveu du passé. Aurai-je donc mal compris ma mission, puisque tout homme a la sienne! Je me fais mille reproches de n'avoir pas su mieux réchauffer ton cœur ! Mais ce sont des regrets intutiles et qui ne peuvent aboutir qu'à te faire de la peine, ce que je ne veux pas du tout. Donc je me tais.

Maman et moi avons causé de ce qui fait le sujet de la lettre que tu m'as écrite. Sous bien des rapports je ne vois pas que ton voyage, et la dépense et la fatigue que cela entraîne soient nécessaires. Pour les objets dont tu as besoin Maman, moi et Joséphine, nous sommes là pour t'envoyer tout ce que tu demanderas. Il ne peut s'agir, d'ailleurs, de faire un déménagement. Tu ne peux loger qu'en garni jusqu'à ce qu'il soit décidé, si tu dois où non revenir demeurer à Nice, c'est à dire d'ici à l'hiver prochain. Tes deux voyages paraissent donc bien rapprochés et ils seront suivis de celui des enfants et de Maman! Eu égard aux dépenses que cela me force à faire et aux fatigues que cela te procure, je crois qu'il te convient de rester. Surtout depuis que Mr. Conneau dit que le climat t'est nuisible.

Quant à moi, tu dois comprendre combien un tel conseil me coûte - surtout après ta lettre! Je pourrais espérer qu'une explication amicable et de vive voix entre nous éclaircirait une situation pour moi des plus pénibles - mais je dois avoir en vue avant tout ta santé, ensuite les intérêts des enfants que je veux soigner maintenant assidûment. Aide-moi à cela, je te prie! Linette a 13 bientôt 14 ans! Le temps passe et que lui donnerons nous?

December 21 (note to himself)

Answer to her letter of the 20th. I cannot make a promise that I am unsure of being able to hold, if the sun further heats our feelings. Is it not an insult to tell me that my affection has to do only with the material bond that she wishes to break? I did not want to mention it, but she says to me again in her letter, "It does not help to say, 'Let us say no more about it.'" I will therefore have to explain myself. Anyway, I am afraid that the more we discuss the subject, the less we will understand each other.

Réponse à sa lettre du 20. Je ne puis pas promettre ce que je ne suis pas parfaitement sûr de tenir si le soleil réchauffe encore nos sentiments. N'est-ce pas offensant de me dire que mon amitié tient uniquement au lien matériel qu'elle veut rompre! Je ne voulais pas lui en parler encore mais elle me dit dans sa lettre : « Il ne s'agit pas de dire : n'en parlons plus ! » Il faut que je m'explique. Je crains, du reste, que plus nous parlerons et moins nous nous entendrons sur ce sujet.

December 24

"Please never say again that 'Only material life makes me happy.' That is offensive. I never said that!"

Prière de ne plus dire que 'la vie matérielle fait seul mon bonheur'. Cela m'offense, et je n'ai jamais dit cela !

Same date (December 24): Letter to Dr. Conneau

"Ask him to please tell me what he thinks of Elise. His opinion is worth more than that of the entire Faculty of Medicine. To those gentlemen, Elise is a patient. To Dr. Conneau, she is a friend.

> *Prière de me dire ce qu'il pense d'Élise. Son avis vaut mieux que celui de la Faculté entière. Elise est un sujet pour ces Messieurs. Elle est une Amie pour Conneau.*

Poor Louis! On top of everything, he has to tell Elise that he has done his end of the year accounts, and that they show them to be in dire financial straits. Letters of January 7 and 8 (1862): "It is a terrible thing to say, but we have eaten up the greater part—almost all—of the capital that we saved at the treasury. We absolutely must economise strictly… Otherwise, I doubt that in six months I will be able to remain Receveur Général. I would be dismissed, and we would be ruined!"

> *C'est affreux à dire, mais nous avons mangé une grande partie - presque tout le capital que nous avions amassé au trésor: Il est absolument nécessaire que nous nous mettions à l'économie, à une stricte économie …*
>
> *Autrement je ne crois pas que dans 6 mois je pourrais rester Receveur Général. On me donnerait ma démission et nous serions ruinés !*

Needless to say, their financial situation reinforces his arguments in favour of Elise remaining in Paris. He also suggests that he send her the children (ie: Linetta, Louise and Josephine), and he summarizes the last part of his letter: "I protest that I love her and that I am more than ever decided to sacrifice everything for her!"

> *Je proteste que je l'aime, et que plus que jamais, je suis décidé à tous les sacrifices pour elle!*

Next day he returns to the problem of their financial situation. It would take several years, he writes, to make up their deficit, and to do this would require their spending not more than 20,000 F per annum. He wonders whether he shouldn't give up his present career and sell the post he now occupies to his successor. Elise's mother has suggested to him that she should take the children with her to Florence, "mais il y a des empêchements. *Lui* en est un grand! » *(but there are some obstacles. He is a big one!)*

Who is Lui? Suzette's husband, Adriano de Larderel? Louis writes that if the children were put in a boarding school, they could see their cousins and aunts (the de Larderel children and their mothers, and by implication - not "Lui)". Elise writes that she must be at Nice for Luisa's First Communion, while Louis tries to dissuade her by stressing the adverse climate and the expense of the trip, but leaving the decision entirely up to her. Elise has been undergoing hydrotherapy recommended by Dr. Arnal.

The identity of "Baby", "Bebe", "Babi" has been a puzzle to me. We know that Elise took "Baby" to Paris with her on November 18, 1861, when she left Nice in order to escape from the climate and receive medical care. I incline to think the "baby" is Adrien, their son, who died in infancy. Unfortunately, the child is never referred to by name, and on the rare occasion when a masculine or feminine personal pronoun is used, the context is uncertain, eg: in his letter to Mme Oleermayer, written on the day Elise left Nice, Louis writes [translation given above]:

Cette fois j'ai peur de tout, d'elle, de sa santé, de son courage absurde, de Baby si un étourdissement la prenait en route…

The *la* could apply to the child, but equally well—or more plausibly in the circumstances—to Elise herself. Then again, in Louis' last letter to Elise in this personal record of his correspondence, he writes on May 3 1862: "Kiss Babi and tell *lui* to give you a good kiss…"

Embrasse Babi [sic] et dis-lui de bien t'embrasser…

This would be conclusive but for the fact that in this context, *lui* is both masculine and feminine. However, if the child were a girl, one would expect this to be made explicit by writing

Embrasse Babi et dis-lui qu'elle t'embrasse bien …

We know that Louis and Elise had three daughters and a last child who died in infancy. It seems to me most unlikely that the youngest daughter, Josephine, should still be referred to as "Baby" in May 1862, when she would have nearly 5 1/2 years old. Moreover we know from Louis letter of December 20, 1861, that Josephine had stayed in Nice when Elise left for Paris in November.

Pursuing his efforts to discourage Elise from going to Nice, Louis writes a diplomatic letter to Dr. Arnal, whose undeclared but discernable purpose is to make it easy for him to advise Elise not to go. However she had been improving and the Doctor allowed her to go, and she left Paris on February 8, 1862 for Lyon where Louis met her on the following day.

Louis continued his efforts to be transferred from Nice. On February 25, he wrote to the Emperor's First Chamberlain, Count Baciocchi, asking for his help to get him appointed to "La Recette de Paris", and telling him that since her return to Nice, "Elise est retombée dans un etat de langueur nerveuse et morale" [Elise has relapsed into a state of nervous and moral exhaustion]. However, Louise efforts were in vain and he remained at Nice for another 5 years or so, when he was appointed to Rennes.

On April 22 Elise returned to Paris, and Louis wrote to Dr.Arnal : "As far as I can tell, it seems to me that her stay here has done her no good at all. However, I admit that there are days when appearances are deceiving—days when she looks less ill than she is, and, moreover, when her limbs are not, I believe, as thin as in other cases of chronic illness that I have seen."

> *Autant que je puisse en juger, il me semble qu'elle n'a rien gagné à son séjour ici. Cependant, je dois le dire, il y a des jours ou l'apparence trompe, où elle n'a pas l'air de souffrir autant qu'elle souffre et, de plus, ses membres ne sont pas, je crois, d'une telle maigreur comme j'en ai vu des exemples dans des maladies chroniques!*

The detailed description of symptoms, which follows, is however not at all reassuring.

The gloomy and pessimistic letters from which I have quoted shed light on Louis' personality as well as on the various problems facing him.

A final note on the dates of Adrien: In 1861 (August), Louis notes that he paid an unnamed painter 230F: "pour le portrait de Baby". Assuming that this portrait was painted in Paris just before the family left for Nice, which was in the second half of 1860, and that Adrien died in 1862, he would then have been about 3 years old - and less than 4.

The last letter we have from Louis in this miraculously preserved record of his letters in 1861-62, is to an underling who had written a letter (as it would be termed today) out of channels. It shows that Louis could crack a whip without worrying about bruising someone's ego:

Dear Sir,

M. Camson conveyed to me the content of your letter. Allow me to say that I find it strange that you should address yourself to my chief clerk for a matter that concerns my office. Your letters on this subject must be addressed to me. It is through me, in person, that all matters for which I am responsible must pass. I invite you to congratulate yourself less on the happy conduct of your own affairs and to waste less time on unofficial correspondence. I trust that you will take care in the future to avoid any further remarks from me.

Monsieur

> *Mr Camson m'a fait part du contenu de votre lettre. Permettez-moi de vous dire que je trouve étrange que vous vous adressiez en particulier à mon Fondé de Pouvoirs pour les affaires de service. Vos lettres de service doivent m'être adressées. C'est par moi, par ma main, que le service doit passer. Je vous invite à vous extasier moins sur la marche que vous trouvez si heureuse de votre service, et à perdre moins de temps à votre correspondence non officielle. J'espère que vous vous attacherez à éviter à l'avenir mes observations.*

The only other letter written by Louis de Castelvecchio that has survived, so far as I know, was sent by him to Elise, then at Bad Ems with the girls, less than 3 days before his death and was thus almost certainly received by her after this event.

Apparently Elise recovered her health and spirits after the dark months in 1861-62. Perhaps she spent part of the time in Paris, for we have a record of an address for her there (8 rue du Luxembourg). The financial crisis which had seemed so catastrophic to Louis at the end of 1861 must also have been overcome, for he remained in his post at Nice until his transfer to Rennes several years later.

I have been able to gather together some information on the family's financial resources, as follows.

The Family Finances

Under the Act of Donation of February 1843, and confirmed in his will, the Comte de Saint Leu gave Louis 100,000 Swiss Francs, equivalent to 150,000 French Francs.

In addition to her trousseau of the value of 7,000 Francs, Elise received in 1847 a dowry of 105,000 Francs from Marcel de Bruges de Camps.

In his will, Marcel de Bruges de Camps left Elise 200,000 Francs, and an additional 150,000 Francs, the interest on which was to be paid to Elisa's mother as life interest. However the estate proved insufficient for all the provisions of his will, and "de graves difficultés" arose in the course of interpreting it. In order to put an end to these, Elise renounced her claim to the second of the two above bequests.

On July 1, 1860, Napoleon III made a gift of 5,040 Francs in "rentes" to Louis, which, the latter notes, "went for the cautionnement [surety bond, guarantee] for the post of Receveur Général de Département des Alpes-Maritimes, awarded to me by decree dated 19 June 1860."

a servi à faire le cautionnement pour la Recette Générale des Finances du Département des Alpes Maritimes à laquelle j'ai été appelé par décret du 19 juin, 1860.

In 1876, Louis' estate was finally settled jointly with that of Marceline. By this time, Elise had settled permanently in Florence. She received (in round figures) 140,000 F, and Josephine 59,000F.

On their marriages, in 1872, and 1874 respectively, Louise and Joséphine each received (according to my mother) a dowry of 500,000F.

While the above would appear to have sufficed to provide a comfortable income for all concerned, Elise spent the last years of her life in painfully straitened circumstances. It seems that "Le Cave", the country house at Pescia which Joséphine acquired at the time of her marriage was paid for by her out of her own dowry. Unfortunately the family's affairs did not prosper: "Wili" Baese's business in Florence was not successful. As for Francesco Palamidessi, his contribution was to gamble away her money within ten years.

Joséphine's career on the stage was by no means a success financially, either in England or in America, and she was troubled by financial problems all her life. As a result, her two daughters, Elisina and Linetta had to go off to England one after the other—Elisina in 1892 and Linetta in 1896, at the age of 17 and 15 respectively, to earn their living by teaching Italian and Italian literature at the Cheltenham Ladies' College. As for Louis, Josephine's son, he was only 12 when he was sent off to sea for the first time. He went off again in 1890 when not quite 14, and returned to London, where his mother was living and pursuing her career on the stage, in 1892. In late 1893, he went off again as a member of the crew of a ship bound for the United States. He jumped ship at San Francisco (having rounded Cape Horn and sailed up the West coast of the American continent) and made his way to the northwest Pacific coast where he established himself as a mining engineer in the state of Washington. Thanks to the initiative and help of Elisina and Grant Richards he emigrated to South Africa, where he settled and had a very successful career in mining, unfortunately cut short by ill health. He died, at the early age of 53, in 1929.

The Title of Count and the Légion d'Honneur

In his notes, René Puaux mentions a visit to Nice by the Emperor in September 1860, but gives no source. He states that this visit gave the newly arrived Louis great pleasure by enabling him to see again some of his former friends at Court. It was also, doubtless, a welcome event, as a flattering start to his tenure of office. Among the friends he saw again were Dr. Conneau, General Fleury and Baron Tascher.

Shortly after the visit, Louis writes (October 26th) to M. Gaudin (Conseiller d'Etat and Ministre Plénipotentiaire au Ministère de la Justice), who is a good friend, asking him for his assistance in obtaining a document officially establishing his right to the title of Count. The operative paragraph in the letter is interesting: "This is the issue. Nothing proves my title of count, for I am in a highly unusual position. However, it is *just* and *true* that, despite having long had it, I never claimed it until [the passage of] the law on titles [*la loi des titres*]. Having no parchment to produce, however, I raised the matter with the emperor in an audience that His Majesty was kind enough to grant me, and His Majesty was good enough personally to ask Monsieur le Comte Walewski to have me listed in this manner in the register of personnel of the Ministry of Foreign Affairs. Would it be possible for me to request some sort of document that could *prove* in the future, and in the interest of my children, that this title is mine? There lies the whole question."

Voici de quoi il s'agit. Mon titre de Comte n'est prouvé par rien, car je suis dans une position toute particulière et exceptionnelle. Cependant il

> *est juste et vrai et, quoique le possédant depuis longtemps, je ne m'en suis prévalu qu'au moment de la loi sur les titres. Cependant, n'ayant aucun parchemin à produire j'en parlai à l'Empereur dans une audience que S. M. voulut bien m'accorder, et Elle eut la bonté de prier elle-même M. le Comte Walewski de me faire porter sur les Etats du personnel du Ministère des Affaires Etrangères avec cette qualification. Me serait-il possible de demander un papier quelconque qui prouve à l'avenir, et dans l'intérêt de mes enfants que ce titre m'appartient? Voilà toute la question.*

The formal document Louis asked for was rapidly forthcoming under date of November 7, 1860, issued in the Emperor's name by the Minister of Justice.

However I do not understand how it had come about that Louis could write about the title of count, "….le possédant depuis longtemps..." Does this mean that when he was naturalized French on June 14, 1854, he thereby acquired *ipso facto* the right to the title of Count as the son of the Comte de Saint-Leu? Perhaps the "Loi sur les titres" to which he refers would elucidate the matter, but I will have to leave it to someone else to look into this.

René Puaux mentions a visit by Louis to Baden-Baden in 1865 and, in the same year the death of Elise's father in October. There was also a "séjour" at Aix-les-Bains in 1866, and in August of this year Louis at last received the long coveted Cross of Chevalier de la Légion d'Honneur.

Rennes (1867 1869)

Louis was appointed to Rennes in March 1867 as Trésorier Payeur Général des Finances du département d'Ille et Vilaine, far from the climate which Elise had found so harmful to her health, and the family moved there soon afterwards.

The Trésorerie, which was also their residence, was at no. 3 rue de Bel Air, (later re-named rue Martenot) in the Hôtel de

Francheville. La rue de Bel Air, notes M. Puaux, «longe la Motte, place ovale plantée d'ormeaux d'ou l'on découvre la vallée de la Vilaine». Julian Lefebvre, Prefect of the Département, and his family lived next door at no. 1. In 1880 the Hôtel de Francheville was pulled down in order to provide office space for the Préfecture.

In August 1867 Louis also received a letter informing him that the Emperor was sending him two half-length portraits of himself and the Empress "peints…d'apres M. Winterhalter". I don't know what happened to them. The only tangible souvenir we have of these last two years of Louis' life at Rennes is a printed brochure of the text of a "Scène Tragique en deux Tableaux", entitled *La Mort de Brutus,* performed at Rennes on October 25, 1868. The cast, to be seen as a photograph inside the cover, consists of 4 young members of the Lefebvre family, one unknown male, Monsieur Anatol Allavène, and, last but not least, Mesdemoiselles Louise and Joséphine de Castelvecchio, in the roles of Porcie (femme de Brutus) and of Cassius (ami de Brutus) respectively. The latter, next to Brutus, is looking at him. In view of Joséphine's lifelong affair with the stage and of the result of this for the rest of the family, this document is of particular interest.

In René Pueux's notes is the following reference to Napoleon III's cousin, Princess Baciocchi, widow of Prince Baciocchi (d. 1866), nephew of Countess Camerata. After his death, Princess Baciocchi retired to Brittany, where she soon found herself to be the neighbour of Louis and Elise at Rennes. She died in 1869, a few weeks before Louis:

> "Princess Baciocchi, a cousin of Napoleon III, lived during the second empire in the former Barrin du Boisgeffroy residence, nos. 10 & 12 rue de Corbin (the present army headquarters building). Her Highness had as one of her chevaliers d'honneur the Marquis de Piré, deputy and chevalier de la Légion d'Honneur. His name was Alexan-

dre de Rosnyvineu, Marquis de Piré.... Princess Baciocchi was said to be so capricious that she was on bad terms with almost the entire imperial family. It is therefore difficult to state with confidence that, while in Rennes, the Comte and Comtesse de Castelvecchio were able to attend social receptions at her residence."

La Princesse Bachiocchi [sic] cousine de Napoléon III habitait sous le second empire l'ancien hôtel Barrin du Boisgeffroy, nos. 10 + 12, rue de Corbin (l'hôtel du Corps d'Armée actuel), son Altesse eut pour l'un de ses chevaliers d'honneur le Marquis de Piré, Chevalier de la Légion d' Honneur, député... Il s'appelait Alexandre de Rosnyvineu, Marquis de Piré... on disait de la Princesse Baciocchi que son caractère fantasque l'avait brouillée avec presque toute la famille impériale. On n'ose donc affirmer à la légère qu'étant à Rennes, le Comte et la Comtesse di Castelvecchio [sic!] aient pu assister à des réceptions mondaines, rue de Corbin ...

A letter to Louis from the Cabinet de l'Empereur, dated April 1, 1868, implies that the good lady had hoped to be able to get some money from her cousin through Louis: "I conveyed to the Emperor the confidential letter with which you honored me, concerning Her Highness Madame la Princesse Baciocchi's request for money. His Majesty is of the opinion that you should do nothing for her that you would not do for anyone else."

Some six years earlier, Louis had written to Princess Baciocchi's husband, then the Emperor's First Chamberlain about his hopes—not to be fulfilled—of being transferred to Paris.

Louis de Castelvecchio's Death and Burial

The performance of *La Mort de Brutus* is the last recorded event we have prior to Louis' death, described as follows in *Le Journal d'Ille et Vilaine* of May 29, 1869:

"An unfortunate event has made a painful impression on our city and plunged a distinguished, honorable family into grief.

This morning, Monsieur le Comte de Castelvecchio, Treasurer General [Trésorier-Payeur Général] was taking a bath in his residence and had been in it for rather a long time when he was at last discovered, dead.

Found half-way out of the bath, he had been suffocated by gas from a heater, which had spread through the bathroom because of an undetected fault in the device.

The best and most devoted efforts proved in vain. This is a sad loss. Endowed as he was with the most winning qualities, attractive and elevated in character, M. de Castelvecchio enjoyed the esteem of everyone who knew him. We share the pain of his devoted family."

Un déplorable évènement a douloureusement impressionné notre ville et plongé dans le deuil une famille aussi honorable que distinguée.

Ce matin, M. le Comte de Castelvecchio, Trésorier-Payeur Général, prenait un bain dans un appartement de son hôtel ; il y était depuis assez longtemps lorsqu'on y pénétra. Quel spectacle ! Il n'était plus qu'un cadavre.

M. Castevecchio qu'on a trouvé à demi sorti de sa baignoire, avait été asphyxié par les gaz du fourneau, qui s'étaient répandus dans la salle de bain par suite d'une dégradation inaperçue dans l'appareil du chauffage.

En vain, la science et le dévouement lui ont-ils prodigué les secours les plus empressés tout espoir était perdu de rappeler à la vie le corps qu'elle avait déjà abandonné. Cette perte sera vivement sentie. Doué des qualités les plus sympathiques, homme du monde affable et d'un caractère élevé, M. Castelvecchio était estimé de tous ceux qui le connaissaient. Nous nous associons à la douleur de sa famille qui l'adorait.

On June 1, at 10 am, "...a solemn service was celebrated in the church of Notre-Dame for M. de Castelvecchio. Clergy accompanied to the station the remains of the deceased, who is to be taken to Paris."

Louis was buried on February 14, 1870 in the family vault on a plot in the Père Lachaise cemetery, which Elisa acquired on 7 November, 1869. Other members of the family buried there are: Marceline, on July 2, 1870; Suzanne Marie, Veuve Pasteur d'Etreillis, Elise's mother, on November 23, 1879, St. Aure d'Etreillis, Elise's brother, July 23 1885; and Elisina Tyler, who died July 11, 1957. The ashes of her husband, Royall Tyler, who died March 2, 1953, are also there. Elise, however was not buried there, but in Pescia where she spent her last years, and died on October 5, 1894. Joséphine had wanted to be buried in Pescia, but was buried somewhere in New York City. Elise's mother, Suzanne Marie Longuet de Breuil, left behind holograph wills, which were found to be invalid for legal reasons. In one of them she specified that she wished to be buried in Florence, next to "mon meilleur ami" (Marcel de Bruges de Camps) but, this was not to be.

We have Louis' last letter to Elise written on May 26, 1869, less than three days before his death, and presumably read by her after his death. She was at Bad Ems with her mother, Marceline (who had only a little more than one year to live), Louise and Joséphine. His last lines to her: "... Good-by, dear Elise, I kiss you, the children, and mother. Give me your news, which I am always anxious to have, especially since I know that all of you are far away and alone. Your Louis.

P.S. Tell me especially about Lina... Do you know that in Paris some nobody [*un homme du peuple*] struck Mr. Paixham, who was on his way home from the theatre in an open carriage with his mother and two other ladies, and that Mr. Paixham lost consciousness and bled a great deal? Is this another fruit of liberty? Did my two other letters reach Ems?

Mr. Paixham's misadventure symbolizes the increasing social turbulence which was to culminate, after the disasters of the Franco-Prussian war, in the "Commune", and the emperor's abdication—the passing of the order of things which had hitherto so greatly favored the fortunes of the Castelvecchio family. Elise was to live on for another quarter of a century, increasingly beset by family and financial troubles, and finally by blindness. Her letters to Joséphine reveal—though she never complained—how utterly wretched her last years were. In retrospect one feels it was fortunate that Louis died when he did—for her as well as for himself.

Napoléon III writes to her from St. Cloud on September 12, 1869:

"My dear Madame de Castelvecchio,
It is with sorrow that I receive your congratulations this year, on the occasion of the 15th of August, for they recall a sad event. At least I gain from them the comforting satisfaction of rediscovering in you and in your children the noble sentiments that animated the unfortunate Castelvecchio. I am deeply touched, and I thank you. With my most devoted regards, Napoléon."

Ma chère Madame de Castelvecchio, c'est avec tristesse que je reçois cette année à l'occasion du 15 août, vos félicitations, car elles me rappellent un douloureux évènement. J'y puise du moins cette consolante satisfaction de retrouver en vous et dans vos enfants les nobles sentiments qui animaient ce pauvre Castelvecchio. J'en suis très touché et je vous en remercie. Croyez à mes sentiments, Napoléon.

We have a seated portrait of Elise by Winterhalter, painted in Paris in 1869. She is in mourning relieved only by a dulled carnation in her hair, on which (my mother told Betsy) Winterhalter had insisted. Her eyes are reddened, her expression is sad and wan. One wonders how it came about that her portrait was painted at such a sad moment in her life. I find it hard to believe that the idea originated with her. Then there is the matter of the cost. After all Winterhalter, patronized by the Emperor and the Court, was the most fashionable portrait painter of the time, commissioned by everybody who was anybody. We know from a letter from him to Elise written shortly after this period, that he and his wife were close friends of the family. All this leads me to wonder whether Winterhalter insisted on offering Elise and the family the portrait as a friendly gesture in memory of Louis, after his death. Certainly the idea of her spending a lot of money on her portrait at a time like this is preposterous.

We also have a fine profile portrait drawing of Elise's mother by Winterhalter, signed and dated December 22, 1870, which was copied one week later by Louise—at a time when the Germans were besieging Paris, and many people were eating horses and rats!

After Louis' death Elise returned to Paris where she lived first at 50 Bld. Malesherbes and then at 23 Boulevard des Batignolles with her mother and her three girls.

The summer brought Marceline's death on June 30, followed by the disasters of the Franco-Prussian war and capitulation. By early September Napoléon III had been forced to abdicate and had taken refuge in England. Within a period of fifteen months the Castelvecchio family had lost its founder, his eldest child and its chief protector and source of support, the Emperor. One can imagine what the future must have looked like to poor Elise. The contrast between the family's position and prospects before Louis' death and the outlook after the fall of Napoléon III is beyond description.

The Return to Italy

In the circumstances Elise took the only course open to her. She left Paris with her two remaining children for Florence, but without her mother. In the letter from Winterhalter mentioned above, he expresses his surprise that Elise's mother had not accompanied her to Florence. "I was greatly surprised to learn that Madame Decamps remained behind, alone, in Paris, she who showed such impatience to return to Florence and rest at home."

> *J'étais bien étonné d'apprendre que Madame Decamps [sic] soit restée toute seule à Paris, elle qui témoignait tant d'impatience de rentrer à Florence et de se reposer chez elle…*

However, one can understand her not being able to face the prospect of returning to live in Florence again, with so many memories of her former life there with Marcel de Bruges de Camps. There may also have been financial considerations. Half a century later, on August 28, 1921, Countess Minerbi wrote to A.P. from her house (Villa Emilia, Belgirate, Lago Maggiore):

> *Mi cara Linetta,*
>
> *Mi chiedi come vecchia, vecchia amica della vostra famiglia qualche informazione sui tuoi Nonni di Castelvecchio, e volotieri ti dirò quello che me ricordo.*
>
> *Li conobbi, se non erro, nell'anno 1857 a Parigi, quando essi avevano une brillante posizione sotto l'Impero. Si disse che il Conte di Castelvecchio era figlio del Re Luigi di Olanda, ma di madre ignota. Napoleone III, generoso verso I suoi parenti, lo vedeva volotieri a Conte con la sua bella consorte, nata Decamps. ed in appresso lo fece nominare 'Receveur Général' a Nizza. Piu tarde ebbe la stessa posizione a Rennes in Bretagna ed è là dove per disgrazia mori accidentalmente.*
>
> *La tua Nonna Elisa gli sopravisse per molti anni, ma con crollo dell'Impero assa perdette oltre la posizione anche gran parta della fortuna, benchè l'Ex-Imperatrice Eugenia s'interessasse ad essa. Ecco*

per il momento quello che to posso dire, abbracciandole con affetto.
Cssa Emilia H. de Minerbi

The Marriages of Louise and Joséphine

On arriving in Florence Elise first lived in the Paluzzo Canigiani, Via S. Jacopo 1. In 1875 her address was Via Guelfa 5, and in 1878 Via della Scala 25, according to M. Puaux, where her son-in-law Palamidessi and Joséphine lived.

On March 21, 1872, Louise Marie Hortense Eugénie de Castelvecchio was married in Berlin to Wilhelm Christophe Emil Baese ("sujet prussien") born in Magdeburg. He was at the time a businessman in Florence, and lived at No. 2 Via de Palestro. Subsequently he and Louise lived at 17 Via Cittadella.

On May 7, 1874, Joséphine Marie Suzette Juliette de Castelvecchio was married in a civil ceremony in Paris to Francesco Alberto Giovanni Vito Palamidessi ("sujet italien") born in Pescia in 1849. They had met at the Music Academy in Florence where he was a professor. Four or five months later they were married in a religious ceremony at Pescia.

According to A.P.'s letter to Gioia of 1958, Louise "always blamed grandmother very bitterly for having insisted—so she said—on marrying her, very young, unwilling, and in 1871 to (of all things!!!) a *German*"...... It was also from Louise ("and from nobody else") writes A.P. in the same letter, that "I heard that the reason for his (Louis de Castelvecchio) leaving the Foreign Office was a 'scandal' about Grandmother and one of their friends, "mon bon Bosino", of whom I know nothing else at all, except a carte-de-visite size photograph that there was, like so many others, in a family album"....

At the time of her marriage to Palamidessi, Joséphine bought, with money from her dowry, a property consisting of a house and grounds called "Le Cave", then near Pescia on the west as you drive north to the town from the road to Florence, but now absorbed within it. Elisina, her eldest child, was born in Florence in 1875, but Louis and Linetta were both born at "Le Cave", in 1876 and 1880 respectively.

I have been able to discover very little about the Baese family, but enough for it to be clear that Louise's marriage was not a success. Wili's business in Florence did not flourish, and there are references to Louise being financially unable to help her mother. Except for one or two brief ones, I have come across no letters from her to her mother, or to Joséphine. That Louise and Elisina were on bad terms is clear from letters to A.P. in the years 1909-14, and according to A.P.'s notes, Louise once told her that she would never see Elisina again.

Louise and Wili had four sons, of whom one died in infancy. Giulio, the eldest, is said to have married in the United States and to have had a son there, but I have found no trace of either. Paolo, the second son, did not marry and died in Florence. The youngest son, Carlo, whom I met with my mother in Florence in December and early January, 1932-33, married in the latter year Genovetta (Jenny) Mori. He died childless in Milan in 1943, while "Jenny" died in Florence soon after the end of the war.

Louise died in Florence in August 1929, but I do not have the date of death of her husband. AP had kept up with her, and saw her just before her death. Elisina never mentioned her to me, and from her references to her in her letters to AP there was no love lost between them, Louise having told her that she would never see Elisina, to which AP adds "Why?"

Elisina was born in Florence, in 1875, probably at Via Guelfa 5; and in the following year, Louis was born at "Le Cave". On November 15, 1878, a son, Giuseppino, was born, at "Le Cave" or in Florence He lived for only one year and three months and the following inscription was prepared by Joséphine for his tombstone:

A Giuseppe Palamidessi, il Babbo, la Mamma, la Nonna, disperati di non poter fare più per lui. Nato il 15 Novembre 1878, morto il 21

Febbraio 1880.

On October 13, 1880, Linetta Adolfina Giuseppina Palamidessi de Castelvecchio came into the world at "Le Cave".

Joséphine de Castelvecchio at about 19

The Move to England

In 1882, Joséphine—by then 25 years old—took the entire family off to London in order to further her ambitions for a stage career. They took a house on Westbourne Terrace, W.8., and also took on a Scottish nanny. It may have been during this visit that Joséphine met Ellen Terry who was impressed by her and became a good friend, as the following letter shows:

Lyceum Theatre, 17 April (no year)

My dear friend,

 I am indeed sorry to hear of your continued illness - I expected little Elisena (that's not right) on Thursday night to see Becket and fear since she didn't come, that it was because you were too ill to let her leave you. I intended coming round to see how you were getting on today, but had to go down to the theatre about some business of Mr. Irving's, and could not contrive to go to *both* places. Tomorrow I must spend some hours at a hospital, so fear shall find no time again—but I do hope you are much better my now. Send your little girl to me at the Lyceum some evening if she wants to see Becket. I hope you will come back very soon—*quite well* though—not before.

  Yours affectionately,
    ET

I cannot be sure that this letter was written in the mid-eighties. However, Elisina entered Santa Anna with Auntie Pitzy in 1888, and left for England to teach at Cheltenham in 1892, by which time she was 17, and "your little girl" no longer sounds appropriate.

Now comes the sad story of little Giuseppina who was born and died in London within the calendar year 1883, by drowning in a foot-bath (according to Auntie Pitzy's notes). Joséphine had sent the nurse out on an errand, and the baby was left unattended with the bath for her ready in the same room, long enough for the accident to happen. The undertaker's bill for the funeral is dated January 5, 1884.

Left to right: Elisina, Linetta, Louis

The Break-up of Joséphine's First Marriage

It seems that Francesco Palamidessi had been engaging in speculation with the family money, which turned out badly—not for the first time. Things came to a head in the early months of 1885 (as near as I can make out) while Palamidessi was about to return to London from a trip.

"Mother and me" writes AP "and probably nanny, were being put for the night when we moved out of the house [28 Westbourne Terrace] because mother was leaving my father, who was expected back from a journey on the following day, and she—or so she told me once very proudly—had emptied the house and torn up (or destroyed) every photograph of him. We were probably on our way back to Italy". The marriage had almost gone on the rocks once before, in 1882, but had been patched up. However, this time was the end.

Their first stop was Paris, where Josephine took the three children with her to see her uncle, Elise's brother, St-Aure Pasteur d'Etreillis. If one accepts his age, as given on his death certificate, as 65, he was about 6 years older than Elise, and born in or about 1820. I have somewhere come across the date November 24, 1825 for the marriage of their parents, but have no confirmation of this, and am inclined to accept 1820 as the year of his birth, Elise having been born in the summer of 1826. He is said to have been attractive and socially active, an excellent shot and a very good horseman. He was a friend of the Duc d'Aumale and often went to stay with him at Chantilly. He wrote articles over many years for the magazine *Le Sport*, a highly social weekly, published in large in folio size between 1855 and 1893. Its sub-title was *Chronique des haras du turf et des chasses*. He must have used a pen-name because his does not appear in the magazine which Vincent Laloy unearthed in the archives of the Bibliothèque Nationale. He was also said to have written articles on the circus and circus life, which interested him particularly. Fiammetta Gondi kindly sent me a photograph of a painting depicting St. Aure on horseback but we do not know the whereabouts of the original. Except for some personal bequests, he left his entire estate to Louise Baese.

In the course of the visit already mentioned of Joséphine and her children, he gave Louis a tie-pin, which the latter long kept and remembered as the only thing he owned which he associated with any member of the family. A few months later St Aure died in Paris, as a result of having been kicked by a horse while in England.

According to AP's notes Louis was dropped off at the Pension Sillig at Vevey, in Switzerland, where his grandfather had been educated, on their way back to Italy. I don't know how long he studied there. According to her notes, he was sent to the Dulwich College after the Sillig boarding school, but was soon taken away again "I should think by reason of the expense, but under the pretext that he had been caned".

Meanwhile Joséphine had joined her mother in Florence and Pescia, whereas Elisina and Linetta stayed for some time with "Uncle Sciamanna" at his Palace "Alla Giornata" in Pisa.

In 1886 the "Tribunale" of Lucca handed down a decision on the the separation of Joséphine and Palamidessi. According to A.P. it is dated August 17-19, and was registered formally on September 4th of the same year. A.P. wrote as follows about this business (in a letter dated July 22, 1958) to Gioia, which, thanks to Tommy and Gillian, I was able to consult at Gragnano in March 1983:

"I was only 5 years old when the definitive legal separation between my parents was decreed...and Aunt Lucciola told me once that it had been preceded by an equally conclusive suit, which however ended in nothing because at the final interview between the parties, demanded by Italian law, mother made a dramatic reconciliation—to the *fury* of her counsel, Enrico Barsanti of Florence. But even on my birth certificate (Pescia) mother's maiden name is given as 'Countess de Castelvecchio' [mere courtesy? snobbishness?], and I don't remember ever having heard her called anything else. This altho' of course, my birth certificate also gives my father's name as *'Prof.* Francesco Palamidessi' and says they are husband and wife...."

"My mother told me that the *sentence of separation* had given her the right to use for herself and for us 'de Castelvecchio' as our surname". When A.P. wrote in

1920 to the Pescia lawyer, Giuntoli, to ask for a copy of the relevant passage, there was none.... She goes on in her letter to Gioia:

"By the way, do not delve into these proceedings for separation. I believe that Mother, in order to make her case, practically slandered Grandmother, and said she had been forced into marrying my father—whereas from Sofia del Vaso—a humble but constant and adoring friend of mother's from early days—as well as from Aunt Lucciola emphatically—I know that mother insisted on it against *everybody's* wishes, and fell ill and said she would die if she wasn't allowed to marry him. You will note that at her marriage in Paris, only Grandmother and 'picked up' witnesses were present. The sentence of separation did give her the custody of us children".

Sofia del Vaso, mentioned above, was the daughter of Antonio and Carolina del Vaso, in whose house in Pescia Elise spent the last years of her life "en pension". She had room and board for 5 Francs a day. Sofia had a brother, Ugo, married with two children, who lived in Pisa. Antonio del Vaso was a "sensale", or real estate agent.

Thanks to my old friend George Picard through Italian friends of his, I have been able to obtain a copy of the text of the Decision of the Lucca "Tribunale", granting Joséphine's request for separation from her husband, and the continued use of the name Castelvecchio, instead of or in addition to Palamidessi, in the case of Joséphine. However the text does not mention the question of use either of the name or of the title, which Joséphine and Elisina used freely. A.P. also used it but much more sparingly. Louis de Castle, having partially changed his name while still in the United States, and emigrated to South Africa in his mid-twenties, never used it at all. While the civil separation of man and wife (particularly in the case of this couple who were married in church in Italy as well as civilly in France) fell naturally under Italian civilian jurisdiction—as did the issue of the use of a family name—I could not believe that an Italian court would consider itself competent to pass on the use of a foreign title. Moreover, the conditions under which the title of Count were to be hereditary are explicitly in the Imperial Decree of November 7, 1860, of which we have an original: "We have conferred, and we do confer, upon M. de Castelvecchio (François-Louis) the hereditary title of Count, for himself *and for his direct, legitimate descendants in the male line, in order of primogeniture.*" [underlining mine]

> *Nous avons conféré et conférons à M. de Castelvecchio (François-Louis) le titre héréditaire de Comte pour en jouir lui et sa descendance directe, légitime, de mâle, par ordre de primogéniture.*

Since no male descendant of Elise and Louis survived infancy, the title lapsed with Louis' death and that of his widow.

The Gower Strain

From June 15 to August 29, 1886, and again from January 20, 1888, to March 14, 1889, British Acting Consul at Livorno was Abel Anthony James Gower, who had retired from the Foreign Service in 1876. His career was spent entirely in the Far East. He went out to China in April 1856 as Private Secretary to the Governor of Hong Kong, and from 1859 on, he was appointed exclusively to posts in Japan until his retirement in 1876 (F.O. Staff list, 1896, pp. 118-119).

I mention him first because for two years after 1981, when I first spotted his name and *curriculum vitae*, I thought I had identified the mysterious Gower who had floated into Joséphine's life for about six years (1888-1984), marrying her (though I have found no evidence of the marriage) and leaving her with a son about whom I know almost as little as about him.

However it only goes to show how insidious coincidences can

be, particularly when bolstered by locations and dates which appear to confirm their implications. Was it not obvious that he was the one? After all, Gower is not a rare name in Wales, or even in England, but it is surely exotic in Tuscany. Moreover the geography and the time were right, and who could doubt that the Acting British Consul was socially active in the Livorno-Pisa-Florence area, where Josephine would have been so likely to meet him? True, there was one slightly disturbing factor: his age. Suppose him to have gone out to China first as a Private Secretary in 1856. Would he not have been at least 25 years old? He would then have been born in say 1830 or 1831, which would have made him some 26 years older than Josephine, who was still just in her twenties in 1886, while A.A.J. Gower would have been 56 or 57. While I, for obvious reasons, would be the last person to consider someone of this age as being automatically senile, the gap in age did seem rather larger than one might expect. However I recalled that it was in 1886 that Josephine had won a separation from Palamidessi in a civil court of Law, so that she was now free to pursue another man, and this one had the advantage of being an Englishman, to whom the disapproval or displeasure of the Church of Rome of a union with Josephine could be only a matter of total indifference, if not a positive incentive. Besides, the evidence was overwhelmingly in favour of this being the Gower.

I picked up what I took to be his trail in references to him and later to his and Josephine's son in letters from Elisina and from Elise, but Gower remained nebulous, and just wouldn't come to life. Uncle Bob was unable to help me. He said it did "appear" that Gower and Josephine had married but he did not exclude the possibility that the marriage "may have been contracted only to help Josephine in some way" (quoting from notes taken during a conversation with him). There had been, he told me, a letter written by Josephine in the nineties in which she asserted that "she did not love him". As Joséphine left for the US in 1894 without Gower, it is reasonable to assume that this letter was written earlier than—or at least not later than—this year. There is also a reference in one of Elise's letters to Joséphine about Gower having gone off to Japan in early 1892, and not being due to return to London (where he and Joséphine were then living) until September. Then, at about this same time, or perhaps in 1893, there is mention of the problem of disposing of a Japanese wooden "idol" by Joséphine.

The rest is silence save for a reference by Joséphine to her son in a letter to Elisina in 1902, and a lively account of her feelings about him and his wife, Minette, written to AP 29 years later on July 24, 1931 (see below).

It was not until March 1983, while we were at Gragnano, that I found the following statement in AP's long letter to Gioia of 1958, in which Leon Gower is referred to as the..."son of a brother of the then British Consul in Leghorn called Sir Abel Gower". So much for coincidences!

I have discovered even more recently, thanks to Valynseele, that Sir Abel had a brother with the initials E.H.M. As of this writing, this is all I know, but let us assume that it is likely that he was younger than Abel, and that he was Josephine's Gower. I wish I knew more about the Gower phase in Josephine's life. As it is I can only propose the following. In 1886 or 87 she meets a younger brother of the then Acting British Consul at Livorno. A 'marriage" of sorts is arranged, which enables Joséphine to accompany him to England in 1889 in order to pursue her aspirations of a career on the stage, Elisina and Linetta having entered the Reale Conservatorio of Santa Anna in Pisa in late 1888. At some point, after Joséphine's departure, Elise became a boarder at Pescia in the house of Antonio del Vaso and his wife, whose daughter, Sofia, was a close friend of Joséphine. This was probably in 1889 and Elise died there 5 years later.

Joséphine's son was never referred to as Napoleon—at least in the letters we have—but only as "Nappie", "Nappy", or "N".

The marriage seems to have gone on the rocks before 1894 when Joséphine left on her first trip to the United States. "Nappie" was left behind in Peterborough, which seems to have been the family's home; and he finally joined his mother in New York, perhaps in 1903 or 1904, after her marriage to Antonio Frabasilis. He later married "Minette" which is all we know about her; and they are said [by whom, where?–RT] to have had a son, about whom I know nothing either.

I know nothing more about the father. Leon re-emerges briefly in England during World War I as a member of the Canadian armed forces, when he turned up at King's College, London, where A.P. was teaching, without any prior warning, announcing himself as the brother of "Miss Lilly Gower". Understandably, this meeting proved to be a most painful and nerve-wracking experience for AP.

In her notes A.P. gives 1898 as the year of Leon's birth, in London. This is obviously wrong for many reasons, among which is the fact that Joséphine was in New York from 1894 to 1896, then in Europe (Italy and England briefly) before returning definitively to New York in 1897. Probably A.P. inverted in her notes the last two digits of 1889. At any rate, we read about "Baby", "Nappie" and "N" in letters Elisina writes to her mother from Santa Anna as early as 1891, as we shall see.

I assume that Napoleon Gower was born in 1889, possibly in London, or perhaps in Peterborough, with which the Gowers and Elisina seem to have had some connection. Elisina and Linetta had gone to Santa Anna in 1888, and Louis, who had been sent off to sea at the age of 12, could also have been out of the country. We know for sure that he went off to sea again on a four-masted ship from Liverpool in the summer of 1890. He gives the date June 10 of that year himself in the account he wrote of the voyage for his grandmother, Elise.

Linetta de Castelvecchio

Elisina de Castelvecchio

Louis de Castle

Santa Anna and Cheltenham

During their years together at Santa Anna (1888-1892), Elisina and Linetta made, each of them, a close friend. Linetta tells in her notes that she "lost her heart" to Signora Vera Badoglio, a widow, who was her French mistress, and who lived with her elderly father ("Italian, very deaf, tall and retiring—I think only because of his deafness") and her children. Elisina made close friends of Ginerva Aldrovandi and her younger brother Luigi, known as "Bubi", who lived with their mother, Countess Aldrovandi, near Santa Anna. He entered the diplomatic service and ultimately became ambassador in Berlin, where his career suddenly came to an end because of a security breach in the embassy for which he, as the Ambassador, had to shoulder responsibility.

The sisters were very close to each other at Santa Anna and remained so for many years afterwards, but they were different from each other in many respects and the course of their lives drew them apart, not only physically. However they never completely lost touch. A.P.'s comment on Elisina, in one of her letters to Gioia is charming and suggestive: "…pretty, witty, clever, and very dear when she was young…"

In addition to numerous letters from Elisina and Linetta to their other in England, we have the printed program of the prize giving ceremony for the academic year 1890-1891 in which both the Signorine de Castelvecchio figure prominently. The first to appear is Linetta, then just eleven; and she performed a "Divertimento per pianoforte a due man sopia l'opera 'Nabucco' del Maestro Verdi". Later on, she and her sister oblige with a "Serenata a 4 mani". In the second half of the program, Elisa (as her name appears in print) performs an "Intermezzo della Cavalleria Rusticana a due mani" and shortly thereafter, Linetta recites a poem entitled "La Châtaigne". Elisina brings the program to a close with a "Divertimento a 4 mani sull'opera 'Saffo' del Maestro Pacini," which she plays with the music master, Maestro Barsanti. Poor Maestro (Giovanni) Pacini! He was, I find, a "famous teacher of composition and himself composer of about 90 operas, orchestral works, chamber music, etc…" (*Concise Oxford Dictionary of Music*) He was born in Catania in 1796, and died in Pescia in 1867. The latter suggests that Elisina herself may have selected a composition by him for this event, but it did not suffice to ensure the survival of his fame!

We also have a small double sheet of paper on which Elisina has written a "Racconto", and two poems "Ideale and "L'Ultimo Desiderio", in her fine hand.

In her letters, Grandmother Elise records other aspects of the Santa Anna years, in particular the academic successes, as will be seen below.

In 1892, Elisina left Santa Anna for England "where mother had already gone" notes AP, in order to teach at the Cheltenham Ladies' College, a well-known and highly regarded institution presided over by Miss Buss and Miss Beale about whom one of the young ladies there had composed the following quotation:

Miss Buss and Miss Beale
Cupid's darts do not feel.
They are not like us,
Miss Beale and Miss Buss.

It seems likely that Elisina obtained her position at Cheltenham thanks to her mother's friendship with a Lady Samuelson who lived there, and with whom Elisina stayed, *au pair*, looking after the two daughters, Helen and Caroline (address: "Helenslee", Hewlett Road). Her husband, Sir Bernhard Samuelson, I know nothing about. Lady Samuelson's maiden name was Serena, and this name was to play an important role in Linetta's future, for, in 1921, she won a most coveted appointment to the newly endowed "Chair of Italian" at Birmingham University. (See the obituary notice in the Appendix by Professor M J McNair).

From Elisina's letters to her mother, I also have the impression that she was a very happy with the Samuelsons and her two charges.

We have a good many letters to Joséphine between 1891 and 1894—mostly from Elisina—written first from Santa Anna and then from Cheltenham.

There are also one or two long ones from Linetta to her mother, written after Elisina had left Santa Anna. Joséphine was in England all this time, presumably with Gower, living at 30 Walpole Street, Chelsea, and then at other addresses in London. The last letter we have (May 17, 1894) is addressed to her at St. John's Lodge, 50A Westbourne Street S.W. The earliest letters contain references to "Daddy" and "Nappie". There is also mention of "Elisina Lodge" which Gower had rented—but no indication of where it was.

The following extract from a letter to Joséphine from Elisina, dated November 20, 1891 (i.e. while she and Linetta were still at Santa Anna together) describes an incident in the form of an announcement to her and Linetta of what could only have been the death of Palamidessi:

> "I will also explain to you, as it happened, the affair of the letters. When Grandmother learned the sad news, she immediately wrote Madame la Directrice [their school principal], asking her to do everything possible to keep it from us, at least for the time being. That is just when your letter arrived. Under the circumstances, the Directrice felt justified in opening it. Seeing that you had informed us, she waited before sending it to us, especially since Aunt Lucciola too, apparently, didn't want us to know yet because she hoped to lighten the blow by coming to tell us in person. However, when Madame la Directrice read your letter, she immediately called us in, and I think she understood that this business had somewhat annoyed you.
>
> Yes, dear Mummy, the news certainly did impress us somewhat, since nothing could have been further from our thoughts. And since God allowed it to happen, my darling mother, let us thank him for this [word omitted; presumably 'death'], which seems to me, simply from the material perspective, a deliverance. But now that pity draws a veil over the unhappy past, I pray for him with all the strength of my heart. May God forgive him everything, everything that he may ever have done or thought against us. I am sure that you feel just as I do, my darling Mummy!…"
>
> *Je vais aussi t'expliquer l'affaire des lettres comme elle s'est passée. Quand Grand Mère a su la triste nouvelle, elle a tout de suite écrit à Mme la Directrice en la priant de prendre toutes les précautions pour*

> que nous n'en sachions rien du tout, pour le moment au moins. Juste alors, ta lettre est arrivée ; avec ça la Directrice a cru bien faire en l'ouvrant, et voyant que tu nous en donnais l'annonce, elle a attendu avant de nous l'envoyer d'autant plus que tante Lucciola aussi, à ce qu'il paraît, ne voulait pas que nous sachions encore parce qu'elle croyait nous en rendre moins frappant l'émotion en venant nous donner elle-même cette nouvelle. Cependant quand Mme la Directrice a lu ta lettre, elle nous a tout de suite appelées, et je crois qu'elle a compris que cette affaire t'avait un peu agacée…
>
> Oui, ma douce Mémère, la nouvelle nous a un peu frappées, car c'était certainement celle à laquelle nous aurions le moins pensé. Et, puisque le Bon Dieu a permis ceci, remercions-le, ma douce adorée Mémère de cette [word omitted—*mort?*] qui me semble, sous le point de vue seulement matériel, une délivrance. Seulement, maintenant que la pitié couvre d'un voile tout le triste passé, je prie pour lui avec toutes les forces de mon cœur ; et que Dieu lui pardonne tout, tout ce qu'il a jamais pu faire ou penser contre nous. Je suis sûre que tu penses ainsi, aussi bien que moi, n'est-ce pas, mon adorée Mémère !

The offspring of the—for want of a better word—Joséphine-Gower union, "Nappie", seems to have been brought up in England, in Peterborough, until he joined his mother in New York in the very first years of this century. What happened to his father, I do not know. At any rate the letters which Josephine wrote to Elisina and Grant Richards in November 1902 from New York, imply that there was no contact between her and Gower.

In a letter to her mother dated September, 1893, Elisina writes: "Mummy, would you be kind enough have Mr. G asked whether he recently received a letter from me, since my return? He has not answered me, and I find that thoroughly impolite of him."

> Petite mère, aurais-tu la bonté de faire demander à Mr G si il a reçu une lettre de moi tout dernièrement, depuis que je suis revenue? Il ne me répond pas, et je trouve cela très peu poli de sa part.

I cannot imagine who "Mr. G" could be other than Mr. Gower. The "faire demander" can only mean that Joséphine and he no longer communicate with each other directly. Moreover, Elisina's sharp comment presupposes that "Mr. G" is no longer *persona grata* in the family, and that this tone in writing about him is what her mother would expect from her.

Through these letters we learn of Louis de Castelvecchios' departure in December 1893 or January 1894 for some unnamed destination. He was then 17 years old. There are also echoes of Joséphine's theatrical activities, of her recitations of poetry, and even of concerts accompanied by a Countess van den Heuvel; but these all filter through to us indistinctly from brief and vague references, like occasional words and remarks, half-heard in and out of context, from a conversation in a neighbouring room. Thus, it seems as though by 1893, Gower was fading—or had already faded—out of Joséphine's life. I have come across no further mention of him.

In 1894, the year in which Elise died (October 5th), Joséphine went to New York to try to further her career. Linetta was left all alone, with her sister in England, her brother on the high seas, and her grandmother dying. It is not surprising that she fell very ill from some unspecified nervous illness in 1895. Fortunately, Aunt "Lucciola" (Louise) took her into her house in Florence, where she remained until she had recovered.

Joséphine returned to Europe in 1896—first to Italy, where Elisina and Linetta joined her. She attended to family business, following her mother's death, and sold "Le Cave". It was bought by a Pescia family, named Magnani, whose name in mentioned in one or two of Elise's letters. A.P. mentions in her notes that she had kept all her grandmothers letters "but when I came to England", (to succeed Elisina at Cheltenham) "I was not allowed to bring them with me, and when 'Le Cave' was sold and had to be emptied, my letters were all burned, and some family photographs—mostly duplicates—were burned too by Sofia del

Vaso and Elisina together". I can imagine whose idea this was...

George Slythe Street

At this time Elisina had become engaged to George Slythe Street, a highly regarded figure in literary circles in London. I remember him coming to dine with my mother at The Burlington Hotel in Cork Street, where we always stayed before I returned to school at the end of my holidays, which were of course spent in France.

This must have been in 1921 or 1922, because in 1923 I started crossing the Channel by myself. There are two reasons why I remember George Street clearly. One is that he wore a patch over one eye. The other is that when he left he gave me a crackling one pound note. In retrospect, this is all the more touching, when one considers that nothing came of the engagement because he had no money, and conceded that he could not undertake to support my mother on 2 pounds per week. However, through friends, he did obtain a government position which afforded him some security in later life. When Elisina told Miss Beale of her engagement to George Street, she was told she must choose between him and the College. As Linetta was ready to take Elisina's place there (Miss Beale apparently never even inquired about Linetta's age!), Elisina left Cheltenham. Though she did not marry George Street, she did marry Grant Richards in the spring of 1898.

Elise's Last Years (1890 - 1894)

The earliest letter written by Elise from Pescia is dated September 1890. She is *en pension* with Antonio and Carolina del Vaso, and their daughter Sofia. Josephine is in England. Elise has written to ask her for some financial help, but she cannot afford the 150 Francs a month (5F. per diem for room and board). At

Josephine's suggestion, Elise has written to Louise Baese, who has explained why she cannot help either.... These last years are haunted by the specters of poverty and loneliness. She yearns for love and affection from Joséphine to whom she writes adoringly; but one has the feeling that this is not reciprocated. In a postscript to her letter of April 24, 1891, she writes: "If you could, my Fifimienne, send me a few extra francs this month, I would be very grateful... Everything, everything is madly expensive, and *here* it is impossible really to save anything. I am so sorry and so ashamed to make this request of you, but I just do not know what to do!"

> *Si tu pouvais, ma Fifimienne, m'envoyer quelques Francs en plus ce mois-ci, je t'en serais bien reconnaissante... tout, tout coûte un argent fou - et ici il est impossible de faire des économies réelles – je suis désolée et honteuse de devoir te demander, mais je ne sais comment faire !!*

On five occasions in 1891, Elise asks Josephine to convey messages to Gower:" "...My regards to Gower—and to you."

> *Mes souvenirs à Gower - et à toi.*

"...My Fiferl and her three angels are my whole life, and I pray to God and the Virgin morning and night for you four...even for *you five* [including Gower, or, more probably meaning 'Nappie', Leon]. Give Gower many messages from me and wish him today the happiness that we did not wish him when we should have. It is from the heart that we do so, but late!"

> *Ma Fiferl et ses trois anges sont toute ma vie - et je prie Dieu et la Vierge, matin et soir, pour vous quatre... même pour vous 5.*

"Give Gower many messages from me, and wish him today the good fortune that we did not wish him in good time—we do so from the heart, but late!"

> *Dis tant et tant de choses à Gower de ma part - et souhaite-lui aujourd'hui le bonheur que nous n'avons pas souhaité à temps - c'est de cœur que nous le faisons, mais en retard.*

"...I am so glad that Gower's affairs are going well!"

Que je suis heureuse que les affaires de Gower promettent bien!

There are several other mentions of Gower in 1891 with warm messages from Elise.

She sends Josephine two wrappers for nightdresses, which she has herself knitted. "But what will make you accept them more gladly still is that the little pieces of lace around them were made by your beloved sister Linette [Marceline, d. 1870]."

Mais ce qui te les fera accepter bien plus volontiers, c'est que les petites dentelles qui sont autour ont été faites par ta sœur bien aimée Linette

On July 26, 1891, Elise sends Josephine a glowing report of the results of the examinations at Santa Anna, in which both Elisina and Linetta starred: "The teachers are delighted with them, and la Directrice...praised them to the skies to me. Your Elisina wrote so magnificent a composition that la Directrice of Santa Anna came on purpose to ask la Directrice to let her have this composition, which she did not want to leave Santa Anna. [WRT note: This presumably means that the school was separate from the convent.] The subject was Italy. Lisy [Elisina] began with a description, of the kind she is so good at, of Italy in general; then she spoke of your 'Le Cave.' She described the view from there, then she ended her composition with a description of Italy that is truly admirable—a real apotheosis. La Directrice told me that the examiners kept her almost half an hour longer than they should have, asking her all sort of questions, and were delighted, really delighted, by her answers. Your beloved Lilly [Linetta] distinguished herself wonderfully, and she said to me, 'I was calm on the outside, but trembling on the inside!' Both are first among the first, each in her class, and they were glad to think of the happiness that they would give to their blessed and excellent mother—to *You*, my thousand-times darling angel."

Les maîtresses sont enchantées d'elles deux, et la Directrice ... m'a fait

> *leur éloge autant que possible. Ton Elisina a fait une composition tellement magnifique que la Directrice de Sta Anna est venue tout exprès prier la Directrice de lui confier cette composition qui ne devait pas sortir de Sta Anna. Le sujet était l'Italie – Lisy (Elisina) a commencé par faire une description comme elle sait les faire, de l'Italie en général ; puis elle a parlé de vos « Cave ». Elle a décrit la vue qu'on y a… puis elle termine sa composition par une description de l'Italie – qui est réellement admirable – c'est une véritable apothéose. La Directrice m'a dit que les examinateurs l'ont tenu [sic] presque une demie heure de plus qu'ils n'auraient dû en lui faisant toutes sortes de questions, et enchantés, véritablement enchantés de ses réponses. Ta Lilly [Linetta] aimée s'est distinguée autant que possible, et elle me disait : «Ero tranquilla di fuore, ma tremavo di dentro» Elles sont toutes deux premières de premières, chacune dans sa classe, et elles étaient heureuses en pensant au bonheur qu'elles donneraient à leur sainte et si excellente mère - à Toi mon ange mille fois adorée…*

In this same letter, Elise refers to Josephine's interest in considering selling "Le Cave", and buying or building a smaller place, and suggests "it would be better if you could manage to get what you want, even if it is outside here [Pescia] because of the Palamidessi."

> *qu'il vaudra mieux si tu peux réussir à avoir ce qui tu désires, que ce soit hors d'ici [Pescia] à cause des P [Palamidessi].*

Joséphine has been buying State lottery tickets….The press reviews about her performances on the stage—which Elise had sent on to Elisina to read—are termed "fair, without excessive praise, but one feels that they are true"…..

> *justes, sans trop d'éloges, mais on entend qu'elles sont vraies …*

in other words, less than glowing. We also read that Louise Baese has been having difficulties with her children: Paolo has to change schools because he hadn't even been given grades in his present school, and had not been considered worthy of appearing for an oral examination. As if this wasn't trouble enough, business has been bad for the Baeses. Louise was about to leave for Viareggio to spend the month of August there, and the "two angels" (Elisina and Linetta) were going to be there with her.

In another letter, Elise expresses her worries because Ugo del Vaso, the brother of Sofia, as asked her whether it was true that Josephine was on the stage; and a Madam Magnami (presumably the one who later bought "Le Cave") had also asked whether it was true that Josephine had married [obviously Gower, though is name was not mentioned]. Elise writes that she had replies "*Non*" flatly. The letter concludes: "My loving regards to Gower, who, I hope, is with you and helps you to get through all your worries."

> *Mes souvenirs affectueux à Gower qui, j'espère, est auprès de toi et t'aide à passer toutes tes inquiétudes.*

From a letter of July 30, 1891: "...seeing the portrait of your dear, handsome Louis, I wondered whether it was not a portrait of my dear Fiferl dressed as a naval officer. Lord, you both have the same beautiful, noble looks. And it seems to me that your beloved Louis has written in the middle of his forehead, 'Comte de Castelvecchio'.

> *en voyant le portrait de ton cher, beau Louis je me suis demandée si ce n'était pas le portrait de ma Fiferl habillée en officier de marine. Dieu, que vous avez la même belle et si noble figure – il me semble que ton Louis aimé a écrit au milieu du front, 'Comte de Castevecchio'* ...

The rifts and tensions within the family are revealed by the following passage in a letter from Elise to Joséphine of August 3, 1891, while Elisina and Linetta are at Viareggio with the Baeses: "Lucciola told me that her husband really loves your daughters! May God open her eyes! I *cannot*, I *will* not believe that Lucciola is so little the daughter of her blessed father!! She is very far from resembling him as you do, darling daughter of his. But she is his daughter, too, and surely she will feel it in the end. Unfortunately, she lived for a *very* long time with Mother [i.e. Suzanne Sophie, Elise's mother].

> *Lucciola m'a dit que son mari aime beaucoup tes fillettes! Que Dieu lui ouvre les yeux ! Je ne puis, je ne veux pas croire que Lucciola soit si peu la fille de ton saint Père!! Elle est bien loin de Lui ressembler comme Toi, chère belle enfant à Lui – mais elle est sa fille aussi et elle doit finir par le sentir. Malheureusement, elle a vécu très longtemps avec Maman...*

A poignant letter from Elise of August 31, 1891, reveals how unhappy she is and how she yearns for the love of her children and family. She hasn't heard from Joséphine for a long time, and begs her "not to leave me without letters from you and without telling me what I am to do"

> *de ne pas me laisser sans lettres de toi, et sans me dire ce que je dois faire*

about difficulties with Lucciola. Then, "Elisina has stopped writing, too. It is three weeks since I had any word from my dear daughters. Sophy has no letters from you either."

> *Elisina aussi a cessé de m'écrire, voici trois semaines que je n'ai plus un mot des chères Fillettes. Sophy aussi est sans lettres de toi*

There are hints of Gower getting into trouble over some wine business: "this unfortunate business in which Gower has found himself involved..."

> *cette affaire malheureuse dans laquelle Gower s'est trouvé mêlé ...*

in London. The rest of the letter is extremely tormented and pathetic—almost hysterical at the end, in its misery: "Good-by again, angel blessed by me... I love you and I kiss you, and I wish that I had treasures to give you, instead of costing you *so much* money. Why cannot love count in place of money? Be sure that no one in the world could give you more of it that I. I love and kiss and adore you, and I thank God who, in his compassion, made me your mother. May God keep and bless you, together with all those whom you love. Your adoring mother,
Elise de Castelvecchio"

> *Adieu encore, Ange à moi bénie*

> *Je t'aime et je t'embrasse, et je voudrais avoir des trésors à te donner au lieu de te coûter si si cher. Pourquoi ne peut-on pas mettre l'affection au lieu de l' argent ? Je t'assure que personne au monde ne t'en apporterait autant que moi. Je t'aime et je t'embrasse et t'adore, et je remercie le Bon Dieu qui, dans sa miséricorde m'a faite ta mère – que Dieu te garde et te bénisse ainsi que celles et ceux que tu aimes.*
>
> *Ta mère qui t'adore*
>
> *Elise de Castelvecchio*

Josephine has been writing to her mother about her plans to go to the United States. Elise, in a letter of September 12, 1891, suggests that before thinking of leaving Europe, Josephine should call on the Princess Mathilde in France.... "[Princess Mathilde] also showed and, I believe, even felt much affection for your father, whom she had known at the residence of the Comte de Saint-Leu. She never liked the Empress, nor did the Empress like her. That should encourage her to like you. Her tastes and her understanding of life are quite unlike this Empress's. Anyway, I could send you the letter that she personally wrote to me and that I copied when Prince Napoleon, her brother, died. She has no children, and she is as kind as any Princess could be. I am quite certain that she would like you."

> *elle a toujours témoigné et je crois même ressenti beaucoup d'affection pour ton Père qu'elle avait connu chez le Comte de St. Leu. Elle n'a jamais aimé l'Impératrice et n'a été aimée par elle. Ce serait donc une raison pour qu'elle t'aimât. Elle a des goûts entièrement autres, et comprend la vie d'une façon contraire à cette ... Impératrice - enfin, vois - je pourrais t'envoyer la lettre qu'elle m'a écrite elle-même, et que j'ai copiée lorsque le Prince Napoléon son frère, est mort... elle n'a pas d'enfants et elle est bonne autant qu'une Princesse peut l'être - et ta nature lui plairait, j'en suis certaine.*

In 1891, Elise's sight was already failing rapidly: "Don't answer on the subject of what I am about to tell you, because Sophy sometimes helps me to read your letters..." and in another: "...when it comes to numbers, I can't see them very well."

> *Ne me réponds pas à ce que je vais te dire, parce que quelquefois Sophy m'aide à lire tes lettres…*
> *moi en fait de chiffres, je n'y vois pas assez physiquement.*

Moreover, Elise is also practically penniless. She writes on January 1, 1892: "I can send you neither your Elisina's drawing, nor the two certificates that your beloved children received when the prizes were awarded. It is the fault of the postal system. They wanted 2.70 francs to send them; it is impossible to do so for less. For me, at the moment, 2.70 francs makes a considerable sum. I had nothing from the two months that Lucciola paid for, and I hardly know how I have managed so far, and it is probably Mr. Antonio [del Vaso] whom I have to thank. I hope that you will forgive me if I delay sending you this drawing by your Elisina and the two certificates that bear witness to the excellent behavior of your two angels. I suffer, believe me, from being unable to send you what your believed daughters had put aside for you, our beautiful angel."

> *Je ne puis t'expédier ni le dessin de ton Elisina ni les deux feuilles que tes enfants aimées ont reçu à la distribution des prix – et la faute en est à la poste. On m'a demandé 2 francs 70 pour les expédier, et on ne peut les envoyer à moins. 2 francs 70 sont une vraie somme pour moi dans ce moment-ci. Je n'ai rien eu des deux mois que Lucciola a payés – et je ne sais comment j'ai pu arriver jusqu' ici – et c'est dû pas mal à Mr Antonio [del Vaso]… J'espère que tu me pardonneras si j'attends à t'envoyer ce dessin de ton Elisina et des deux feuilles qui attestent à l'excellente conduite de tes deux anges. Je souffre, crois-le moi, de ne pouvoir t'envoyer ce que tes Aimées avaient mis de côté pour toi, notre belle Ange …*

This, on top of a painful experience when she was about to leave Pisa in order to return to Pescia: "I have something very painful to write, something that I would never have told you if I had been able to hide it. Yesterday evening I was about to leave Pisa when the administrator of Santa Anna came to tell me, in the name of the Operajo [administration?], and to ask me to inform you by letter, that you must send the fees due for you beloved children, and that if you do not, the school will have no choice but to dismiss them. Apparently there was a girl for whom 500 francs were due, and who was dismissed; and that led to greater severity. I would never have wished to be responsible for delivering this painful message, but the Treasurer told me that if I did not, they would have to send you an official letter... He came purposely to see me yesterday evening at the station and very nicely, with every mark of civility, laid this painful burden on me. I thought that you might perhaps write, and that you would certainly know how to resolve the issue in one way or another."

> *J'ai une chose bien pénible à t'écrire, et que je n'aurais pas accepté de te dire – si j'avais pu la cacher. Hier au soir, j'allais quitter Pise, lorsque l'administrateur de Santa Anna est venu, au nom de l'Operajo, me dire, me prier de t'écrire que tu envoies ce qui est dû pour tes aimées enfants, sans quoi ils seraient forcés de les envoyer. Il parait qu'il y a eu une jeune fille pour laquelle cinq cents francs étaient dus, qui a été renvoyée – et cela a amené plus de sévérité. Je n'aurais pas voulu être chargée de cette bien pénible commission, mais le Caissier m'a dit que si je ne le faisais pas, on devrait t'écrire une lettre officielle.... Il est venu exprès hyer [sic] au soir à la gare et, bien gentiment, et avec toutes les préparations oratoires, il m'a chargé de cette pénible commission. J'ai pensé que, peut-être, tu pourrais écrire, et que tu saurais bien sûr t'en tirer d'une façon quelconque.*

She adds messages for Gower:

"Tell him that I pray to God from the bottom of my heart that he open for You All a new era, a fresh, new era [in your lives]. That would give me only happiness possible for me. This miserable problem of money is so burning on all sides that it is terrifying!! Let us hope that God will remedy it."

> *Dis-lui que je prie le Bon Dieu du fond de mon âme pour qu'il veuille*

> *qu'une ère nouvelle, toute nouvelle, commence pour Vous Tous. C'est là le seul Bonheur que je puisse avoir. Cette malheureuse question d'argent est si tellement brûlante, arrôtissante de tous les côtés, que cela devient effrayant !! Espérons que le Bon Dieu y apporte un remède.*

And a last note:

> "It has been quite a few days since I last received a letter from Lucciola. That surprises me, since for Christmas and the New Year a letter is so heartening."
>
> *De Lucciola je n'ai plus de lettres depuis pas mal de jours. Cela m'étonne, car pour Christmas and New Year, une lettre fait tant de bien.*

Elise describes in a letter of November 24, 1891, the success of Elisina and Linetta at the prize-giving ceremony: "We were all there: Lucciola, myself, Sophy, and even Ugo's two little girls. Your darlings both played the piano perfectly. Lilly also recited a little fable in French, and perfectly well. She first played solo; then Elisina, too, played solo; then they played a piece for four hands; then, finally, Elisina and the teacher played a piece together, to applause."

> *Nous y étions toutes: Lucciola, moi, Sophy, et jusqu'aux deux fillettes d'Ugo. Tes Aimées ont joué toutes deux parfaitement bien du Piano. Lilly a aussi récité une petite fable en français, et parfaitement bien. Elle a joué d'abord toute seule, puis Elise a joué aussi seule, puis Elles ont joué un morceau à quatre mains – et enfin Elisina et le Maître ont joué un morceau ensemble difficile et qui a été applaudi.*

The letter ends on a somber note:

> "Now, my angel, I must give you a sad piece of news. For some time this eye that was operated on has not been doing well. We went with Lucciola to the oculist, who said that the eye needs another little operation—one not at all like the first, but that would requite a fifteen-day rest in the hospital. There is no hurry. I just wanted to let you know, in order to keep nothing from

you. Lucciola said that she will do what she can, but she, too, is terribly short of money. Actually, the hospital is no more expensive than a____ [perhaps she refrained from writing, "a room in Pescia"?], but you have to put down a month in advance. I am sorry that I had to bring that up, my darling daughter. Please believe that I am not suffering at all. It is just that I see so poorly—enough, though, that I could go there alone; and that is already a blessing from God."

> *Maintenant, chère Ange à moi, il faut que je te donne une nouvelle qui m'ennuie. Depuis quelque temps cet œil qui a été opéré n'allait pas. Nous sommes allées avec Lucciola chez l'oculiste et il a dit qu'il faudrait une autre petite opération, qui ne serait pas du tout comme la première, mais qui nécessiterait un repos de 15 jours à l' hôpital. Cela ne presse pas du tout. J'ai seulement voulu te le dire à fin de ne rien te cacher. Lucciola a dit qu'elle ferait ce qu'elle pourrait – mais elle est très tourmentée aussi pour l'argent. Au fond l'hôpital ne coûte pas plus cher qu'une ---- [sic! Perhaps Elise meant «a room in Pescia»...] mais il faut déposer le mois complet. Je regrette tant d'avoir du te parler de cela, Fille adorée mienne – crois que je ne souffre nullement, seulement j'y vois peu, mais assez pour aller seule, et c'est déjà une grâce du Bon Dieu...*

News of Gower in a letter dated February 9, 1892: "The day before yesterday we had a very surprising letter from Ugo [del Vaso]. He said that Gower has left for Japan, where he is to stay until next summer; that by September he will be back; and that your marriage can then take place!! He said nothing about where and how he had learned all this—on the contrary—and he asked us whether it was true! But then, my darling angel, you will be all by yourself in the vastness of London?"

> *Avant hyer [sic] il nous est venu une lettre d'Ugo [del Vaso] qui nous a bien étonnées. Il disait que Gower était parti pour le Japon, où il demeurerait jusqu'à l'été prochain – que le mois de septembre il serait déjà revenu et ton mariage aurait lieu!! Comment et où il avait appris*

> tout cela, il ne le disait pas, au contraire, et il nous demandait si
> c'était vrai ! Mais alors, Ange bien aimée, tu serais seule seulette dans
> cette immensité de Londres ?

We learn from the same letter that Gower had been involved in a "malheureuse affaire" of oil and wine, with the result that friends of Josephine in Pescia are not well disposed toward him: "The name of Gower is never spoken in my presence, but I know that he [Cardini] has no praise for him."

> Le nom de Gower n'est jamais prononcé devant moi – mais je sais
> qu'il [Cardini] est loin d'en faire des éloges.

From this letter we know that Gower and Josephine were *not* married in early 1892; and that Gower's business activities had *not* met with success in every respect. If he *had* left for Japan for 8 months or so, it may have been due to both personal and business factors which led to what seems to have been his eclipse in 1893. However, the question whether they ever actually married is not conclusively answered, in my mind, even though A.P. implies in one of her letters to her mother, nearly 30 years later that she had pressured her mother into making a scandalous statement in order to make the marriage possible. At any rate I have found no record of a marriage;[2] and if Josephine ever answered this particular letter of Elise's, her answer has not survived.

On December 19, 1891, Elise wrote Josephine a Christmas letter in English and French: "My own beloved darling—I hope, my darling, God will grant thee and thy dear beloved ones a Merry Christmas and a very happy New Year, and many, many others to follow—et tout le bonheur que Dieu si bon peut accorder—tant à toi, my darling beloved, qu'à celles et ceux tous qui te sont chers..

"It is real Christmas weather today, cold, grey, and

---

[2] See Appendix on E.H.M. Gower, p. 263. He and Joséphine were married in a church in Westminster in December 1890. (RT)

threatening snow. We may not get it, but it makes me think even more of you, my darling angel, and of the grey sky—mainly *moral*—that you must feel. A merry Christmas, my own beloved one and a happy, as happy as possible New Year."

> *Il fait aujourd'hui un vrai temps de Noël, froid et gris, promettant de la neige que, peut-être, nous n'aurons pas, mais qui me fait penser doublement à toi, Ange adorée, et au ciel… surtout moral… gris que tu dois ressentir ! A merry Christmas, my own beloved one – and a happy, as happy as possible New Year.*

There seem to be a good many "sous-entendus" in this message—perhaps allusions to Palamidessi's recent death... and/or to some aspect of Josephine's relations with Gower?

On April 6, and again in an incomplete letter of May 22, 1891, Elisa writes about divorce. The second letter contains a most unexpected and startling definition by Elisa of the cornerstone of marriage. This preoccupation with the subject of divorce must have been related to the situation in which Josephine and Palamidessi found themselves since the 1886 decree of separation of the Lucca Tribunal. Since they had been married religiously in Pescia, as well as civilly in Paris, they were not divorced in the eyes of the Church, and Josephine could not have married Gower without committing bigamy—no light matter, at least in those days!

> There are articles written by Mr. Naguet, the man who saw to the establishment of divorce in France. He next came to Italy, where he preaches the same doctrine. They say that, here, the Queen is adamantly opposed to divorce—in truth, I do not know why, because, to my mind, divorce is the cornerstone of marriage. Here, though, husbands are either against this law, or they throw it in the wastebasket, since they do whatever they want without it. Still, despite everything, it seems to be being taken seriously…when there is nothing else to do.

Anyway, if you want this book [*Il Divorzio*], let me know, and I will send it to you. ... Next Sunday Sophy and I will go to see Monsignore, and I will write you, my darling angel, what he has to say. As for me, I hold divorce to be essential, and I would give everything in the world to see it established. So answer me, my darling...

> *Il y a des articles écrits par Mr Naguet, qui est celui qui a fait établir le divorce en France. Il est ensuite venu en Italie, où il prêche les mêmes doctrines. On dit qu'ici, la ... Reine est excessivement contraire au divorce – je ne sais en vérité pourquoi, car, selon moi, le divorce est la pierre fondamentale du mariage. Mais ici, les maris sont ou contraires à cette loi, ou ils la jettent dans le panier des oubliettes, car ils font tout ce qu'il veulent sans elle. Toujours est-il que, malgré tout, on semble s'en occuper.... quand on n'a pas autre chose à faire. Enfin, si tu veux avoir ce livre [Il Divorzio, of which she includes an advertisement clipped out of a newspaper] dis-le moi, et je te l'enverrai... Dimanche prochain, Sophy et moi, nous irons chez Monsignore et je t'écrirai, Ange aimée, ce qu'il nous dira... Pour moi, je ne tiens qu'au divorce, et je donnerais tout au monde pour qu'il soit établi. Réponds-moi donc, chère Aimée...*

On April 6, 1892, "Ma Fifinette a moi" is expected at Pescia shortly, and everything is being done to put "Le Cave" in order for her. It was a brief visit, for on May 5, Elise writes to her in London to say she is happy to learn that she has arrived there safely.

On May 26, 1892, Elise writes to tell Josephine that the doctors have said that if she is to retain the little sight she still has, she must undergo "this little, leftover bit of surgery,[she adds]: It does not mean any increase in expense, I know, because it costs the same five francs a day that you pay here; but one has to put down 150 francs in advance. It is true that I will get the balance back, but the 150 francs have to be paid first. I have written to Lucciola about this at the same time as to you. You will tell me what I am to do." The letter ends on a painful note of remorse:

"...... I wish I had been all my life what I am now. I have loved you, but *badly*. Forgive me, and love me."

> *... je voudrais avoir été toute ma vie ce que je suis maintenant. Je t'ai aimée, mais je t'ai mal aimée – pardonnes-moi et aime-moi.*

Elise (probably after the eye operation, given the date of early August in a letter) had suggested to Lucciola that it might perhaps make things easier for everyone if she were to come and live with her, or at any rate leave Pescia. When her "Ange bien-aimée" learned of this, she reacted very strongly and wrote a letter scolding her mother soundly. The following passages from Elise's reply to this letter give one an idea of what the tone of Josephine's letter must have been. August 6-7 1892:

> My good, kind Fifi, I have just received your, despite everything, very kind letter. Please, my dear daughter, believe that you are quite wrong about what I wrote you... I should have written to you before telling Lucciola what I wrote to her. You are a thousand times right. Absolutely all I had in mind was the thought of how much I cost you... that alone prompted me to compose the letter that I wrote, and I am sorry that I did so, since it hurt you so badly. I was wrong, and I ask you again to forgive me for having written as I did to Lucciola without telling you. Love me, my dear, kind daughter, that is all I ask; and believe that I would have to be mad and bad not to be perfectly comfortable here. I am not and never will be tired of Pescia. I made a terrible mistake, writing to Lucciola as I did, without at least telling you beforehand. Send me a single word of forgiveness, dear and beloved daughter of mine, and believe that in your letter you were severe toward me. I asked you that I might come here, and I am happy to stay. Absolutely the only thing that troubles me is that I cost you so much money. I assure you that I am telling you what I have in my heart. I promise never to write about any

serious matter without informing you in advance. Tell me that you forgive the hurt that I caused you without ever wishing to do so. I was utterly stupid to write without letting you know, but it will never happen again. Good-by, my dear, kind, beloved daughter, from the bottom of my soul.

Your idiot mother,
Elise de Castelvecchio

Ma chère et bonne Fifi,

Je viens de recevoir ta, malgré tout, bien bonne lettre. Crois, chère enfant, que tu t'es entièrement trompée sur ce que je t'ai écrit… J'aurais dû t'écrire avant de dire à Lucciola ce que je lui ai écrit – tu as mille fois raison. Ce n'était absolument que l'idée de te coûter si cher… qui m'a fait faire la lettre que j'ai faite, et que je regrette puisqu'elle t'a fait tant de peine; et je t'en demande pardon… J'ai eu tort et je t'en demande pardon de nouveau d'écrire comme je l'ai fait à Lucciola sans te le dire. Aime-moi, chère et bonne fille, c'est tout ce que je désire ; et crois qu'il faudrait que je fusse méchante et folle pour ne pas me trouver parfaitement bien ici. Je ne suis et ne serai jamais fatiguée de Pescia. J'ai fait une atroce bêtise d'écrire à Lucciola ce que je lui ai écrit, sans te le dire au moins avant… Ecris-moi un seul mot de pardon, chère et si aimée enfant mienne, et crois que ta lettre a été sévère pour moi. Je t'ai demandé de venir ici, et je suis heureuse d'y rester. La seule et unique chose qui me fait de la peine, c'est de t'y coûter cher. Je t'assure que je te dis ce que j'ai dans le cœur … Je te promets de ne jamais écrire quelque chose de sérieux sans te le dire à l'avance. Dis-moi que tu me pardonnes la peine que je t'ai faite bien, bien involontairement… J'ai été une immense bête d'écrire sans t'en prévenir, mais cela n'arrivera jamais jamais plus… Au-revoir chère, bonne, aimée – du fin fond de mon âme.

Ta mère imbécile, Elise de Castelvecchio"

Another equally pathetic letter of August 16, 1892, tells Joséphine that she has not heard from her since she wrote begging her pardon. Elise prostrates herself again, beseeching her daughter over and over to forgive her—and begging for just one word from her, telling her that she has forgiven her mother, and that she loves her.... A renewed plea for forgiveness and for her daughter's love is contained in a letter of September 4, 1892. I have found no letter from Elise subsequently which indicates that she had received a reply from Josephine to her appeals.

On December 19, 1892, Elisa writes to Joséphine to tell her that she is sending her some jewellery for Elisina and Linetta in two little boxes, and one little box for Louis containing two mother of pearl buttons which had belonged to Louis de Castelvecchio. It seems likely that the small wooden box I have, with brass edges and the monogram EC engraved in brass on the lid, is one of these "petit boîtes".

Her eyesight is failing increasingly: "Would you be kind enough, my blessed child, to help Louis make out my hieroglyphic scrawl? But I should stop writing to you if I cannot do better; and since you manage to divine my meaning, I prefer to paddle along with you."

> *Veux-tu, chere belle enfant, aider Louis à déchiffre 'mei linei hyerogliffi' – autrement dits 'scarabocchi'? Mais il faudrait ne plus vous écrire du tout si je ne sais pas faire mieux; et puisque vous me devinez, j'aime mieux barboter avec vous.*

In January 1893 she writes affectionately to Louis, thanking him for the long account he wrote for her of his voyage to Calcutta. She tells him how pretty "Lilly" is and that [to WRT's astonishment] "she resembles, especially in character, your angelic mother." She writes to Elisina who has written to thank her for the jewellery.

A number of letters from Elise cover the period from January 1893 to march 1894, the year in which she died. They become less and less legible, and seem not to have been mailed by Sophie del Vaso singly, but all together in a package addressed to Joséphine—after Elise could no longer write—at 30 Walpole Street, Chelsea.

Elise, as has been already noted, died in Pescia on October 5, and was buried there, not next to her husband in the family vault at the Père Lachaise cemetery which she had built for him and for the family. At the time of her death, the family was widely scattered. The only adult member nearby was Lucciola Baese in Florence. Linetta was at Santa Anna in Pisa, Elisina was at the Cheltenham College for Ladies. Joséphine was in New York, and Louis, who had gone off to sea again nearly one year before, was by then in, or nearing the State of Washington.

Linetta's Notes on Louis de Castle and Elisina

When they were together in England (1892-93), they were "very great friends and so proud of each other". I happened to be alone at Antigny with my mother in early September, 1929, when the news arrived of Louis' death. She was very deeply affected. A.P. writes that he had changed his name to de Castle while he was still in the States. She states he did so for "purely practical reasons, among uneducated people when he lived in a mining community"... before Elisina and Grant Richards brought him back to London and helped him to emigrate to South Africa. She adds... "He used the same initials as myself [L.P.C.] because they were on his trunk; but in his last letter he asked me for information about the family and said that he did not know what the P stood for—and that at his marriage, being asked, he had suddenly improvised and said 'Percy' ! (which was the cause of much worry to Francis' mother, as I gathered from a letter she wrote me)."

When Louis set off to sea again late in 1893, he missed his Merchant Navy ship purposely (according to A.P.), in spite of the fact that the Captain would have been a friend, and was then sent off on another whose Executive Officer was a brute. "At S. Francisco," she writes, he deserted. He had some very rough years, but learned all about mining of different kinds. Only lack of transport stood in the way of developing what he considered very good mines; and about 1902 he asked Elisina and your [i.e. Gioia's] father whether a company could be floated on the London Stock Exchange. They then paid his journey to London, and a few months later from there to S. Africa. He passed the highest exams and made a very good career."

He died on September 1, 1929, at Elim Hospital, Bandolier Kop, near Pietersburg, Northern Transvaal, and was buried in the Mission Grounds.

He had met his future wife, Frances Wahl, at a hospital ball given by the town of Germiston, Transvaal, in early 1916. They were married at Sunnyside, Pretoria on December 24, 1917. Frances Wahl's uncle and aunt, Mr and Mrs Edenborough, sponsored her because her mother was living in Capetown, a thousand miles away. Mrs Edenborough was from Blankenberg—hence the B in G. B. de Castle. Gerard Blanckenberg was born on September 30, 1918, at Roodepoort, where Louis was Manager of Roodepoort United Mines.

At the bottom of the typed notice of Louis' death in the *South African Mining and Engineering Journal,* Johannesburg, of the first week of September, 1929, A.P. has written the following:

"Louis knew hardly any details about the family and his own childhood—only what he could remember. He had never been back to Italy since we all, including my father, came to London c. 1884 [sic, but this date is wrong. Josephine took the children to London with her in 1882—as far as I have been able to work out] and I am sure he did not know in what Italian district he was born. Being Italian would not suit his environment in the Western States and I suppose he improvised his birthplace on first being asked about it in S. Africa. He wrote to me—his last letter, I think, from hospital—asking for information, which he said Billy was then getting old enough to be given, and said he could not account for his initial P, and that for his wedding papers he was driven to invent 'Percy'! I had written to him, some time before about a small inheritance from a Palamidessi uncle, but he would have nothing to do with it."

A.P.'s notes (now at Gragnano) provide interesting information on Elisina's life at the Cheltenham Ladies College (1892 - 1896). Her College salary was 40 pounds a year guaranteed, and a *little* more if there were more Italian students.

She gave mother all her money each term, and was sent back with 10/- a term in her pocket... She became engaged to George S. Street in London, and Miss Beale said she must choose between him and the College—mother having meanwhile gone to the United States to make a success of her acting. I was ready to come and teach too (1896), so she got Miss Beale to accept me in her stead and went to London. But George Street, tho' an excellent writer, did not make a living, and there couldnt be a future. Time passed..." In a marginal note to the page on which the foregoing was written, A.P. has added: "After mother had gone to America [this departure must have been in 1897] Elisina boarded with a family of friends, the Swanson's, and Dorothy Swanson, the youngest daughter, was my first friend in England."

A.P. adds that Elisina met Grant Richards at the home of the G. W. Rawlinsons in Notting Hill Gate, and that they were married [in 1898] "with every likelihood of happiness." A.P. was subject to a nervous illness which kept her in hospital more than once, in this period. She writes that Grant Richards was "awfully good" to her, then and for a long time after: "But he *did* gamble. And he grew to have enemies. He was a pioneer in good publishing....and they used to discuss the form and contents of series of books, together. When the bankruptcy came [this was the first in 1906, I believe. The second came in 1909, when my mother left him] she helped him all she could, and ran the business, going to the office until he was discharged. She did love you children very very much. Frankly, I don't know what to say. And I cannot imagine what made her change so completely. You remember what she did in the first World War; and how she was given at a ceremony held for her alone (a great honour) the Légion d'Honneur?"

The Twentieth Century

The Twentieth Century opens with Elisina (married to Grant Richards since 1898) living in London; AP still at Cheltenham; Louis de Castle making his way in mining in the State of Washington; Gioia born May 28, 1900, in London; "Tante Louise" (Lucciola) Baese in Florence; and Josephine pursuing her stage career in New York City.

According to the obituary notice in the NY Herald Tribune of Dec. 20, 1932, Joséphine was brought to the United States "thirty five years ago" (i.e. 1897), and had appeared in W.A. Brady's production of "Trilby" and with James A. Hackett in "Plot and Passion". She had also played in "Romeo and Juliet" and in "Quo Vadis". According to the same obituary, she had intended to stay in the US for six months, but had made it her home, becoming a US citizen. While I do not know whether the account of Joséphine's stage activities is correct, the dates conform to those I arrived at independently. The obituary also states (correctly) that she married Antonio Frabasilis in New York in 1903.

On November 28, 1902 Joséphine wrote Elisina and Grant Richards a bitter letter which I quote here because it not only sheds light on Joséphine's feelings toward her elder daughter, but reveals the unhappy state of family relations:

As you have written me in English" (so she writes to "My dear Daughter"), for both of you, so will I answer too, in English, and for both of you (i.e.: Grant Richards and Elisina). Since I wrote Grant, asking for immediate help, for the first time in my life (and for the last too, happen what may), 24 days have elapsed.

In that time, I could have gone to heaven several times. Of course, you must have been sure that I would not write except under exceptional pressure, but the haste has been rather slow just the same; it is no more than I expected, so I do not either grumble or reproach.

A few days ago, I have signed an Engagement for Christmas, and as I have lived up to now, so shall I manage a little longer.

I have asked my children for help, once in my life, and I have received a beautiful letter, telling of anxieties insufferable etc....., and offering me to bargain the very liberty of my thoughts and actions, of my hopes and aspirations, for board and lodging....perhaps. These are at least the outsketched premises.

I expected nothing and am not disappointed.

I did not ask for a further hindrance; I was asking for a momentary and urgent help.

You have dear Lilly (Linetta) under Doctors for months, against my will and you have given way to my idea, which proved to be the right one for her, only after having spent a lot of money which would have done wonders if spent wisely, or with more sense.

You have had your way with Louis too, and he is now far from everybody in a strange land, when half the money you have spent on that whim would have seen him through in the country where I am, and where he had already made friends and with whose business methods he was well acquainted.

Now you can be perfectly sure of one thing: I shall not be your puppet too, and I will not give up my profession until it pleases me to do so.

If you think that you tell me something new when you

speak of doubts about my eyes, I will tell you in answer to that, that you cannot have thought very much about it, or at any rate not the tenth part of what I have had to think about it...

I am in God's hands, and He will see me through.

I suppose I ought to thank you for the professed expressions of affection, but I am not in a mood to dissimulate, and I think frankly they count for very little.

I am not in need any more, and I thank you, but will not sell my right of living or thinking as I please: No, I will not take to type-writing or companionship or anything of that kind just now.

You need not write any more, either of you, at least on this subject, for it would be absolutely useless. I know now, at least, where I shall not go if ever I want help again.

I feel very much roused and indignant, that is true, but I am not angry. I am myself astonished at feeling this so much, for I certainly thought I was no such fool as to have some doubts left about business matters between us, but it bites sharply enough to show me I was not quite as wise as I thought to be; all this will blow over soon, I dare say…. it's only one more cord snapped, that's all.

Only don't do me the injustice of comparing me with my dear Father, for that implies that my conduct might have somewhat resembled yours, which I selfishly thank God on my knees could never have been the case.

You do not answer in any manner or form the letter I wrote you personally, Elisina, or tell me anything about Nappy. I asked you also to let me know who had bought my Solitaire ring, my Father's watch-chain and the laces; but, of course, thinking you saw a good opportunity of starving me out of my dignity, you omitted to answer any such trifling questions.

Well, my dear Children, I wish heartily I had never applied to you, but as it is, I find myself wiser instead of foolishly happier.

Wishing you a very happy New Year and a very merry Christmas, I remain,

Your Mother

Joséphine de Castelvecchio

In the undated draft of the letter written by Grant Richards to Joséphine about this time, no doubt (though not in reply to the preceding letter from Joséphine), he defends Elisina and, incidentally, reveals the fact that Joséphine must have already left England by the time he and Elisina were married.

My dear Mother: we do not know one another, so it is the more difficult for me to tell you how much the character of your letter surprised me and how difficult it is for me, having just read it, to answer it with patience. Elisina is your daughter, but she is also my wife. Is it possible that you do not know how she has worked for you, how she has spared neither time nor money in her love for you, how she has given all her energies to keep what you value against your return? She has told me very little of what happened in regard to your property before our marriage, but I can only imagine from the many demands for the payment of interest on this loan and that, which have come to us that for many months she must have been paying on your behalf. Since our marriage too on more than one occasion considerable sums have been paid—until I have had to refuse to let her pay anything else...."

Three days after her previous letter, on December 1, Joséphine received a letter from Grant Richards, sending her some money, and she writes to Elisina and Grant to thank them, and tell them she wished she could have recalled her first letter.

When one considers her situation in New York at this time,

her worries are understandable. She is 45, and has been in the States 5 years since Daly had recruited her, doubtless with high expectations which had so far shown no sign of being fulfilled. She has serious financial problems. However she has now been engaged for Christmas, "and that settled my mind at rest [sic] for the future, but the present didn't improve much until my new Manager, having all faith in me, apparently, has advanced me the money to save my things that were in Storage, and enough to live day by day. I owe him now $100, and am to repay him at so much the week, as soon as our work begins…" The implications for Joséphine's prospects of such a state of affairs require no elaboration.

In addition to this, she has other personal worries: "Meantime I received the news of poor Paci's death, and of course of my Nappy's now terrible position…" I don't know why the news of Paci's death was a blow to Joséphine, nor why Nappy's situation was "of course" now terrible, but in a letter of April 27, 1927 to Linetta, Elisina writes as follows: "I was left in England, alone, at the age of 19", (i.e. 1894, when Josephine went off to America for the first time)" with no provision for my holidays save what I could make myself. I had to take care of N's boarding expenses, and had to go down near Peterborough, where I found him in a dreadful condition of physical and moral neglect. I was encouraged to undertake the journey to Italy, from Paris, under the escort of a most dissolute and horrible old man, Professor Paci, who on the journey tried to come and go freely in my bedroom and explained that with M's knowledge, *he* was paying my ticket and hotel bills. Eventually, after his death, his nephew tried to extort money from me by saying that he had found a lot of compromising letters from Mother to his uncle, which proved that his uncle had 'lent' money to Mother, and he, as executor of the will, must exact reimbursement from me, or these letters would be given about to be read".

This is one of three references to Paci I have come across. I do not know whether there was any connection between him and "N". However, the juxtaposition without transition of the mentions by Elisina of her visit so see "N" and of Paci suggests to me that there may have been. Since there is no mention of Gower, was Paci supposed to be looking after "N" during Joséphine's absence? Where was Gower at the time? All this increases the nebulousness of the Gower element in the family history! There seems to have been a sort of tacit conspiracy within the family to avoid, or erase any discussion of the man— to obliterate him, as it were, as though he had never been. In AP's letter of Jan 7, 1927 to her mother, she refers to "Paci's tardiness to operate, when he knew perfectly well that in a case of dropsy it is essential above all to operate at the right moment….." this being in relation to Elise's final illness.

Then, in a letter to A.P. from Elisina from Budapest, on April 1, 1933, obviously in response to a question: "I knew nothing whatever about Leon's date or place of birth". In the circumstances, the "nothing whatever" weakens the credibility of the assertion. So far as Elisina was concerned, Gower must have been a non-person, and Leon even more so.

In her letter of December 1, 1902, Josephine makes it clear that the most sensitive topic, and the source of her strongest resentment, is any suggestion that she should give up the stage and earn her living in other ways. In this letter she makes her feelings perfectly clear:

> We know each other, my Elisina, we know that we are, all of us, trying to do our best for the short little while we have to spend on this Earth…. Why will you then put conditions to me, which you know to be the most onerous ones that anybody could try to impose on me, and which you ought to know I will always resent as incompatible with my dignity, my self-respect as I understand it, and with what I know I could do were the

proper chance to offer at last? Why will you insist on saying to me, ever and always: 'Do *any* mortal thing except one' and that ONE being the only one I care for? Had you written to me that you could not help me now, upon my honor I say to you, I would have had no other thought than fear *for you*, for I would have believed it implicitly and would only have been sorry and frightened at your not having that much to spare; but it was not hearing from you for so long, and then hearing like that, that wounded me to the quick......

As for your offer my darlings, both of you, let me thank you for it but, dears, I do not feel that life would be worth living for me, had I to give up the struggle before the battle is over. Now, with your help, and with that of my new Manager, Mr George H Brennan, I am in the position, for the first time in my life, to be free from daily, nay, hourly cares. I have made certain arrangements with him by which I hope his scheme of starring me next season may be facilitated. If this comes true, then it will be 'up to me' and, should I prove a failure to my contentment (?) [sic], I would not only give up the stage, but come back to live as near you as I could, an doing there, as you say, any other mortal thing rather than that for which I believe I was born.

Still, my eyes would not, I am afraid, let me do any translation, dress-making or much else, but I could still be a chaperone, or a companion, or... well... any other mortal thing!

Antonio Frabasilis (1854 – 1927)

The barely visible Chinese characters are from an edifying poem attributed to the Confucian philosopher Zhu Xi (Chu Hsi, 1130-1200)

Most fortunately for Josephine at this critical moment of her life, when she can no longer have really believed in her own professional future she married in 1903, Antonio Frabasilis (b. 1854, near Naples, d. in Naples while there on a trip with Josephine, on March 31, 1927). An obituary notice in the form of an article in a periodical published in Naples, states that he was a Marquis, and that his father was Duke of Castelsarraceno. His life is defined as having been *venturosa e luminosa*. His principal career was that of interpreter for the New York City Law Courts.[3]

---

[3] The Ellis Island National Monument web site states that he went to America in 1899, was naturalized in 1906, and was employed as an official Ellis Island interpreter in 1908. He made possible the arrest of a smuggling ring by translating a letter written in Armenian, Turkish, Polish, and three dialects of Russian. (RT)

Before emigrating to the United States at about the turn of the century, he had lived in Athens for several years where he had held several minor teaching positions, and had been teacher of foreign languages to members of the Greek royal family, and of the Diplomatic Corps. He was both a polyglot and a polygraph, and had hoped to see published before his death many volumes of his writings on all kinds of subjects, including art, philosophy, politics and literature, as well as mathematics. The obituary closes with his last literary effort: a sonnet to Benito Mussolini introduced to the reader with the words *Eccolo, splendido nella sua attica compostezza classica, che par fatto dallo scolpello di Fidia.*

The only document by him I have is an affectionate letter from him to A.P. whom he had met, with Joséphine, during her lecture tour in the United States in 1922 under the auspices of the American Federation of University Women.

One wonders what would have happened to Josephine had she not met, and married him in New York in 1903. Though he was certainly not wealthy he gave her some security and enabled her to settle down in New York and live an active life there, in spite of the relative failure of her stage career.

I was amazed to discover that Joséphine became a Christian Scientist while in America. I would not have believed this were it not for her own letters. On April 20, 1927, she writes to AP from Naples, less than a month after the death of "The Professor" (as she always referred to her husband): "It is strange for me, a Christian Scientist—is it not, my dear—to find myself in a convent of nuns combined with a children's hospital."

> *C'est drôle pour moi, C.S. de me trouver dans un couvent de religieuses, doublé d'un hôpital pour enfants, n'est-ce pas, chérie ...*

On May 1, she writes again to A.P. that she is recovering from a bout of illness: "I was so ill that I had to write to the [American] Vice-Consul here, a Christian Scientist, to ask him to send a cable to my practitioner [is this a technical CS term?] in New York."

> *J'allais tellement mal… que j'ai été obligée d'écrire au Vice-Consul ici [the American V-C] qui est un C.S., et de le prier d'envoyer un cable à mon Practitioner à N.Y.…*

Then, further on in the same letter: "I think that I will be able to leave, one way or another, because my cable to my practitioner said, 'Please treat me health supply peace' [what does this mean?], and I *know* that after such an S.O.S. he will give me a good 'treatment'……"

> *Je crois que je pourrai partir d'une manière ou de l'autre, parce que mon cable à mon Practitioner disait "Please treat me health supply peace" – et je sais qu'avec un S.O.S. pareil il me donnera un bon "treatment"…*

and she adds further on: "These last eight or nine months—I could say without exaggeration these last 24 years—could have driven mad heads far far stronger than mine. If I managed to hold out, I can attribute my doing so *only* to Christian Science. You see, my dear, that my 'privacy' does not hold up very well with you."

> *… ces derniers 8 ou 9 mois, je pourrais dire sans exagération ces dernières 24 années [ie: since the year of her marriage], auraient fait devenir folle mille et mille et mille fois des têtes bien plus fortes que la mienne. Si j'y ai résisté, je ne puis l'attribuer qu'à la C.S. Tu vois ma Chérie que ma 'privacy' n'est pas forte avec toi…*

Joséphine's feelings toward her son Leon and his wife, Minette, are revealed in a letter to A.P. of July 24, 1931: "Last month I had Leon and Minette here with me for a whole week. But I had to accept even more than before, alas, that both of them are absolutely *impossible*. Eating with both elbows planted on the table, fork held in fist, etc., etc. Mon Bon Plaisir [the farmhouse Josephine had bought in New Jersey] was far from deserving its name while they were there. I was in a constant agony of apprehension that some of my neighbors might drop in, because I would have been ashamed of them. I took them to see just one farmer, and the farmer himself, Pietro, his Italian wife, and even their four-year-old girl were shocked. What to do? Leon has completely given up any form of religion, and Minette never had any. Thank God they have no children.... Venezuela is in the season of torrential rain, which, according to their usual itinerary, should last about two more months."

> *J'ai eu le mois dernier Léon et Minette une semaine entière chez moi. Mais j'ai dû me persuader encore plus que hélas ! je ne l'étais, qu'ils sont tous les deux absolument impossibles. Mangeant avec les avant-bras cloués sur la table, la fourchette dans le poing, etc. 'Mon bon plaisir' était loin de mériter son nom tant qu'ils y étaient. J'étais dans des transes continuelles que quelques-uns de mes voisins paysans ne vinssent me voir, car j'aurais eu honte d'eux. Je les ai conduits seulement chez un paysan… et le paysan lui-même, Pietro, sa femme italienne aussi, et même leur petite fille de 4 ans, ont été choqués de leur conduite. Q'y faire? Léon a quitté entièrement n'importe quelle forme de religion – et Minette n'en a jamais eu. Dieu merci, ils n'ont pas d'enfants. Venezuela est dans la saison des pluies torrentielles qui, selon leur itinéraire annuel, devraient durer encore environ deux mois.*

This reference to Venezuela may explain the reference in Joséphine's will to Venezuelan securities (which did not fulfil expectations). It suggests that Leon had business connections there which required an annual visit.

The same letter blames A.P. for having allegedly been scatter-brained and having "spoiled everything" with regard to Joséphine's efforts to sell or let "Mon Bon Plaisir" by sending someone a letter from Joséphine, intended for her eyes only.

Louis de Castle had been dead nearly two years, and this escapes her attention, but she makes critical remarks about his widow, Frances, and about Gerard (for not writing to her). "I don't demand a letter every week, but I certainly am entitled to require one every month—twelve letters a year—from the only grandson who can possibly count for me.... since all my other grandchildren belong to the 'brood' of the most unnatural daughter who has ever breathed God's sweet air."

So far as I know, Joséphine was not in correspondence with Louise Baese. The only significant reference to her I have come across is in a letter to A.P. of March 16, 1928, in which she indirectly accuses her and Elisina, "ces tendres enfants" [these sweet children', of scheming to put her into an Old Ladies Home..... "as Aunt Louison[Lucciola] wanted me to do for my—*our*—mother." She adds: "I will walk alone to the cemetery gate, to wait for you to stuff me through it, but I will not go to an old ladies' home, or, if I do, I will choose it myself, and I will *not* allow Elise [Elisina] to 'sacrifice herself' in order to provide for me in that way."

>...*comme Tante Louison voulait que je fasse pour ma – notre Mère.*
>*Je marcherai seule jusqu'à la porte du cimetière, attendant que vous*
>*me fourriez dedans, mais je n'irai pas dans un Old Ladies Home –*
>*ou, si j'y irai, je le choisirai moi-même et ne permettrai pas à Elise de*
>*'se sacrifier' pour faire de telles 'provisions' pour moi!*

Light is shed on the nature of relations between Joséphine and her two daughters, Elisina and Linetta between 1925 and Joséphine's death by the following extracts from letters written in those seven years.

Elisina to Linetta, May 12, 1925, from Antigny

"I am extremely sorry you had another abusive and horrid letter. Do let me see all she writes. It is much better that I should be aware of everything, and it helps me when I have to give advice. Believe me, dearest Pitzy, there is no way of saving one's soul alive if one keeps a spark of tender natural feeling for her. No one has ever worshipped their mother as I did mine, nor ever suffered more in consequence. The only way to see her is with a clear eye, and to say to oneself that she cannot help it. For practical purposes it is necessary however to take precautions of every kind, as she can do a great deal of harm and never scruples to use her capacity for that purpose. If I can keep her off Peter and Bill and Babie (i.e.: Gioia, pronounced Barbie), I shall thank my stars. When I told her Babie's married name, I spelt it Outram on purpose; and now that Babie is out of London, the danger is less great".

Elisina to Linetta, March 3, 1926, from Geneva
"…if you can induce Mother to keep quiet in America, do. If she once gets over here, Frabasilis may put obstacles in the way of her returning, and then we should have a peck of troubles".

Joséphine's Visit to Antigny

Elisina's apprehensions about a visit to Europe by Josephine proved justified. She came over by herself in late June 1926. She informed neither Elisina, nor Linetta of her plans—not even of her departure. She made no attempt to get in touch with Linetta, let alone see her; but, instead, she turned up one day at Antigny……without warning. This memorable event is recorded in a letter from Elisina to Linetta which is worthy of the occasion—indeed it is a minor masterpiece.

Antigny-le-Château
Par Arney-le-Duc
(Cote d'Or)
July 16th, 1926

"Darling Pitzy,
 I was in the cellar at Antigny putting wine away, when the servant came to announce that 'un monsieur et une dame étaient arrivés en auto' [a gentleman and a lady had arrived by car]. I went up, and saw one of the

auto-owners of Arnay waiting to be paid by a stout lady whose face was not familiar, and yet who reminded me of someone I knew very well…in a second I recognised mother.

I don't know how she got my address, but it may have been simply out of the 'Tout Paris', which she may have consulted after having ascertained my name from Henrietta Dreyfus, whom she went to see in Paris.

I embraced her, I confess without emotion, and asked he how long she intended to stay (as it was a holiday and I had to make arrangements to get her taken back). She said: 'Well, that depends on you dear'. So I said at once, kindly but firmly 'In that case I think you had better go back this afternoon', and I told the auto-man to come and get mother at 4 p.m.

She followed me into the house, and I set her down in the drawing room and she said 'I have only come to get an explanation of the reason why you never wrote to me'. I said 'Dear Mother, you have come to see me after all these years, and we are going to spend a pleasant day together and not lose ourselves in quite needless explanations and discussions. I then asked her where she had come from (It was Lyon, where she had been to see one of her nephews by marriage), and the reason of her coming to France. She has been given the Médaille de Vermeil de la Reconnaissance Française, a good decoration, and that enabled me to ask her about her war-work, and so on to her ordinary life. She is perfectly fit and seems remarkably strong. She has grey hair, cut short and looks at times very handsome. Indeed she is a powerful and also touching figure. There were no high jinks of any kind. The only nonsense was when she told me that at the Bellevue hospital they had started giving her the 'black pills' which they usually give to those whom they intend to destroy. It is much more likely that the legend was set about so as to decide troublesome patients to remove themselves voluntarily! She walks quite well, and is very gallant about getting in and out of a motor without my help. I heard all the tales about Frabasilis; the past matters little now, but what is good is that on October 10th he retires with a small pension, and they both go to Italy to his people's place and stay there. She is very keen to do it, and feels she will find plenty to keep her busy. There is an estate to manage, a buried Greek town to excavate, and even salt mines to work. She realizes that the right and dignified thing for him to do, and for herself too—is to be there.

I couldn't possibly be unkind to her, or even make her [see?] the extraordinary incongruity of her behaviour in turning up like that, especially as I happened to be alone, and no harm was done. But can you conceive the frame of mind of someone who parts from her daughter for 27 years, blackens that daughter's character right and left, never writes, never answers a letter for two whole years, and then knowing quite well that for her own reasons that daughter wishes to be unmolested, forces a visit on her without warning and then pens the enclosed note? [I found no trace of that note.]

She never asked about Charlie nor Geoffrey. She wanted to go to London to see the Ameses! And Miss Ellen Terry. I told her all the Ameses she knew were dead, and Ozzie lives in the country in Norfolk. I also told her that England was very expensive. I cannot quite make out her state of mind. She has a good deal more sense than one might expect, and at the same time she is so utterly bereft of tact and consideration, and it makes one feel uncomfortable to think of her exposing herself to rebuffs when she might so easily keep quiet and avoid them.

She said the motor fare from Arnay was more than she expected and would I give her 15 francs for which she made out a cheque. Needless to say I shall not cash it. At the station at Arnay she showed apprehension about not having quite enough change for the hotel expenses in Paris, so I asked her to accept a small note, and put 100 francs where she told me to put it, in her folded cheque book in her handbag. She is leaving France on August 4th or 5th and I cannot deny that I shall be easier in my mind when she is safely in New York once more.

I hope that the quiet and pleasant day we spent here together will have had the effect of preventing her from going on the war-path to reach me, and also that she won't try to see Babie. She said nothing about it, just asked what her name was now.

I don't regret her coming—and I am satisfied that she is all right, if she has the wisdom not to mess everything up by a 'coup de tête'.

I feel sure you will be glad to know of all this at once.

She spoke of you with real admiration, and there we both agreed.

My very tenderest lov—ever your devoted Zi".

In the above letter, E.R.T. writes about Joséphine having "parted from" her daughter "for 27 years". This would take us back to 1899. However by then E.R.T. had been married to Grant Richards for over a year. Yet, in his letter to Joséphine of 1902, he tells her that they had never met, which suggests that Joséphine was in the US when they became engaged, and married, so that the words "who parts from her daughter" are to be taken as referring to written communications only. Joséphine left for America for good in 1897.

Joséphine's recollections of her visit to Antigny, one year and eight months later had not been softened by time, as her letter to AP of March 16, 1928 shows:

"When I went to see my elder daughter, nearly two years ago, and surprised her—because otherwise I would not have seen her at all—how did she receive me? 'Ah! Mammina!' (with the kind of kiss that I would give to a little dog) When will you be leaving? [This exchange is in Italian.] 'Well, I don't know. I might stay until tomorrow.' 'There's a good train at 4. You had better take it. Driver, come back for Madame in time for the 4 o'clock train.' I had brought my nightgown, my combs and brushes, etc…, because I had just spent two nights and three days with the Professor's nephew and his family at Lyon. Despite their 'squalid' poverty they had not wanted to let me go.

At the home of my own daughter, after years of separation, when despite everything I had gone there to see her, that is the reception I got. How touching!"

Quand j'ai été voir ma fille aînée, il y a deux ans bientôt, et que je l'ai surprise – car sans cela je ne l'aurai pas vue – comment m'a-t-elle reçue?.. 'Ah ! Mammina !' (un baiser comme j'en donnerais à un joli petit toutou…' …… 'Cocher, revenez reprendre Madame pour le train de 4 heures.' J'avais apporté ma chemise de nuit, mes peignes et brosses, etc…, parce que je venais de passer deux nuits et trois jours chez le neveu du Professeur, à Lyon - qui, malgré leur misère 'squallida' ne voulaient pas me laisser repartir.

Chez ma propre fille, après des années de séparation, étant allée la voir malgré tout, voilà comment j'ai été reçue - c'est touchant !

Correspondence Concerning Joséphine

Elisina to Linetta, July 27th, 1926, from Antigny
"If she ever provokes me to speak out the truth I will do so, and tell her that the publicity she has chosen to give to private affairs, and the ruthlessness with which she has placed us over and over again in an awkward position by flaunting *our* maiden name with her present husbands name, make it impossible for me to have anything to say to her… I shall tell her quite plainly that I intend to keep my happiness and my peace of mind, and that if she attempts to destroy them, I shall retaliate. I believe there is no other way with her at all. I cannot say I feel anything but animosity when I read the word 'adored' applied to me by mother. She has some very trying trick - words…"

Elisina to Linetta, December 5th, 1926, from Antigny
…"As to mother's eccentricities, my view about her position and ours is perfectly clear. We have, all three of us, attained in our different spheres a position which we value, and which we have achieved without the slightest help from her. [i.e: Elisina, Linetta and Louis] She has *no right at all* to damage, or attempt to damage our position. That is the long and the short of it, and we are perfectly justified in exacting from her the observance of certain special measures, when the opposite course does us harm."

Elisina to Linetta, April 24, 1927, from Antigny
"It is bad enough that I should have to be trumpeted all over the world as a bad daughter who takes no care of a devoted and suffering parent…. If she again accuses me you might perhaps say to her that, viewed fairly, the

position is as follos: for 27 years she gave me no sign of life [25 actually: see her 2 letters of Nov. 28 and Dec. 1, 1902]. At a crisis in my life, she certainly showed no tenderness or understanding; having ascertained my address she should have written and asked me if I wished to see her, and not risked a dramatic scene with strangers present. So far you may go. Let the rest lie."

On April 30th and May 7th, 1927 there follow two more letters from Elisina to Linetta, written at Antigny, which are both autobiographical to the point of not needing to be quoted separately:

I am very much annoyed at the threatening tone of mother's last letter (of April 20th) concerning me, and I think it is best for me to speak my mind plainly. I had better make myself perfectly plain on the subject though it is painful for me to write, and it will be painful for you to read—but these are the facts: since I can remember, Mother's conduct towards me has been cruel and selfish in the extreme. I will give as an instance the terrors I suffered as a little child in having a padlock brought on the table at Le Cave, with which she threatened to lock Louis' mouth if he spoke at table, her persistent refusal to allow me a nightlight when I was terror-stricken by the tales she used to tell me—a child of 7 or 8—about my father's threats on her life; her unkindness to Grandmama, whom I loved so dearly. While I was at Sant' Anna, I was fairly safe.... But when I came out at the age of 17, I was sent to Cheltenham, where *every penny I earned was taken by her*, and she actually gave me 10/- for my pocket-money on going back at the beginning of term!" [The next few lines have already been quoted in connection with Prof. Paci].... "I had to meet the interest on mortgages of Mother's furniture till I could do so no longer, and it was sold. I had to pay the interest on

Mother's jewellery pawned in Italy till Grant Richards refused to go on doing so, and had it taken to London and sold. I had been married one year when Mother came back to England, stayed with us at Cookham Dene, and so definitely and ruthlessly started making mischief between Grant and me that even to the last time I saw him, he continued to throw in my face her conduct at that time. That was 28 years ago.

[This would make it 1899. Josephine had left England in 1897. Elisina and Grant were married in 1898. It is thus possible that Josephine returned to England on a visit in 1899, though I have no other indication of it. In this case, Grant Richards's letter, of which the draft has been quoted above, was written in that year, before J's visit.]

'I went on writing to Mother for two whole years during which, being 'angry' with me, she never answered me once. I then stopped writing, and heard no more from her till she appeared last year on my doorstep, giving no warning of her intention and having practically deceived you in order to carry it through in spite of us both." [In view of the two letters from J. in late 1902, one must assume that Elisina has got the date of her mother's visit to England muddled up, or that she had forgotten about those 2 letters.]

"The passionate devotion I had for her and which carried me through so much that was iniquitously guilty conduct on her part towards me is long since dead. I have helped you to help her, time and time again, because I felt that the burden she continues to impose on you is really too heavy for you, darling Pitzy. But I will not be bullied by her, and if she makes the slightest attempt to write to me, or if I hear of her having gone and taken away my character by telling things in her own way, I shall consider myself at liberty to write to the people to whom she has maligned me, to tell them the truth......

> Since my children have grown up, I understand better the utter heartlessness of Mother's conduct. I have no scruples whatever in saying all this, and I want you to write to her, quoting me exactly, so that she may hear the truth, and avoid being shown up to her friends, as she has the good fortune to have some. Make it clear that I shall tell the truth about her to Tante Emilie and to Tante Henriette as well as to anyone else, *if* she provokes me by scattering tales about me. She will never bring anything but evil to me and I must guard myself..."

Tante Emilie is Emilia Hierschel de Minerbi. I don't know who Tante Henriette was—perhaps Emilia's daughter. A Henriette Dreyfus is mentioned in the correspondence as having perhaps been the person from whom J. obtained Elisina's address at Antigny.... Joséphine is still at Naples in late April—early May, 1927. Elisina has offered to buy her a third class ticket from Naples to New York—through A.P.—but refuses to send her money. In her second of these two letters, her resentment breaks out again; but she applies the brake a little:

> I am glad you didn't send your angry letter, and don't trouble to write what I said. Tell her that *I* claim the right to say whether *my* child shall or shall not now be worried and unnecessarily distressed by receiving letters from someone whom she has never seen, who has never bothered to hear about her when it was easy to do so, when she was little. As to my writing to mother now, did she write to me when darling G. died? My reasons for not writing to her are that her correspondence brings me endless trouble and vexation; but what was her reason for not writing to me then?.... Do you know that when she went to America (I was 19) and she took every penny I had, including a present of £20 which Lady Samuelson suddenly and unexpectedly sent *me*, as I had lived with Caroline and Helen for two years at Cheltenham? I was

left with £1-16-0 in all, and no plans at all made for me from August 19th to the end of the holidays. It was of course always 'Mon Enfant Adorée' and my 'Toute Belle Enfant' in every letter.

Elisina to Linetta, February 19, 1928, from Budapest
If God will grant us that the curse of the mother's temperament will not appear again in generations to come in our family, I will find courage to bear with it as long as possible! But she is really a devastating influence.

With this combined invocation and lamentation, I will end my quotation of extracts from Elisina's letters concerning her mother. However, at the risk of lengthening unduly the part of my text devoted to Joséphine, I shall now turn to some letters from Linetta to her. These are particularly interesting because she had continued to correspond with her all her life, and had seen her again during her American lecture trip in 1922. Moreover—as will be seen—Linetta made valiant efforts to ignore her mother's sharp words and criticism, and to keep up an attitude and tone of filial respect and affection, however great the provocation. She also remained loyal to Elisina, rejecting their mother's harsh accusations against her, and never responding to Joséphine's attempts to woo her over onto her side, and against her sister, by professions of special affection for her. The difference between Elisina's and Linetta attitudes and reactions toward their mother reflects in part a difference of temperament, and in part Elisina's fear of her as someone who might—and she felt sure, would if she could—wreak havoc with her life, family happiness and position in society. Elisina was the more pugnacious of the two partly—perhaps largely—because her past made her more vulnerable. Linetta, on the other hand, being still single and having no money, was out of reach and thus felt no fear of her. This makes Linetta letters both more interesting in substance and more useful as a revelation of Josephine's nature. Her tone is much more deliberate, more relaxed, than Elisina's and thus lends greater weight to her statements.

The following passages are from 4 letters from Linetta, written to her mother, who was then in Naples. "The Professor", as Josephine always called her husband in her letters, had fallen ill shortly after their arrival in Italy in late 1926, and died there on March 31, 1927.

January 7, 1927:

My dear mother,

I have just received your second letter, the one dated the third of this month, after receiving the other the day before yesterday—the one in which you told me about the awful difficulties surrounding you arrival in Naples, and all the rest. Thank you for both letters, dear mother, but not for the tirade or the threats in the second. It is not the children [who?], whose address you discovered by means that you yourself regret, who either requested or desired the details; it is I, whose address has always been available to you. Besides, it is absolutely impossible to grasp the general situation, apart from the details, when you give such different accounts of it at different times. From New York you always told me that you lived in poverty, and unfortunately I believe that to be so; but now you tell me that you had bought there "Mon Bon Plaisir and other small parcels of land." On June 1st (the date of your letter) you wrote that you could no longer come to Europe because the concert had not brought in enough money. Then, on July 4th, there you are in Paris; and you write that you funded this trip with money that you, personally, had earned. You also say that it is with that money that you bought Mon Bon Plaisir. In the past, though, you told me that Leon and Minette had wired you [the money?] in order to save it for you, and I do not believe it possible that you should have returned it over the course of these last few years [without?] very great difficulty. Regarding the procedure you adopted in order to discover the name and address of Elisina, I can more or less imagine what it may have been, and what surprises me above all is that someone as intelligent as you—quite apart from all the feelings that should have been involved—should have failed to understand that it is precisely this kind of behavior that makes everyone close to you seek to avoid you. You claim to love your children, but you see no need to grant them the most elementary consideration. And for the love of God, do not speak to me of how you are treated as a grandmother. What I have seen during my life, and the horror that it has inspired in me, is the only thing that has twice prevented me—a year ago, when you told me you had sent Louis Elisina's address, which he had asked for (you knew perfectly well that he had had it for ages), and especially later on, when I heard from Elisina that you had visited her unannounced, whereas to *me*, during you whole stay in Europe you never wrote a single word, knowing as you did what I would think of your behavior—the only thing that has prevented me from breaking off all contact with you. I am firmly resolved not to treat you the way you treated your mother, from the awful declaration you forced her to make in order to be able to marry Gower; to the cigarettes that you made her return to Uncle Florestano during the last months of her life, when she was penniless, blind, and terribly alone, despite the three people in whose house she was lodging—all of whom made noise eating their soup; and Paci's delay in operating, when he knew perfectly well that in a case of dropsy it is vital to intervene at the right moment... For the love of God, never mention these things to me again. And Miss Haydn told me herself that she would have liked so much to have Grandmother with her...

But let us leave the past behind. And let us hope that the Professor will soon be better now that he has no more family troubles; and that the Italians to whom he lent all that money in New York will decide to return it; and that his inheritance at Episcopia—what he is to inherit from his father—will come back to him little by little...

Please tell the Professor that he must get well soon and thoroughly; that he will then be able away to write a lot of interesting things; and that life will then smile on you both.

And you, my dear mother, go on loving me, and may God bless you. I hope to send you two sterlings [silver shillings?] as a gift for your name day [*fête*], and I hope that the Professor's pension will soon start coming in. Do please keep me abreast of your affairs. You know that no idle curiosity prompts me to ask you to do so.

Your devoted daughter,
L

Ma chère Mère

Je viens de recevoir ta seconde lettre, celle du 3 courant, après avoir reçu avant-hier l'autre, dans laquelle tu me racontais les affreuses péripéties de votre arrivée à Naples et le reste. Merci des deux, ma chère Mère - mais pas de la tirade ni des menaces de la seconde. Ce ne sont pas les enfants, dont tu as trouvé l'adresse par des moyens que même toi tu regrettes, qui t'ont demandé ou qui désirent des détails – c'est moi dont tu n'as jamais eu aucune difficulté à savoir l'adresse. Du reste, il est absolument impossible de comprendre la situation en général à part les détails, lorsque tu la racontes si différemment à diverses époques. De N. Y. tu me disais toujours que tu étais dans la misère, et malheureusement je crois que c'était vrai ; mais maintenant tu me racontes que tu y avais acheté 'Mon Bon Plaisir et d'autres petits terrains'. Le 1er juin tu m'écrivis (c'est la date de ta lettre) que tu ne pouvais plus venir en Europe parce que le concert n'avait pas eu, financièrement, assez de succès, puis pour le 4 juillet tu es à Paris, et tu m'écris maintenant que c'est avec l'argent que tu as gagné toi, personnellement, que tu as fait ce voyage ; tu dis aussi que c'est avec cela que tu as acheté Mon Bon Plaisir, mais tu m'avais raconté autrefois que Léon et Minette t'avaient télégraphié pour te le sauver, et je ne crois pas possible que tu les leur aies rendus pendant ces dernières années de très grandes difficultés [sic in the text, but the meaning is not clear]. *Et pour ce qui regarde les moyens dont tu t'es servie pour savoir le nom et l'adresse d'Elisina, je me les imagine à peu près, et ce qui me surprend plus que tout le reste c'est qu'une personne de ton intelligence – à part tous les sentiments qui devraient entrer en jeu - ne comprenne pas que c'est justement ce genre de conduite-là qui force tout le monde de tes intimes à tâcher de t'éviter. Tu dis aimer tes enfants ; mes les égards les plus élémentaires, tu ne crois pas les leur devoir. Et pour l'amour de Dieu, ne me parles plus de ton traitement de grand-mère. Ce que j'en ai vu de mon vivant, et l'horreur que j'en ai, sont la seule chose qui m'a empêché à deux reprises – il y a un an – quand tu m'as dis que tu avais envoyé à Louis l'adresse d'Elisina qu'il t'avait demandée (tu savais très bien qu'il l'avait depuis longtemps) et surtout plus tard quand j'ai su d'Elisina que tu avais été chez elle de surprise, tandis qu'à moi, pendant tout ton séjour en Europe tu ne m'avais pas écrit un mot, car tu savais bien ce que je ne pourrais manquer de penser de ta conduite –qui m'a empêché, dis-je, de cesser d'avoir rien à faire avec toi. Je suis bien, bien résolue à ne pas te traiter comme tu as traité ta mère – depuis l'horrible déclaration que tu lui as fait faire pour pouvoir épouser Gower, jusqu'aux cigarettes que tu lui as fait rendre à l'oncle Florestano pendant les derniers mois de sa vie, quand elle était pauvre et aveugle, et bien seule, malgré les trois personnes chez lesquelles elle demeurait, et dont toutes les trois faisaient du bruit en mangeant leur soupe ; et le retard de Paci à opérer, quand il savait bien qu'avec l'hydropisie il est question surtout* d'opérer au moment juste… Pour l'amour de Dieu, ne m'en parle plus jamais. Et Miss Haydn m'a dit elle-même qu'elle aurait tant voulu garder grand-mère auprès d'elle…

Mais laissons là le passé. Et espérons que le Professeur guérisse vite, maintenant qu'il n'a plus de bouleversements en famille, et que les italiens à qui il a prêté tout cet argent à New York s'avisent à de le lui rendre, et que son héritage à Episcopia – ce qu'il doit hériter de son père – lui revienne peu à peu…

Dis au Professeur, je t'en prie, qu'il faut qu'il se guérisse vite et bien ; qu'il pourra écrire tout de suite un tas de choses intéressantes, et que la vie vous deviendra belle à tous les deux.

Et toi, ma chère Mère, continue de m'aimer – et que le Bon Dieu te bénisse. J'espère t'envoyer deux Sterlings comme cadeau de ta fête – et espère bien que la pension du Professeur commence bientôt à vous arriver. Dis-moi toujours comment vont vos affaires – je t'en prie – tu sais bien que je ne te le demande pas par pure curiosité.

Ton enfant encore dévouée,

L

Linetta to Josephine, April 7, 1927
[Note on top left of first page: "revoyée par maman" [returned by mother]

…What you say of all these boxes sounds very serious. And when I think that the Professor had not even paid for all your tickets when he left New York, and that now you tell me he had left his boxes for someone else to send him! Even if it was someone who owed him money, I wonder whether he has really never had any notion of responsibility. How could he expect Elisina and Louis to make sacrifices for a reason like that? They have never even met him; and as for you, Elisina sacrificed herself for you when she just a girl at Cheltenham, and for the last twenty-seven years you have done nothing but speak ill of her, especially after her new marriage; and last summer you went to her home without telling her you were coming, at the risk of finding her in the company of strangers and making some dramatic scene. No, really, quite frankly, *how* could you expect that of them? And I, unfortunately, simply *can't*….

Good-by, my dear mother, I will send you Friday at the latest the five sterlings for the 1st of May. May Heaven keep you and bless you.

Your wholly devoted daughter
Linetta

Ce que tu me dis de toutes ces caisses est bien grave – Et quand je pense que le Professeur n'avait même pas payé tous vos billets quand il est parti de N. Y., et que maintenant tu me dis qu'il avait laissé ses caisses pour que quelqu'un d'autre les lui expédient – même si c'était un de ses débiteurs, je me demande si vraiment il n'a jamais eu aucun sens de responsabilité. Comment peut-on s'attendre à ce que qu'Elisina et Louis fassent des sacrifices pour une raison pareille? Lui, ils ne l'ont même pas vu; - toi, Elisina s'est sacrifiée pour toi quand elle était bien jeune à Cheltenham – et pendant les derniers 27 ans tu n'as fait que dire du mal d'elle, surtout depuis son nouveau mariage; et l'été dernier, tu as été chez elle sans l'avertir, en risquant d'y trouver des étrangers et d'y faire une scène dramatique – non, écoute, franchement, comment veux-tu t'attendre à cela d'eux? Et moi, malheureusement je ne peux absolument pas!…

Au-revoir, ma chère Mère ; je t'enverrai vendredi au plus tard les cinq Sterlings du 1er mai – et le Ciel te garde et te bénisse.

Ton enfant toute dévouée

Linetta

Linetta to Josephine, May 1, 1927

(We have a draft with corrections, and the words "pas expédiée" [not sent] on the top left of the front page. The other text, only slightly modified, is marked "copy". In Elisina's letter to Linetta of May 7, 1927, she writes—obviously referring to this letter which Linetta must have destroyed "I am glad you didn't send your angry letter, and don't trouble to write what I said…."!)

My dear mother,

I received yesterday your letter of April 25. It begins and ends with expressions of affection, but the remaining four pages… are so full of sarcasm, of quotations from *my* letter, of reproaches, etc…. that I will answer it only as briefly as possible; but I have no intention of entering, just for that, into a quarrel with you. However, I understand that Elisina and Louis should do all they can to avoid these continual alternations of affection and nastiness, which, like it or not, are upsetting and hurtful….

Concerning Leon and your anger with him, I have heard only one voice, and that voice has been yours. He and I exchange a Christmas *card* once a year and that is absolutely all. You were angry because Minette had refused to go to live with you at Mon Bon Plaisir to make jam and canned fruit. If I believed that they had given you 400 dollars, that is because you wrote me quite simply that they had wired the money to you, and hitherto you had said nothing to me in this connection about loans, but rather about interest. You are right, under the circumstances, to tell me that I insult you by concerning myself with this money. But I only did so in response to a letter from you, in which you announced that they would have *nothing* from you—which you wrote in large letters, underlined.

Regarding Elisina and Louis—and me at King's College—if you had said that you approached strangers in order to punish us and seek vengeance, I might understand your motive; but to impose respect for you—you really are much too intelligent to believe in any such result. And I repeat that you have done all three of us a great deal of harm.

I write all this because it strikes me as necessary to do so, and I beg you again, for the love of God, not to speak to me of all you did for your mother!

But remember that I do not love only those who seem to me infallible—for whom, then, would one love?—and that whatever you may do or say, and force me to do or say, at bottom I will love you *always*!

Your daughter,

Linetta

Ma chère Mère,

J'ai reçu hier ta lettre du 25 avril. Elle commence et finit affectueusement, mais le reste des 4 pages… est tellement plein de sarcasme, de citations de ma lettre à moi et de reproches, etc., que je ne vais y répondre que le plus brièvement possible; car je ne vais pas, même à cause de cela, me quereller avec toi. Seulement je comprends qu'Elisina et Louis fassent leur possible pour éviter ces continuelles alternances de tendresses et de méchancetés qui, vouloir ou non, bouleversent et blessent…

Quant à Léon et à ta colère contre lui, je n'ai entendu qu'une cloche, c'est vrai, mais cela a été la tienne. Avec lui, nous nous échangeons une fois par un par un une carte de Noël; et voilà absolument tout…

La raison de ta colère était que Minette avait refusé d'aller avec toi habiter « Mon Bon Plaisir » pour y faire des confitures et du « canned fruit ». Si j'ai cru qu'ils t'avaient fait cadeau de 400 dollars, c'est parce que tu m'as écrit simplement qu'ils te les avaient télégraphiés, et tu ne m'avais jusqu'ici jamais parlé de prêts, mais d'intérêts à ce propos. Tu as raison, vu les vraies circonstances, de me dire que c'est une insulte de m'occuper de cet argent. Mais je l'ai fait en réponse à une lettre de toi, où tu disais qu' ils n'auraient rien de toi – et tu l'écrivais gros et souligné.

Quant à Elisina et Louis – et moi à King's College – si tu disais que tu t'étais adressée à des étrangers pour nous punir et te venger, ce serait encore une raison – mais pour exiger le respect – tu es vraiment beaucoup trop intelligente pour croire à ce résultat-là. Et je répète que tu nous a fait à tous les trois énormément de tort.

Je t'écris tout ceci parce que cela me semble tout à faire nécessaire – et je te prie encore une fois, pour l'amour de Dieu de ne plus me parler de ce que tu as fait pour ta mère!

Mais souviens-toi que je n'aime pas seulement les personnes que je croirais infaillibles – car alors, qui aimerait-t-on ? – et que quelque chose que tu fasses et dises, et m'oblige à faire et à dire, je t'aimerai, au fond, toujours !

       Ton enfant, Linetta

Linetta to Joséphine, May 6, 1927

My dear mother,

I received today your letter of the 2nd. Naturally it made painful reading, but although my previous explanation—for which you had asked me at least three times—concerning the attitude we all take toward the famous question of addresses gained me nothing but mockery and sarcasm, I shall still answer your new question.

You ask *what* I say you expected from Elisina and Louis, and what it is that I "simply *can't*…." So here it is. On the subject of the boxes, and especially because you felt obliged to return to New York; and after telling me in this connection that you hope to reclaim them with the proceeds of selling Mon Bon Plaisir, you continue: "and I will always have something left in hand, and in a country where such things have an agreed value, not in one, like here, in which people expect to buy everything for nothing! No! The only thing to do would be—*if* at the start I were to need a little help—to make Elisina and Louis understand that under such circumstances they are strictly *duty-bound* to help their mother, toward the goal also of enabling her to reimburse *everything* that they might advance her now, instead of sending inadequate little crumbs that would be lost as much to them as to me, and that would only end up (if they *did* send such little crumbs) prolonging an agony of poverty."

I have copied your words precisely, including the underlinings. And the subject was the large sum that the boxes would cost you to reclaim and to transport, and the importance for you of reclaiming them. Naturally, that is the sum that I understood you expected from Elisina and Louis *if* Mon Bon Plaisir failed to sell or did not bring in enough. Even now, I do not see how to interpret otherwise the passage that I just copied. But for the love of God, let us not quarrel, too.

I had written a four-page reply to the sarcasms that you sent me on the subject of 'privacy'—and I did not send it. As far as I am concerned, there will be no quarrel between you and me if I can possibly prevent it. But what would be the point of pretending that I see things in some other way than what appears to me to be the truth? I will never do that for anyone, and while I inevitably have my own opinions, I will not, either, claim that anyone believes me to be infallible. With respect to those whom I love best, I am content that they love me, too, despite my failings and my errors—something that is very difficult to do when the love is genuine and free of hypocrisy. (What hypocrisy do you mean in your letter of today? I certainly would never have believed that it was a defect of the neapolitans!)

Your daughter, who will always love you,

Linette

Ma chère Mère, j'ai reçu aujourd'hui ta lettre du 2 courant. Elle me fait naturellement beaucoup de peine ; mais quoique mon explication précédente – que tu m'avais demandée au moins trois fois – sur notre attitude à tous vers la fameuse question des adresses ne m'ait procuré que boutades et sarcasmes, je vais cependant répondre à la nouvelle question que tu me poses.

Tu demandes à quoi je dis que tu t'attends de Elisina et de Louis, et ce que c'est que moi « je ne peux absolument pas ! » Voici ! En me parlant des caisses, à cause surtout que tu sentais devoir rentrer à New York ; et après m'avoir dit à ce propos que tu espères les retirer avec ce que tu pourras gagner par la vente de « Mon Bon Plaisir », tu continues : 'et il me restera toujours quelque chose en main, et ce sera dans un pays où ces choses-là ont une valeur reconnue et non où on veut tout acheter pour rien comme ici ! Non ! la seule chose à faire serait – si j'avais besoin d'un peu d'aide tout au commencement, de faire comprendre à Louis et à Elisina qu'il est de leur stricte devoir d'aider leur mère dans une circonstance comme celle-ci, dans le but aussi de l'aider à se mettre à même de leur rembourser tout ce qu'ils pourraient lui avancer maintenant, au lieu de lui envoyer d'insuffisantes miettes qui seraient perdues tant pour eux que pour moi, et n'aboutiraient (si ils envoyaient même des miettes) qu'à prolonger une agonie de misère…'

Je cite absolument littéralement, même jusqu'aux soulignés. Et le sujet était la forte somme que les caisses te coûteraient à retirer et à transporter – et l'importance pour toi de retirer les caisses. Naturellement, c'est à cette somme que j'ai compris que tu t'attendais d'Elisina et de Louis, si, ou Mon Bon Plaisir ne se vendait pas ou sa vente ne te rapportait pas assez. Même maintenant, je ne vois pas quelle autre interprétation on peut attacher à ce que je viens de copier. Mais pour l'amour de Dieu, ne nous querellons pas nous aussi.

J'avais écrit une réponse à 4 pages des sarcasmes que tu m'as envoyés à propos de la 'privacy' – et je ne te l'ai pas envoyée. Pour mon compte, si je puis l'empêcher, il n'y aura pas de querelle entre nous – mais à quoi bon prétendre que je vois les choses différemment de ce qui me semble la vérité? Moi, je ne prétendrai jamais cela de personne; et, tout en ayant, inévitablement, mes opinions à moi, je ne prétendrai pas non plus que personne me croie infaillible. Il me suffit, de ceux que j'aime le mieux, qu'ils m'aiment aussi malgré mes fautes et mes erreurs – ce qu'il est très pénible de faire, quand c'est du vrai amour, et sans hypocrisie (de quelle hypocrisie parles-tu, dans ta lettre d'aujourd'hui ? Je n'aurais certes pas cru que c'était là un défaut des néapolitains !)

Ton enfant qui t'aimera toujours,
                                                                Linette

Louis de Castle's Letter about His Mother

We are most fortunate in having a letter to Linetta about their mother from Louis de Castle, written on October 6, 1926 from Johannesburg. In addition to revealing in a most felicitous way Josephine's outlook on life and the trouble it could cause to members of her family, it concludes an account of a visit by Louis to the spot where his uncle the Prince Imperial had been killed in 1879:

… Really Mother is an extraordinary person. I think I told you when I last wrote, how she had been writing to all sorts of people out here asking for me, and telling them peculiar cock-and-bull stories which made rather a fool of me, and which in any case, would have been of interest to nobody even if they had been true. You will also remember that either I wrote to her direct, or asked you to write to her and ask her to send her letters to me through you in the future. This, she point blank refused to do, and I ultimately received a letter from her which was written in her very best melodramatic style, in the course of which she stated that she would allow no one 'not even my sister' to act as intermediary between herself and her Son' (The capital is hers—I wouldn't dare to be so profane). Well I let the matter go at that and didn't answer the letter.

Just before I came down here, that is about two months ago, I called on some friends of mine, the Curtis's and at their house (they are Americans by the way). I met a cousin of Curtis's, one Dr. Rosalie Morton who, it appears, was just taking a pleasure jaunt through this country. She is a rather stout, middle-aged person, but quite vivacious and clever but given to liking the sound of her own voice a little too much. However she talked entertainingly and has had quite entertaining experiences. When I left the Curtis's I called at my Post-Office box, and you can imagine my surprise at finding a letter awaiting me there from Dr. Rosalie Morton telling me that before her departure for this country, my mother the Countess de Castelvecchio, had entrusted her with a letter for me and had asked her to try and get into touch with me, and that if I would call at her cousin's house, or let her know where I could meet her, she would hand me the letter. Really Pitzy, I was d__d annoyed. 'No one not even my sister would be allowed to act as intermediary between myself and my Son', but a total stranger, and a darned talkative one at that, is allowed to carry a letter half around the world so that she can deliver it personally! Really, it's the limit. As soon as I got that letter I went around to the Curtis's again hoping that I would get there in time to stop the good woman mouth, but it was no good. It appears that she had not caught my name when I called there earlier in the afternoon, and I had hardly got out of the house when she asked what my name was. You can imagine the result.....When I got to the Curtis' for the second time the whole story was out, even to the alleged riots in Spokane directed against some imaginary Italians who 'had behaved abominably'. I was annoyed—extremely annoyed—and found it very difficult not to show it. In fact, I am afraid that I succeeded only too well in letting the worthy Dr. Rosalie understand that I thought she would be better employed in her normal activities of setting bones and dishing out pills than turning herself into a sort of perambulating post-office. The worst of it was that Mother had left the envelope of her letter to me unsealed, and in the letter she had enclosed a sort of pedigree of the excellent Frabasilis and also the program and prospectus of a farewell reception and concert that was given in her honour at one of the New York Hotels. You may have seen these precious documents, in fact you probably have, and these, if you please, had been trotted out for the entertainment of the Curtis family. The worthy Frabasilis, it appears, is Duke of a couple of dukedoms, marquis of half a dozen marquisates, count of a score or more counties and baron of, I should say, about all the rest of the provinces, cities, villages and hamlets of Italy so that Mussolini, the Pope and the King ought to have a pretty soft job. I really feel sorry for the poor old Frabasilis and if his lamented sire only left him as many pence as he did titles, he must be a millionaire. In one of these precious documents it stated that mother, with all *her* titles, and Frabasilis with all *his* titles, were going to live in "one of their Castles in Italy" (Let's hope that none of them are in Spain or in the air), after they had made a sort of triumphal but leisurely tour of Europe during the course of which, poor Pitzy, they were going to call on you at Birmingham. Mother's pedigree and history or rather, parts of both were also outlined, and it absolutely beats me why she can't forget them both instead of publishing them broadcast. However, you can imagine how pleased I was at having all this tosh trotted out for the edification of friends of mine who [sic] I have known for eighteen years and from whom I had carefully concealed all that Dr.

Rosalie Morton told them. Incidentally, it appears that this excellent lady had also been commissioned to interview Frances privately and to take back a report concerning all of us. Billy, upon whom Dr. Rosalie Morton seemed to be under the impression [that] a perfect galaxy of honours, estates and titles were to be showered one of these days, was fortunately at school. With regard to mother's mysterious recent visit to Europe, which you are supposed to know nothing about, it would be interesting to know what the object of it was. Dr. Rosalie told me that mother and Frabasilis were leaving the United States for good and all in October and that she hoped to get back to New York before mother left there and tell her all about us out here. She said nothing about any preliminary visit which, of course, may have been decided on or made necessary, after Dr. Rosalie left the USA. However, there appears that there is little doubt about your seeing mother when she comes over to Europe for good, and when you see her I would be extremely obliged if you could impress upon her the facts that firstly, I am *sure* to get her letters if she will only address them quite plainly to L. P. De Castle at Box 4650, Johannesburg, South Africa, and that therefore registering the letters is only a useless expense and the practice of plastering her own name *and* titles on the front and back of the envelopes is quite unnecessary and a waste of time, besides which, it so complicates the appearance of the envelope that it reduces, instead of enhancing, the likelihood of my receiving the letters. Secondly, as long as it is necessary for me to hustle my own living, and as far as one can see this is going to continue being a necessity as long as I have any living which will need maintaining, I prefer to be addressed as I have stated, and object, strongly object, to having the past family history broadcasted amongst my friends. Not only do I object to having it broadcasted but I even object to having it known, and she will be doing me a favour and, further, rendering communication between us much easier and more possible, if she will only refrain from communicating with me in any other way than simply writing to me direct, and stop this thing of raking up everybody she can who either has or is about to have any communication with this sub-continent, and unburdening herself of all our past history to them and charging them with all sorts of epistles, messages and powers of investigation. I am, after all, old enough to know my own mind, and, I consider that I have a right to have my wishes observed. If mother does not admit these facts then it will only result in making communication between us impossible, and I shall, in future, go out of my way to be extremely rude to anyone she appoints as an embassador [sic] or embassadress' [sic] of hers; and if that does not stop her, then I shall have no other recourse but to shift out of the country and not tell her where I have gone to. I do not suppose that it is her deliberate intention to persecute me and render it harder than it already is for me to make a living, but that is actually what her actions amount to. I am perfectly willing, in fact I shall be glad, to keep in touch with her, but this must be done on the lines I have stated and no others. If you can make all this perfectly clear to her, I shall be glad, and you will be rendering us both a service. If she wants me to meet friends of hers when they come out here I certainly have no objection provided she tells them the true position addressed as I have stated it above (instead of concocting all sorts of silly stories) and asks them to respect my wishes regarding my family connections, etc. Impress upon her, if you possibly can, that writing to admirals, consuls, Presidents of Chambers of Mines, Mine Managers and all the rest is absolutely unnecessary, as letters addressed as I have stated are certain to reach me, and if she receives no replies, it is because I haven't sent any, and not because I haven't received her letters. Also, she will have a much better chance of receiving replies if she will stop plastering her name etc. on the envelope. When she does that it puts me in a frame of mind that does not make replying to her letters any easier.

Well, old Pitzy, I think I have told you just about all there is to tell. The difficulty about your writing to Billy direct is again the question of how he is going to reply to you as you have retained the name in full. Sometimes I think it is too bad that when I decided to curtail my name I did not decide to change it entirely and call myself Mr. Bill Jones or something equally unobtrusive. It would certainly have simplified matters. Talking about mother... reminds me that the place where I am staying at the moment is only 5 miles from the spot where the Prince Imperial was killed. I went out to look at the place a couple of Sundays ago. The native kraal at which the Prince and his party were resting when they were ambushed has been moved a few hundred yards to one side of its original site and I was fortunate in finding an old native in this kraal who, as a youngster of about fourteen (natives are always hazy about their own ages) had witnessed the whole thing, and he described it to me in detail, at the same time pointing out the different places where everything happened. It appears that the Prince and a party of four others—two officers and two troopers—left the main body of troops, principally to enable the Prince to do some sketching. Whilst the prince was sketching from the side of a hill, he and his party were seen by a body of about 70 natives who were out on a foraging expedition. The way the old native told me that part of the story was rather interesting. What he said amounted to: "When the native chief in charge of the 70 natives saw the five white men, he decided to attack them in view of the fact that the forces were about equal". Which shows what the natives think of the white man. At all events, when the natives first sighted the Prince's party, they were at the top of a hill some five or six miles from the place where the Prince was, with a small shallow river intervening. The grass, however, at that time of the year (June) was long and dry and offered excellent cover to the natives. By the time the natives had reached the river, the Prince and his party had come down to a native kraal, abandoned at the moment, but the women and children who occupied it had only left it a few hours before when they first saw the white men approaching. The native who told me the story was one of these. The Prince's party were apparently about to prepare some refreshments when they were attacked, because they had sent a native attendant who was with them to fetch some water from the river which was only a few yards away. When the natives made their rush, the whole party of white men made for their horses. The story of the Prince's saddle turning is quite wrong, according to the native who saw the whole thing. The Prince was riding a very tall white horse. According to the native's account, the horse must have stood about 16 hands high. When the Prince tried to mount this horse, he reared and shied at the on-coming natives and the Prince's hands slipped off the pommel of the saddle, but as he already had one foot in the stirrup, he fell on his back on the ground and before he could recover himself, the horse had run away. The two troopers came back to the Prince's assistance and were killed with him; the two officers (!) escaped. The native who told me all this said that the white men killed a lot of natives before they were killed themselves and that the white men would have probably killed all the natives if they had only had big guns instead of little ones (probably revolvers). Another interesting statement made by the native was that the natives were very sorry when they heard that one of the white men they had killed was an "inkose" (chief) who belonged to another nation than the English, but they did not know that because he wore the same clothes as the English soldiers. One can forgive these natives a lot when one of them makes a remark like that……

When you see mother, please tell her what I have asked you to tell her but, for the love of heaven, do not mention my whereabouts or Curtis or Barklie or Waterman. If you do, she will move Heaven and Earth but she will get in touch with them somehow and write them one her melodramatic letters appealing to them to get in touch with her Son, giving them a lot of irrelevant details and a few imaginary ones by way of trimmings to give the thing an artistic 'ensemble'.

Joséphine's Death, and René Puaux

I happened to be staying with my mother over Christmas, 1932 at the Hotel Aurora at Fiesole, when she received from A.P. the news of their mother's death. However I did not learn of this at the time; nor was I even aware of Joséphine's existence. On December 29, my mother wrote to A.P: "The news saddened me as the last farewell is always painful. At heart, though, I am grateful to Providence for having spared mother a long agony."

La notizia mi ha attristata perchè è sempre una cosa dolorosa il senso dell'ultimo addio. Sono però in fondo al cuore grata alla Providenza che ha risparmiato a mamma una longa agonia…

The immediate and overriding concern of both Elisina and Linetta was to discourage, and if possible prevent any publicity about their mother. However this was impossible because the New York press, in particular the *N.Y. Times* and the *N.Y. Herald Tribune*, published substantial obituary notices (See Appendix…). These had rapidly come to the attention of René Puaux, editor of the foremost Paris newspaper, *Le Temps*, who happened to be interested in the Castelvecchio family. He wrote to A.P. for information shortly after Joséphine's death.

At first my mother was very apprehensive, fearing that René Puaux would publish stories in the French press. However he turned out to be a very understanding and friendly person with whom she established excellent personal relations of mutual discretion and respect. We have Puaux's notes, which have been very valuable to me. It is also thanks to him that we have the letters about Joséphine quoted below. The earliest of these, dated January 20, 1933, from the French Consul Général in New York, Charles de Pouhers, is in reply to a letter from Puaux of Jan. 7, i.e: less than 3 weeks after Joséphine's death: "I learned of her death only from the press, which the next day published a rather brief account of her life."

Je n'ai été informé de sa mort que par la presse qui le lendemain faisait paraître un curriculum vitae assez sommaire…

The letter mentions the death "in Africa" of her son (Louis) and the marriage at about the same time of her daughter Linetta. It continues: "She had indeed founded and presided over Le Salon, a philanthropic and cultural enterprise with a distinctly social character. '

This is an inexcusably sloppy and unfair piece of reporting on the part of the French Consul General in New York, or of the underling who, I suspect, was given the job of preparing it for his signature. In any case he bears responsibility for it.

The obituary notices in the *New York Times* and the *New York Herald Tribune* cannot possibly be describes as "sommaires"; and to have characterized *Le Salon* as having primarily a social function is both untrue, and unfair to Joséphine and her husband. It was founded in the first World War in order to stimulate interest in, and sympathy for the cause of the Allies, as well as to raise funds for war victims, particularly in France.

Evidently the French Government did not share the Consul General's opinion, when, in 1926, it awarded Joséphine the "Médaille de Vermeil de la Reconnaissance Française", which Elisina herself termed "a good decoration".

However it was thanks to this letter that René Puaux obtained the names of Madame Carlo Polifème and (through her) that of Miss Marguerita P. Williams, both close friends of Joséphine in her last years. Their letters to René Puaux are vivid, and have the ring of sincerity. They are invaluable in that they give us an idea of how Joséphine appeared to two people who were not members of the family. For this reason I am including interesting passages from them in this text, rather than placing them in the Appendix.

Letter from Mme Polifème, March 3, 1933

…The Countess and Linetta, on an occasion when the latter was in New York, had delegated Margaret Williams—an American who speaks a little French, an unmarried lady between 45 and 55 years old—to see to our friend's last needs. Linetta had long been sending generous monthly remittances to her mother. During these final, cruel years it was Miss Williams who received them. The Countess also had a pension from her husband, Marquis de Frabasilis, who passed away in Naples five or six years ago. He spoke 14 languages and had long served as a preceptor to the children of the Greek royal family. They had met in society in New York some thirty or forty years ago. I deeply loved them both, because to me both were beautiful—physically so, no doubt, but also intellectually, for all that they knew.

The Nurse, or the nurses, would no doubt say the same to you, but they would also say that she was very difficult, etc., and that is certainly true. Well born as she was, the Countess had been brought up to heed and to command; and then, a nurse is not someone able to analyse the intimate feelings of a patient who pays nothing. No, I do not believe that we could receive any help from them. No doubt she was difficult with them. Saint Luke's hospital wanted no more of her, but everyone loved and respected her, and it was the hospital chaplain who gave her the supreme unction [*derniers hommages*]. Everyone acknowledged her worth, her mind, her smile, and her laugh even while she was in the greatest pain. She was admirable!

No, the Countess spoke to no one of the past. She did speak of it to me, but not fully, I could feel that. With respect to her children, she spoke of Linetta and of her son Louis, who died in Africa two, three, or four years ago—I am not sure how long. Of her success in the theatre, yes, she had had a great deal to say, *to everyone*. She spoke to me a good deal of her youth, but never clearly, and I did not seek to discover more.

I believe that she has a daughter in Paris or in France. I never heard of any other child. However, I know that the Countess left Italy with four children. One, named Leon, is married and lives in New York. I have known him only by the name Leon. "My son Leon," his mother used to say. It is at the time of his mother's death that I learned that his last name was Gower.

No, I never knew the Countess's address, West Eleventh Street.

No, she was never considered a pauper. Besides, she was too regal to be a pauper. However, she never had anything.

Properly speaking, Mr. Frabasilis was an interpreter for the American courts. I do not know whether he had become a naturalized citizen.

Louis… Palamidessi died in Africa. The Countess was shattered!

No, I cannot tell you now where Louis died—in central Africa, I believe. I do not know what he did, but I believe that he enjoyed the prestige of a good position. He died several months before his mother heard of his death. He was married and had a little son, who must be in England with his Aunt Linetta. The mother—married or not married, according to [how?] the law [defines it?], went home.

It is true that the Countess appeared on the stage beside Irving and Ellen Terry. She came to America with them and had success there.

The Countess's "Le Salon." Here, she gathered artists from the theatre world. She brought together a great many people, and once a year she gave a "Bénéfice" [a benefit event]. Miss Williams and Maître [the title for a lawyer] Doremus were in charge of organizing the events you mention.

Miss Williams is a gift from God. Maître Doremus, too, I would say. In any case, the Countess trusted them implicitly, and I believe that she was right to do so. These things are deposited, if I remember correctly, in the office of Maître Doremus, who is, I believe, a distinguished lawyer. I believe that I am named in the Countess's will, according to a letter from her that I received in France last August, at a time when already she foresaw her eternal departure. I think I remember that the portrait—I can give no further details, and I do not have the letter before me, but a portrait at any rate—was to go to me, and another to His Excellency General Gouraud, whom I was never able to see in Paris, as she had asked me to do. I was unable to accomplish that mission. Concerning the portrait of her father, I do not remember.

I never heard the Countess mention a brother or sister. It is true that I never paid attention to these discrepancies, being aware than I would never know the truth; and I would never have allowed myself to be indiscreet toward her. The Countess had many women friends more valuable to her cause than myself. She saw them far more often than she saw me, and they naturally knew her better than I did—I mean, as far as her financial situation was concerned. As for myself, I and many others observed with deep sorrow how this proud and greatly loved woman suffered from desperate, although concealed, need. I was her true friend in her worst days, the true frenchwoman who answered her call in the last hours before her imminent death. In October, hardly back from France, I rushed from afar to the side of this most gracious, dying lady. She lay, radiant, upon a pallet, and I said to her: "Dear friend, how beautiful you are! I have never seen you so beautiful." With her great black eyes still shining and smiling she replied, "My dear, you know (lifting her gaze to the heavens) that it comes to me from on high!" My visit had transformed her! The next day, however, she was worse, then better, then worse again. It was impossible to keep her here. Hospitals do not take such cases free. It was Hell. It will never be said, I told myself, that this adorable person, this frenchwoman, this woman of France, was forgotten in darkness.

The president of our French hospital admitted her, despite the hospital's normal practice. She was treated kindly there, but unfortunately it was impossible to keep her. She was therefore sent to the Metropolitan Hospital with an urgent recommendation from Monsieur Lucien

Gouvant. She was kindly received there as well, and she died shortly afterwards.

Miss Margaret Williams works for the Sage Foundation, 130 East 22nd Street. She has been sublime and deserves our highest respect.

Please forgive me for having run on this way….

Madame Carlo Polifême (née Wanecq)

La Comtesse et Linette dans un passage à New York avaient délégué Marguerite [sic] Williams – américaine parlant un peu français, demoiselle entre 45 et 55 ans pour répondre aux besoins derniers de notre amie. Linette, depuis longtemps, envoyait chaque mois une obole généreuse à sa mère. Dans ces dernières et cruelles années c'est Miss Williams qui recevait cette obole. La Comtesse avait aussi une pension de son mari, M. le Marquis de Frabasilis, décédé à Naples il y a cinq ou six ans. Il parlait 14 langues et avait été pendant de longues années précepteur des enfants de la Maison Royale de Grèce. Ils s'étaient rencontrés dans le monde à New York il y a … 30 … ou 40 ans, je ne puis préciser aujourd'hui. Je les aimais tous deux, profondément, car, pour moi, ils étaient beaux de front sans doute, mais surtout par leur savoir, leur intellectuel, etc, etc…

La Nurse, ou les nurses, vous diraient sans doute comme moi, mais elle vous diraient aussi qu'elle était très difficile, etc., etc., cela est évident. La Comtesse, bien née, avait été élevée à obéir et à commander – et puis une nurse, ce n'est pas une personne capable d'analyser dans l'être intime d'un patient qui ne pay [sic] pas! Je ne crois pas que nous puissions obtenir à ce sujet aucune aide. Certes elle était difficile avec elles.

L'Hôpital St Luc ne voulait plus lui donner abri, mais elle était aimée et prisé de tous, et c'est le chapelain de cette maison qui lui rendit les derniers hommages. Tous reconnaissaient sa valeur, sa mentalité, son sourire et son rire même dans les plus grandes douleurs. Elle était admirable !

Non, la Comtesse ne parlait du passé à personne. Elle m'en a parlé à moi mais pas entièrement, je le sentais. De ses enfants elle parlait de Linette, de son fils Louis mort en Afrique il y a deux, trois ou 4 ans, je ne puis préciser aujourd'hui. De son succès au théâtre, oui, elle parlait beaucoup avec tous. De sa jeunesse elle me parlait assez, mais jamais au clair et je n'insistais pas.

Je crois savoir qu'elle a une fille à Paris ou en France. Je n'ai jamais entendu parler d'une autre fille. Je sais cependant que la Comtesse a quitté l'Italie avec 4 enfants. Un fils du nom de Léon, marié, habite New York. Je ne l'ai jamais connu que sous le nom de Léon. 'Mon fils Léon' disait sa mère. C'est lors de la démise de sa mère que j'ai appris qu' il s'appelait Gower.

Je n'ai jamais connu l'adresse de la Comtesse, West Eleventh Street.

Non, elle n'était pas considérée comme une indigente. Elle était du reste trop royale pour être jamais indigente, cependant qu'elle n'avait rien.

Correctement, M. Frabasilis était interprète auprès des tribunaux américains. Je ne sais si M Frabasilis s'était fait naturaliser américain.

Louis... Palamidessi est mort en Afrique. La Comtesse en fut désespérée !

Non, je ne puis vous dire aujourd'hui où est mort Louis – dans l'Afrique centrale, je crois. Je ne sais ce que Louis faisait, mais je crois qu'il jouissait du prestige d'une bonne situation. Il est mort plusieurs mois avant que sa mère en eût connaissance. Il était marié et avait un fils en bas âge qui doit être en Angleterre chez sa tante Linette. La mère, mariée ou non mariée – selon les lois – s'en est retournée chez elle.

Il est vrai que la Comtesse a joué aux côtés d'Irving et d'Ellen Terry. Elle est venue en Amérique avec ceux-ci et eut bon succès.

La Comtesse 'Le Salon'. [sic] Ici elle réunit les artistes du théâtre. Elle y envoyait et invitait beaucoup de monde et une fois l'an elle y donnait un 'Bénéfice'. Miss Williams et Maître Doremus avaient charge et responsabilité de ces choses dont vous parlez.

Miss Williams est une envoyée de Dieu. Maître Doremus aussi que je sache. En tout cas la Comtesse avait en eux une confiance entière et je la crois. Le dépôt de ces choses sont, je crois me rappeler, dans les bureaux de Maître Doremus, grand avocat, je crois. Je suis, d'après une lettre de la Comtesse reçue en France au mois d'Août, alors que déjà elle prévoyait son départ éternel, sur son testament. Je crois me rappeler que le portrait – je n'ose préciser – et je n'ai pas cette lettre sous les yeux, - un portrait en tout cas, m'était destiné, et un autre à Son Excellence Mr le Général Gouraud que je n'ai pas pu voir à Paris comme elle m'avait chargée de le faire mais je n'ai pu accomplir cette mission. Au sujet d'un portrait de son Père – je ne me souviens pas.

Je n'ai jamais entendu La Comtesse parler de frère ni sœur. Il est vrai que je n'ai jamais tenu compte de ces divergences sachant que je ne connaitrais sans doute pas la vérité, et pour rien au monde j'eusse voulu être indiscrète auprès d'elle. La Comtesse avait de nombreuses amies bien plus nécessaires à sa cause que moi-même : Elle les voyait bien plus souvent que moi, et ces amies en bonnes causes la connaissait mieux que moi, je veux dire dans ses divers moyens pécuniaires.

En ce qui me concerne, je voyais, ainsi que tant d'autres personnes, les vifs regrets de constater cette femme superbe et tant aimée néanmoins dans un écrasant besoin dissimulé. J'ai été la véritable amie des mauvais jours, la véritable française qui répondit à l'appel aux dernières heures du trépas futur. En octobre, à peine rentrée de France, je courus bien loin auprès de la gracieuse mourante qui était radieuse étendue sur un grabat, et je lui dis : 'Chère amie, comme vous êtes belle, jamais je ne vous vis si belle' – ses grands yeux noirs toujours brillants et souriants elle me répondit : 'Vous savez chère – levant les yeux au ciel – cela me vient d'en haut!' Ma visite l'avait transformée ! Mais le lendemain elle était plus mal, et puis mieux et puis pire. On ne pouvait la garder ici. Les hôpitaux ne prennent point ces cas gratuitement. C'était la Géhenne. Il ne sera pas dit, pensé je, que cette adorable créature, femme française et femme de France, soit oubliée dans les ténèbres.

Notre président de l'Hôpital français la fit accueillir, malgré l'usage contraire à son cas. Elle y fut traitée avec grâce et bonté, mais malheureusement on ne put la garder ici. Elle fut donc envoyée au Metropolitan Hospital avec toutes les bonnes recommandations de M. Lucien Gouvant. Elle y fut également accueillie avec bonté et piété, où elle mourut peu après.

Miss Marguerite Williams est occupée dans la Sage Foundation, 130 East 22. Cette Demoiselle a été sublime et mérite notre vénération.

Pardonnez, je vous prie, mon griffonnage et croyez à mes meilleurs sentiments.

Mme Carlo Polifème (née Wancecq)

The letter has an elaborate letter-head:

"Le Lyceum"

Société des Femmes de France a New York, Incorporated

In it appear several names, including that of Paul Claudel as Honorary President, and that of Madame Polifème (followed by the insignias of the Légion d'Honneur and of the Palmes Académiques. She is listed as "President Fondatrice", and the address given is: 321 West 92nd Street.

The second letter, of April 22, 1933, is from Marguerita (not Marguerite, as Mme Polifème writes it) P. Williams, who is obviously a very well educated woman, who writes well and to the point—in contrast to the well-meaning but rambling Mme Polifème. Having acknowledged receipt of M. Puaux's letter of March 23rd, the reply to which has been delayed by a "full Easter season", she proceeds as follows:

> Shortly after its receipt, a letter from my friend Mrs Richardson made mention of a communication she had received from you, making many inquiries, doubtless similar to those in your letter to me. As she was about to reply, I believe, you have probably by now had her answer, and it is much more fitting, as well as satisfactory, that a member of the family itself make answer to these

questions concerning their own personal affairs, I will not deem it my duty to answer your letter in these respects. I shall send your letter to Mrs Richardson, however, with a copy of my reply, so that there will be complete understanding of what you desire to know, and what I have replied.

There are several phrases used in your letter which I beg to correct, in the interests of all concerned, and I am sure you will be glad to have the light I can throw upon them. In the order of mention they are:

1. Your mention of me as 'Mrs Frabasilis' good angel, till the end? This is a lovely title, and I appreciate that fact, but I must disclaim it on one important ground at least - that it seems to imply her desertion by others, which was far from the truth. The Countess for years, and to the end, had a very large circle of friends in this city; but during the last months of her illness, when she sought medical and surgical assistance in hospitals for the painful arthritis which crippled her, and the cataracts which blinded both eyes, she was naturally unable to keep closely in touch with many friends, and when the end came very suddenly from a stroke of paralysis, it was the first intimation many had had that matters had become so serious with her. Having long been an intimate friend, it was natural that I then assumed the moment's responsibilities, but other friends also had been very helpful during her illness. And I should not fail to state that her daughter in England, Mrs Richardson, had all through the years and to the end kept as closely in touch and been as lovingly helpful as such hindrances as distance and her mother's very independent spirit would permit.

2. Your use of the word 'half-legitimate' in connection with the Countess's grandson, for whose education in England Mrs Richardson has taken the responsibility since his

father's death several years ago. I wonder how you came to use this term, as there is no ground for it in fact, and I have personally seen documents that would disprove it—certified copies of the marriage certificate of his father and mother, and of his birth certificate. There was nothing irregular about his birth, and it would certainly be a serious matter if you made further use of this term—its falsity could be too easily disproved.

3. Your reference to the Countess's 'unhappy life'. Despite the many vicissitudes of her life, the Countess's friends can never think of her in terms of 'unhappiness'. Not only her beauty, culture, marked personality and strong character, and delightful charm, made her the centre of attraction wherever she appeared, but there was a radiance, an overflowing vitality, an abounding cheer and wit, with never-failing interest in all the worth-while things of life, that made her an inspiring example to all her friends of a nature that would never admit defeat nor surrender to unhappy circumstances.

The Countess once wrote the following, which I preserved as characteristic of her noble and independent spirit: 'My birth has been made much of (referring to an article), while I regard it only as an accident, and a responsibility, and my paramount thought and wish have ever been to lead a life worthy of it. I am prouder of my efforts in this direction.....and my active part in public life—where it was thought I could do some good......than of a thing for which I am heartily thankful, but the decision of which certainly did not rest with me'.

The Countess's memory of her father, in whose life you seem so interested, was a beautiful one and very precious to her. He died while she was a young girl, but she would sometimes relate anecdotes (which I cannot now recall accurately) that revealed his great devotion and fidelity to his duties as Treasurer General of Finances, under the regime of the Emperor Napoleon III.

For other information I beg to refer you to the Countess's daughter, Mrs. Richardson, but I trust the above statements have made some points clearer to you, and I make them in loving memory of my revered friend, regarding whose closing days, owing to unexpected sudden happenings, unfortunate reports have been circulated.

Very truly yours,

Marguerita P. Williams

P.S. Pondering further over your use of the word 'half-legitimate', the thought comes—may you be referring to his father, Louis—but here again it would be a bad error. The idea might arise from him bearing his mother's maiden name, perhaps. The facts are that when the Countess was granted her divorce, she was also granted the right to resume her maiden name, and give it to her children by that marriage. M.P.W.

Note: Miss Williams can only be quoting Joséphine. The "real facts" are that:

1) The Lucca Tribunale only granted her request for separation, not her divorce.

2) It did not grant her "the right to resume her maiden name, and give it to her children by that marriage".

3) It did not pass on the question of use of the title, which in any case did not lie within its competence.

With these two testimonials, I shall lay Joséphine to rest, and also close this story of the Castelvecchio family, down to the fifth generation of Louis Bonaparte's descendants, i.e: as far as the great-grandchildren of Josephine.

William Royall Tyler

Supplement to Joséphine and her death (RT)

The *New York Times* for December 21, 1932, reported that "The ashes of the Countess will be sent to Paris for Interment." However, Joséphine's grave is actually in Dividing Creek, New Jersey.

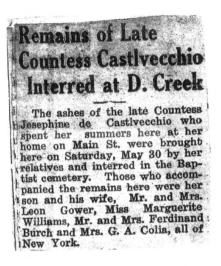

Joséphine, born in 1857, never confessed her real age.

Records of Joséphine on stage are few. One source mentions her joining a production in 1901. In May-June 1903 she appeared in a play entitled *John Henry*. In 1920, she performed in a movie version of *Half an Hour* by Sir Robert M. Barrie. A review of the film dated October 25, 1920 (Ogden, Utah, *Standard Examiner*) states, "A member of an old Napoleon family, the Countess de Castelvecchio, who has had wide experience on the stage and is known to the public as Elouina Oldcastle, but has been absent a number of years, comes back in *Half an Hour*."

APPENDICES

LOUIS BONAPARTE'S LAST ILLNESS
by François Louis de Castelvecchio

Journal de la Maladie de S.M. à Livourne

Wednesday 22 July, 1846

Upon returning from his Ardenna walk at 9:30, His Majesty rested for half an hour or so on a canapé in the sitting room and chatted in a lively manner. At 10 he went to lie down because his nerves were troubling him, and the great heat kept sleep from him that night.

Thursday 23 July

His Majesty was exhausted from lack of sleep during the night. Dr. Micheletti, who had attended him during the previous days, was called back and came about 11. Upon speaking with His Majesty, the doctor found that he had a low fever. He prescribed an ounce [*une once*] of ricin. An hour after having taken the oil, His Majesty drank a little broth, which had very little effect. At about 3 he seemed to fall into a deep sleep; however, his sleep appeared at times agitated or interrupted. Dr. Micheletti returned at about 7, but, seeing that His Majesty was still asleep, he preferred not to wake him and returned two hours later. He then found His Majesty still asleep. This long sleep, quite foreign to His Majesty's usual habits, seemed strange and gave rise to fears that those with him sought to dispel by waking him, with great care; but all attempts to do so were in vain. His Majesty failed to respond and seemed deeply unconscious, breathing hard. Dr. Micheletti therefore agreed that Professor Andreini should be summoned immediately, since he happened to be in Livorno at the time, and since he was perfectly acquainted with His Majesty's general health. Professor Andreini was unable to come earlier than 10. When a careful examination led him to fear apoplexy, he decided, in agreement with Dr. Micheletti, to bleed His Majesty (a task entrusted to Prof. Andreini's assistant,

Bonamici) and at the same time to apply twenty leeches around his ears. When these measures produced no immediate effect, the two gentlemen decided to apply mustard poultices [*sinapismes*] to his legs. During all this time, which lasted until about midnight, His Majesty seemed to experience no significant relief; it is only with the greatest care that it was possible to have him swallow a few spoonfuls of water, because he hardly moved his lips, never spoke, never opened his eyes, and seemed unaware of what was happening around him. The physicians discussed the question of what more they could do and then withdrew past midnight, after noting that His Majesty now had a high fever. It was imperative, they said, to have him drink frequently and to continue to massage his legs. These instructions were followed to the letter.

Mercredi 22 juillet, 1846

>   *Sa Majesté à son retour de la promenade de l'Ardenna à 9h et demie s'est reposée sur le canapé du Salon pendant une demi heure environ et a causé très gaiement. A 10h Elle est allée se coucher des maux de nerfs et n'a pu se reposer de toute la nuit à cause de la grande chaleur.*

Jeudi 23 juillet

>   *S. M. s'est trouvée très fatigué [sic] de ne pas avoir pu dormir de la nuit. Le Dr Micheletti qui était venu les jours précédents a été appelé de nouveau et est arrivé vers les 11h du matin. Le Dr après avoir parlé avec S. M. lui a trouvé un peu de fièvre et lui a prescrit une once de Ricin. Une heure après avoir pris l'huile S. M. a bu un peu de bouillon qui n'a produit que fort peu d'effet; vers 3h de l'après-midi Elle a paru s'endormir profondément, mais son sommeil paraissait agité ou interrompu de temps en temps. Vers 7h de Dr Micheletti est revenu, mais voyant que S. M. dormait encore il n'a point voulu la réveiller et a préféré revenir deux heures plus tard. Il revint en effet et trouva S. M. toujours endormie. Ce sommeil trop prolongé pour les habitudes de S. M. parut fort singulier et fit naître quelques craintes que l'on voulut dissiper en cherchant à éveiller S. M.*

avec précaution mais toute tentative fut inutile, car elle ne répondit pas et parut profondément assoupie, respirant avec force. Il fut donc convenu avec le Dr. Micheletti que l'on appellerait sur le champ le prof. Andreini qui se trouvait en ce moment à Livourne et qui connaissait parfaitement la constitution de S. M. A son arrivée qui ne put avoir lieu qu'après 10h le prof. Andreini après un examen attentive, craignit une apoplexie et se décida avec le Dr. Micheletti à faire une saignée (par le moyen du sous-aide Bonamici) conjoinctement [sic] avec une application de 20 sangsues près des oreilles ce qui ne produisit pas un effet immédiat et détermina ces M.M. à faire mettre des sinapismes sur les jambes. Pendant tout le temps de ces opérations qui durèrent jusqu'à minuit environ, S. M. ne parut pas éprouver aucun soulagement important ; et il ne fut possible de lui faire avaler un peu d'eau à petites cuillerées qu'avec beaucoup de précaution car Elle remuait à peine les lèvres, ne parlait point, n'ouvrait point les yeux et ne paraissait pas avoir la connaissance de tout ce qui se passait autour d' Elle. Les médecins ayant délibéré sur ce qu'ils avaient à faire se retirèrent après minuit, après avoir constaté que S. M. avait une forte fièvre, qu'il fallait lui donner souvent à boire et continuer les frictions aux jambes, ce qui fut fait très exactement.

Friday 24 July, 1846
At 5 a.m. Prof. Andreini came back to examine His Majesty and found his condition largely unchanged. Doctors Micheletti and Capecchi arrived, together with the assistant Bonamici. In agreement with Prof. Andreini they once more bled His Majesty, applied twenty new leeches around his ears, continued to massage his legs, and changed the poultices. However, these measures produced very little change. All these gentlemen returned at 11. Observing that the measures taken hitherto had been inadequate, they ordered a poultice of blister beetle [*vessicatoire aux mouches cantharides*, powdered "Spanish fly"] applied to each arm in order to obtain greater relief. At noon Doctor Bentheso, who had already come at 9, returned and remained beside

His Majesty. At 2, Prof. Andreini ordered new leeches, which Doctor Bentheso [or Betheso?] applied to His Majesty's left temple. Dr. Bentheso stayed with His Majesty until 5. The other doctors then returned, had the poultices changed, and, on instructions from Dr. Micheletti, ordered another *lavement* [enema?]. The fever continues, none of the treatments has produced the desired effect, and His Majesty remains in the same comatose state, without speaking, moving, or giving any sign of life. His eyelids have been raised several times, but his eyes fail to respond to light and remain in a fixed stare; he appears to see nothing. They continue to give His Majesty water to drink; only his lower lip moves slightly when touched with a spoon. His Majesty's illness, which the doctors diagnose a *congestion cérébrale* [stroke], continues to make disturbing progress. At 5:30 they apply new poultices [? François' French is unintelligible here] and administer a *lavement*, which works. An hour later, the fever has varied several times during the day. A priest summoned on the initiative of Prof. Andreini administered the extreme unction and visited His Majesty several times thereafter.

Vendredi 24 juillet, 1846

A 5h du matin le prof. Andreini est revenu examiner S. M. et l'a trouvée à peu de choses près dans le même état que la veille. A 6h les Drs Micheletti, Capecchi et le sous-aide Bonamici sont arrivés et d'accord avec le prof. Andreini ont fait saigner S. M. de nouveau, lui ont fait poser 20 autres sangsues autour des oreilles (regione della mastoide) et ont fait continuer les frictions aux jambes, et changer les sinapismes, mais le résultat n'a donné que fort peu de changement – à 11 heures tous ces Mrs son [sic] revenus et, vu l'insuffisance des moyens employés, ils ont ordonné qu'un vésicatoire aux mouches cantharides serait posé sur chaque bras pour obtenir un plus fort soulagement. A midi le Dr. Bentheso qui était déjà venu à 9h est revenu une autre fois et est resté près de S. M. A 2h le prof. Andreini a ordonné d'autres sangsues qui ont été appliquées à la tempe gauche de S. M. par le Docteur Betheso qui est resté près de S. M. jusqu'à

5h. A cette heure là les Drs sont retornés [sic] ont fait changer les sinapismes et fait prendre un autre lavement d'après l'ordonnance du Dr Micheletti. La fièvre continue toujours, toutes les prescriptions n'ont fait se produire l'effet désiré, et S. M. est restée dans le même état d'assoupissement, sans parler, remuer, ni faire aucun signe. Les paupières ont été soulevées à plusieurs reprises mais les yeux sont insensibles à la lumière, restent fixe [sic] et ne paraissent pas voir – on continue de donner boire à S. M., dont la lèvre inférieure seulement fait un léger mouvement lorsqu'on la touche avec une cuiller. La maladie de S. M. que les médecins traitent de congestion cérébrale, continue à faire lentement des progrès inquiétants. A 5h et demie on fait passer le nouveau sinapisme aux coup [?sic] de pieds et l'on fait donner un lavement qui opère. Une heure après, la fièvre a varié plusieurs fois dans la journée. Un prêtre a été appelé sur l'invitation de Mr. Andreini et est venu faire plusieurs visites à sa M. après toutefois lui avoir donné l'absolution et les saintes huiles.

REPORT ON LOUIS BONAPARTE'S DEATH

Letter of July 25, 1846 to the Foreign Minister, M. Guizot, from M. H. de la Rochefoucauld, French Minister to the Grand Duchy of Tuscany

Livourne, 25 July, 1846

Monsieur le Ministre,

Monsieur le Comte de Saint-Leu (Louis Bonaparte, ex-King of Holland) died a few hours ago in Livorno. Yesterday morning he suddenly had a stroke [*apoplexie*], and no application of the physician's art was able to help him. After thirty-three hours in a coma [*assoupissement léthargique*], he passed away this morning without convulsions or crisis. I believe that he was sixty-seven years old.

His brother the Prince de Montfort, to whom an express letter was sent yesterday, has not yet arrived from Florence. Monsieur le Comte de Saint-Leu had beside him at his death only a young man whom he had brought up, who never left him, and who is generally understood to be his natural son. M. le Comte's visible affection for this young man offended the family of the Prince de Montfort, which explains the steps they took lately to secure Prince Louis' admission into Tuscany. The family no doubt hoped that his presence beside the Comte de Saint-Leu would keep within the Bonaparte family the fortune that he might otherwise, or so they feared, settle while still living on this young man. I do not yet know the content of his will, but I doubt that Prince Louis will have gained much from this course of action, because the ex-King of Holland spoke of him only drily and with displeasure. It is worth noting, among other things, that after his escape from Ham, the Comte de Saint-Leu never once took any steps in favor of Prince Louis.

In any case, the Comte de Saint-Leu leaves only a mediocre fortune, one that I have often heard estimated to amount to fifty or sixty thousand francs in annual income [*50 or 60 mille francs de rente*]. Moreover, there are rumored debts. He lived a very retiring life in Florence, especially in these last years, during which his paralysed condition became more and more cruelly serious. He was a stranger to all political preoccupations. His name was never associated with any intrigue. All in all, one can say that he bore with dignity the vicissitudes of fortune.

Among the brothers of Napoleon, the only one left is the Prince de Montfort, ex-King of Westphalia, now 60 years old.

It is likely that news of the death of the Comte de Saint-Leu will decide Prince Louis to attempt to return to Tuscany, and I imagine that, under these circumstances, at least temporary authorization to do so will be granted. This is only conjecture on my part. Besides, the perfect peace now prevailing in Italy, and the enthusiasm everywhere aroused by the papal amnesty, remove for a long time any chance of the kind of intrigue with which one might imagine Prince Louis disposed to associate himself.

His cousin, M. Napoléon de Montfort, must be at the moment in or near Geneva. It is likely that his stay in Switzerland has something to do with Prince Louis's ambition to return to Italy. There is no doubt that intrigues are afoot to favor this ambition, and in that connection I have reason to believe the information, provided by the Préfecture de Police, that Your Excellency was kind enough to communicate to me in your dispatch #20. However, I believe that the death of the Comte de Saint-Leu will do more than these intrigues to facilitate an admission to Tuscany which, I have reason to believe, was already secretly favored by Florence.

Livourne, 25 juillet, 1846
Monsieur le Ministre,

M. le Comte de Saint-Leu (Louis Bonaparte, ex-roi de Hollande) vient de mourir, il y a quelques heures, à Livourne. Frappé subitement dans la matinée d'hier, d'un coup d'apoplexie, tous les secours de l'art ont été impuissans [sic]. Après un assoupissement léthargique de 33 heures, il a rendu l'âme ce matin, sans convulsion, sans crise, il s'est éteint... il était âgé, je crois, de 67 ans.

Son frère, le Prince de Montfort auquel un exprès avait été envoyé hier, n'est pas encore arrivé de Florence ; Monsieur le Comte de Saint-Leu n'avait auprès de lui au moment de sa mort qu'un jeune homme qu'il avait élevé, qui ne le quittait jamais et qui passe généralement pour son fils naturel. L'affection qu'il lui témoignait portait ombrage à la famille du Prince de Montfort, et c'est ce qui explique les démanches qu'elle a faites en dernier lieu pour obtenir l'admission en Toscane du Prince Louis. Elle espérait sans doute que sa présence auprès du Comte de Saint-Leu retiendrait dans la famille Bonaparte la fortune dont on craignait qu'il ne disposât de son vivant en faveur de ce jeune homme. J'ignore encore quelles sont ses dispositions testamentaires, mais il est probable que le Prince Louis aura peu à s'en louer, car l'ex-Roi de Hollande ne s'exprimait sur son compte qu'avec sécheresse et mécontentement. Il est notoire, entre autres, que depuis son évasion de Ham, il n'a fait aucune démarche en sa faveur auprès du gouvernement toscan.

Du reste, le Comte de Saint-Leu ne laisse qu'une fortune peu considérable que j'ai souvent entendu estimer de 50 ou 60 mille francs de rente. Encore prétend-on qu'elle est endettée. Il menait à Florence une existence très retirée, surtout dans les dernières années, où son état paralytique avait fait de cruels progrès. Etranger à toute préoccupation politique, son nom n'a été mêlé à aucune intrigue, et on peut dire, en tout, qu'il a supporté avec dignité les vicissitudes de la fortune.

Des frères de Napoléon, il ne reste plus aujourd'hui que le Prince de Montfort, ex-roi de Westphalie, âgé de 60 ans.

Il est probable que la nouvelle de la mort du Comte de Saint-Leu va déterminer le Prince Louis à tenter son retour en Toscane et je serais disposé à croire qu'en égard à cette circonstance l'autorisation d'un séjours, du moins temporaire, sera accordée. Ce n'est pourtant qu'une simple conjecture de ma part. Au surplus la parfaite tranquillité dont jouit l'Italie en ce moment, et l'enthousiasme que produit partout l'amnistie pontificale, écartent pour longtemps les chances d'intrigue auxquelles on pourrait supposer le Prince Louis disposé à s'associer.

Son cousin, M. Napoléon de Montfort, doit être en ce moment à Genève ou aux environs. Il serait assez probable que son séjour en Suisse se rattachât aux tentatives de retour de Prince Louis en Italie. Que les intrigues soient nouées pour le favoriser, il est indubitable, et sous ce rapport, j'ai lieu de croire exacts les renseignements émanés de la préfecture de Police, que Votre Excellence a bien voulu me communiquer par sa dépêche no 20. – Mais la mort du Comte de Saint-Leu aura, je crois, plus d'influence que l'intrigue pour faciliter une admission en faveur de laquelle j'ai lieu de croire qu'on s'inclinait déjà secrètement à Florence.

Notes

The two brief final paragraphs of this despatch do not concern the death of the Comte de Saint-Leu, directly or indirectly. It is signed H. de la Rochefoucauld, and is an extremely interesting family document. It emphasizes the Comte Saint-Leu's affection for his son, as well as the understandable—in the circumstances—suspicion, resentment and jealousy of the Bonaparte's toward the latter. I find it strange that de la Rochefoucauld does not mention François' name. He had been living with his father in Florence for nearly two years; and even though the Comte de Saint-Leu lived a very quiet life, it is hard for me to believe that the resident French Minister had never met him, or at least learned his name. Perhaps de la Rochefoucauld wished for political reasons to avoid any implication of even normal social relations with him.

It is also possible that neither de la Rochefoucauld nor Louis Napoléon knew of the Act of Donation which the Comte de Saint-Leu had signed in François' favour in February 1843.

Whatever the situation, François' position must have been a delicate and vulnerable one. It is greatly to his credit, it seems to me that he soon won the confidence and respect of his half-brother, to the point that after the latter became Emperor, he wanted François to come to Paris, and did much to help him and his family socially and materially.

DRAFT LETTER TO NAPOLEON III
by François Louis Castelvecchio

Sire,

From childhood on I received no care but from King Louis of Holland. Thereafter, his paternal affection for me was visible at every moment of my life. His solicitude followed me in the houses of those charged with my care, and he wished to see my circumstances for himself. I remember happily the period of my childhood when he took me on his lap, caressing and kissing me in a very loving manner! When I was at school, he often sent someone he trusted to see me and to make sure of my health and my progress. When he sent me to Switzerland to pursue further studies, he wept as he watched me go, and his letters bear witness to the affection that his noble heart had for me. It was when I had been away from him for two years, and he planned to have me stay away from him another two in order to further my education, that he made me the gift of which Your Majesty is aware, and which is the sole basis of my own fortune.

I admired the depth of his thought, and I was grateful that he had left me nothing further in a last, solemn expression of his wishes. He may have reflected that my position required caution, since I did not bear his name!

After he had recalled me to his side, no demonstration of affection seemed excessive to him, and my relations with him were exactly what those between a good, loving father and his son might have been. As a matter of fact, his deepest feelings escaped through his lips. More than once, when King Louis kissed me, he acquainted me with my origin and with the reason for his affection toward me. More than once he asked me to call him by his rightful name; and the Emperor will surely understand that in calling him my father I sought only to please him, and that my greatest happiness would have been to be able to address as my brother the one who was free to call himself, publicly, his son.

There are other things, too, that I will touch on only briefly. When Prince Louis managed to escape from the shameful prison that held him, the King's only wish was to see his son again, and it pleased him to think that, before he died, he might have been able to introduce us one to the other and insure that we should love each other.

That was his constant desire, and it is natural that, feeling his end approaching, he should have considered those whom he would leave behind in this world and wished happiness both upon the one who inherited his name and the one whom he had loved to the very end.

Sire, I have only a few more words to add. They are these.

The end of this noble life was drawing near.

I was A L O N E among all those whom he loved in assisting him during that sad time; A L O N E I gave him what care it fell to me to give him; A L O N E I closed his eyes; and, finally, I A L O N E accompanied him to the church, where he remained until Your Majesty, in conformity with your father's wishes, had him transported to the soil of his native land.

A few days later I was given to understand my position. No one could say that I was affected by this in any way, or that the small fortune left me dissatisfied me to the slightest degree. It is true that if King Louis had lived a few years longer, he would have wished to insure my advancement and sought in person to provide me with another position. The times made this impossible, however, and my fortune had to suffice. I was content with it, since the idea of accumulating a great deal of money never occurred to me.

Thereafter, following through on a course of action initiated by King Louis, I married. The restricted nature of my resources kept me for some time tied to Florence. When I reached Paris, Your Majesty received me as a brother, and you were kind enough to kiss me. This evidence of affection meant a great deal to me, and I would have given anything to prove to Your Majesty, by remaining in Paris as you desired me to do, how greatly I respected your wishes.

Unfortunately, the sorrow that I would have caused the man who had been as a father to my wife, by taking her away from him, and—on the other hand—the thought that my fortune was too small to allow me to remain in Paris decided me to return to Florence.

The following year Your Majesty gave me the same affectionate welcome, and you and Her Majesty the Empress pressed us to stay on in Paris. Your Majesty said to my eldest daughter, then six years old, "Do you really think you are doing the right thing by your parents by taking them back to Florence?" Not wishing to be a burden upon you, I refused once more, although shaken in my resolve. I changed my mind completely when, the following year, the death of my father-in-law relieved me of the ties that detained me in Florence.

However, despite everything that Your Majesty had said and despite Your Majesty's warm letters—letters that I treasure—I made up my mind at last only upon receiving from Your Majesty a new letter, stating that you would be pleased to see me come in Paris.

Trusting in these promising signs, I made up my mind and came to establish myself here.

Your Majesty received me well, and I should add that, apart from the rarity of the occasions when I am able to see you, I can only be delighted with the goodness that you have shown me.

However, I have always wondered whether Your Majesty so encouraged me to come to Paris in order to give me a position in a ministry, one that will oblige me to travel continually if I am to rise—fortunate though I am to be offered the chance to do so.

I had believed that my relationship with Your Majesty was different in character, and I had hoped that Your Majesty would not leave me dependent upon the good will of a minister.

I have only one further thing to add. I did not want to be a burden on Your Majesty, but reflection on your pressing invitations to come here, and moreover in view of my family's anxiety, I felt that I would fail in my duty to you, since nothing any longer kept me in Florence, and in my duty to my children if, for their sake, I did not take advantage of a position that seemed to promise well. Was I wrong to do so? It is up to Your Majesty to let me know.

Sire,

Dès mon enfance je n'ai reçu de soins que du Roi Louis de Hollande. Depuis, à chaque instant de ma vie, l'affection paternelle qu'il me portait n'a jamais cessé de se montrer. Sa sollicitude me suivait dans les maisons particulières où l'on était chargé par Lui d'avoir soin de moi, et il voulait voir par lui-même l'état où j'étais. Je me rappelle avec bonheur le temps de mon enfance où il me tenait sur ses genoux, me prodiguant mille caresses et m'embrassant de la manière la plus affectueuse! Au Collège, il envoyait souvent une personne de confiance me voir et s'assurer de ma santé et de mes progrès. Lorsqu'il m'a envoyé en Suisse pour avancer mes études, il a pleuré en me voyant partir, et ses lettres témoignent de la profonde amitié que son noble cœur avait pour moi. C'est lorsque j'étais absent depuis deux ans, et qu'il me destinait à rester encore deux ans au loin de lui pour achever mon éducation, qu'il m'a fait cette donation que V.M. connait et qui est l'unique base de ma propre fortune.

J'admirai la profondeur de sa pensée et je lui fus reconnaissant de ne rien m'attribuer de plus dans un acte solennel et dernier. Il peut avoir pensé que ma position exigeait des précautions, car je ne portais pas son nom!..

Lorsqu'il m'eût rappelé auprès de lui aucun témoignage d'affection ne lui parut exagéré, et les rapports que j'eus avec lui étaient tout à fait ce qu'auraient pu être ceux d'un bon et affectueux père avec son fils. Son cœur d'ailleurs s'échappait de ses lèvres et plus d'une fois en m'embrassant, le Roi Louis m'a fait savoir mon origine et les motifs de son affection, plus d'une fois il m'a demandé de lui donner le nom qui lui appartenait, et l'Empereur peut penser qu'en l'appelant mon Père, je ne désirais que lui être agréable, et que mon plus grand bonheur eût été de pouvoir appeler mon Frère celui qui pouvait publiquement se dire son Fils.

*Il y a encore d'autres circonstances que je ne rappellerai que brièvement. Lorsque le Prince Louis put échapper à la prison indigne qui la [*sic, but this is because François had originally written V.M. instead of 'Le Prince Louis'*] renfermait, Le Roi n'eut d'autres désir [*sic, but originally the word had been 'pensées'*] que de revoir son Fils, et il était heureux de penser que, avant de mourir, il aurait pu nous faire connaître l'un à l'autre et nous faire aimer l'un de l'autre.*

C'était sa pensée fixe, et il était naturel que se sentant près de sa fin, il jetât un regard sur ceux qu'il laissait dans ce monde, et qu'il désirât qu'il y eût du Bonheur pour l'héritier de son nom aussi bien que pour celui qu'il n'avait cessé d'aimer jusqu'à la fin.

Je n'ai que peu de mots à ajouter, Sire; les voilà!

La fin de cette noble vie approchait.

Je fus S e u l [with a capital S and letters twice as large, and twice as spaced as in the rest of the text] *de tous ceux qu'il aimait à assister à ces tristes moments, S e u l je lui prodiguais les soins qui dépendaient de moi, S e u l je lui fermai les yeux, et S e u l enfin je l'accompagnai à l'église, où il est resté jusqu'à ce que V. M. selon le vœu de son Père l'ait fait transporter sur le sol de sa patrie.*

L'on me fit connaître peu de jours après dans quelle position je restais; tout le monde peut dire que je n'en fus aucunement touché, et que la petite fortune qui me restait me satisfaisait complètement. Il est vrai que si le Roi Louis eût vécu quelques années encore, il aurait eu de l'ambition pour moi, et il aurait lui-même cherché à me faire une autre position ; mais alors c'étaient des temps contraires et ma fortune devait me suffire : je fus content, car l'idée d'amasser beaucoup d'argent ne me vint jamais à l'esprit.

Depuis cette époque suivant un projet entamé par le Roi Louis, je me mariai.- L'exiguïté de mes ressources me retint immobile quelques temps à Florence. Lorsque je vins à Paris, V.M. me reçut comme un Frère et elle daigna m'embrasser. Ce témoignage d'affection me fut bien précieux, et j'aurais tout donné pour prouver à Votre Majesté, en restant à Paris comme elle voulut bien me le demander, quel cas je faisais de ses désirs.

Mais le chagrin que j'aurais fait à celui qui avait tenu lieu de Père à ma femme, en le privant d'elle, et - d'un autre côté - la pensée que ma fortune ne m'aurait pas suffi pour rester à Paris, me déterminèrent à retourner à Florence.

L'année d'après je reçus de V.M. le même accueil affectueux, et V.M. ainsi que S.M. l'Impératrice, nous pressèrent de rester à Paris ; et V.M. s'adressant à ma fille aimée qui avait alors 6 ans, lui dit : 'Tu crois donc leur faire du bien à tes parents en les ramenant à Florence ?' Ne voulant pas vous être à charge je refusai encore, quoique ébranlé dans ma résolution. Je changeai d'avis entièrement, lorsque l'année suivant [sic] mon Beau Père étant mort, je me trouvais dégagé de ce côté des liens qui me retenaient à Florence.

Cependant, malgré tout ce que V.M. m'avait dit ; malgré les lettres affectueuses de V.M. qui me sont plus chères que bien des trésors, je ne me décidai que lorsque je reçus de V. M. une nouvelle lettre dans laquelle elle me disait qu'elle verrait avec plaisir mon arrivée à Paris.

Comptant sur ces précédents, je me décidai et je vins m'établir ici.

Je fus bien reçu de Votre Majesté et je dois ajouter que sauf le peu de facilités que j'ai de la voir, je ne puis que me louer de ses bontés.

Mais je me suis toujours demandé si V.M. m'a tant encouragé à venir à Paris pour me donner une place dans un Ministère, une place qui me forcera à voyager perpétuellement pour avancer, et trop heureux qu'on m'en offre l'occasion.

Je croyais être dans une autre position vis à vis de V.M., et j'espérais que V.M. ne me ferait pas dépendre du bon vouloir d'un ministre.

Je n'ai plus à ajouter qu'une chose. Je ne voulais pas être à charge à V.M. Mais en réfléchissant aux invitations pressantes qu'elle m'a adressées de venir ici, et d'ailleurs ma famille étant augmentée, je crû [sic!] manquer à mes devoirs envers vous, puisque rien de me retenait plus à Florence, et envers mes enfants en ne profitant pas pour eux d'une position qui paraissait pouvoir devenir belle. Mais suis-je trompé ? C'est à V.M. de me faire savoir.

Notes

This is truly an extraordinary document! Though drafted in the form of a letter, I don't know—and I doubt—whether it was ever sent off. If it was, I doubt even more whether Louis received a reply.

He makes three major points: how close he was to his father, how much the Emperor had urged him to move to Paris, and how disappointing—in view of the implicit prospects—he finds his present situation.

It may well be—indeed, for his sake, one can only hope—that Louis decided not to send off the letter. I can imagine the Emperor reacting explosively to the thinly, if politely, implied charge of bad faith: the last brief sentence is highly provocative! Louis may have drafted the text as an exercise to formulate his grievances, and as a rehearsal for a conversation he was planning to have with the Emperor. At all events he kept the draft and this shows how important he considered it to be. It contains several interesting points, in addition to the main thrust: "King Louis acquainted me with my origin" [Le Roi Louis m'a fait connaître mon origine.] Since François had known his paternal "origine" all his life, I take it that "origine" in this context means his mother.

(1) The initiative of Louis Bonaparte with regard to François' marriage. At that time Elise was known to the world as Mademoiselle de Bruges de Camps, daughter of the highly

regarded and well-to-do (both important!) French businessman, long established in Florence and his wife (as she was thought to be), Madame Marcel de Bruges de Camps.

(2) The letter reveals that Louis (as he was by then known) Castelvecchio, first met his half-brother in Paris in 1853, and that the latter asked him if he would move there. A year or so later (Marceline, born October 12, 1848, already being six years old), the Emperor repeated his invitation. Marcel de Bruges de Camps had died on September 5, 1854, and François now felt free to accept his half-brothers offer.

(3) The letter must have been drafted after the birth of Joséphine (Jan 25, 1857), for François writes "…ma famille etant augmentée", and before he was appointed to Nice and made a Count (mid-1860). He had left the Foreign Office when the Minister, Walewski, resigned in January of that year.

JEAN BAPTISTE FORTUNÉ DE FOURNIER
Painter and engraver, Ajaccio 1798 - Paris 1864

We have two paintings by this artist—one, a charming miniature of Elise, signed and dated Florence, 1851, with a view of the city in the background; the other au aquarelle of Elise's bedroom at 216, rue de Rivoli, inscribed "Souvenir d'Amitié a Madame Elize (sic) par F. de Fournier Juillet 1860. On the mount in ink, and possibly in Françoise Louis' hand: = Juin 1860 =. This was the year in which he was named Count, and Receveur Général des Finances at Nice. On the left can be seen a black wooden box on the floor, which is now at Antigny. In the background is a little girl seen from behind, in a neighbouring room, who must be Louise. She is too young to be Marceline (b.1848) and too old to be Joséphine (b.1857)

We also have the following works by him:

1. A pencil and wash view of the Tuileries gardens, with the palace on the left.

2. A pencil sketch of the rue de Rivoli and the Tuileries gardens looking west to the Arc de Triomphe, unsigned and inscribed "D'apart de Mad 21 juillet 1860"

3. A pencil sketch from the same spot, looking east toward the Palais de Tuileries and the Pavillon le Marsau, and up the rue de Rivoli, unsigned and inscribed "15 aout 1860".

4. A pencil drawing of the drawing-room, unsigned and inscribed "Depart. de Castelvecchio 28 Juin 60".

Note: Although the inscription on #2 above looks like "D'apart" etc...both because the second letter looks like an "a" rather than an "e" and above it and to the left is what looks more like an apostrophe than an acute accent, it certainly makes more sense to read it as "Départ" rather than "D'apart". Just to complicate matters, the "Depart" (de Castelvecchio) has no acute, or any, accent over the "e"! I would take it that Louis left on June 28, and Elise three weeks later.

On March 14, 1861, Louis de Castelvecchio summarizes a letter he has written from Nice to Countess Walewska, wife of the former Foreign Minister under whom he had served:
> [I have not translated this material on de Fourier and his work because it concerns neither me nor the reader of these translations. I do not know what happened to the paintings and drawings mentioned–RT]

Prière de s'intéresser à M. De Fournier, ancien serviteur et ami de la famille Bonaparte à que l'Emp: porte beaucoup d'intérêt. M de Fournier désire être nommé Inspecteur des Beaux Arts au Louvre : cette place va être vacante par la promotion de M. Pasqualini appelé à d'autres fonctions et il prie Mme Wal. d'intéresser en sa faveur M. le C. Walewski.

L'empereur l'aime beaucoup ; il a été visité ses ouvrages, et l'a honoré de commandes importantes depuis 1852, tant pour lui que pour la Reine d'Angl. Et il l'a décoré après l'exposition universelle. 'Si mes souvenirs peuvent lui être favorable je me permettrai de vous dire que je l'ai vu traiter par le Roi Louis comme un ami de 40 ans' et que S.M. lui portait beaucoup d'intérêt. Mad. La Comtesse me pardonnera mon initiative en faveur de ses nobles instincts qui auront par là une nouvelle occasion de faire du bien.

On the same day he writes a letter in the same vein to des Vallières, Attaché au Ministère d'Etat: "I commend Fournier to him and hope that he will intriduce Fournier to Marchand."

Je lui recommande Fournier et le prie de le présenter à Marchand.

Yet another letter on the same day and the same subject to Eugène Marchand, Secrétaire Général au Ministère d'Etat:

Mon cher ami, Permettez-moi de vous recommander tout spécialement un de mes bons amis, artiste distingué, honoré de plusieurs commandes de S.M. l'Emp. et décoré de sa main après l'exp. Universelle. M. de Fournier qui vous remettra cette lettre, et qui est l'artiste en question, désire obtenir la place d'inspecteur des Beaux Arts au Louvre… Je vous serai particulièrement reconnaissant de ce qui vous ferez dans son intérêt, car je le connais depuis au moins 15 ans et j'ai eu lieu d'apprécier l'honorabilité et la délicatesse de son caractère, sa capacité en ce qui regarde la peinture, et le dévouement à la famille Impériale dont il a toujours été aimé.

Thanks to research undertaken, at my request, by Madame Marguerite de Cerval, in Paris, I obtained the following information on this minor and little known artist, whose contribution is of such historical interest:

1) Gerald Schurr, *Les petites maîtres de la peinture* (1820 – 1920) (5 vols. 1980-82), vol. 5, p. 91:

Fortuné de Fournier

Né à Ajaccio en 1798, mort à Paris en 1864, est presqu'uniquement aquarelliste et se spécialise dans les vues d'intérieur ; il les expose au Salon de 1843 à 1864 – accrochant toutefois, en 1859 et 1861 le portrait de Napoléon III, et des projets de panneaux décoratifs en 1863.

Plusieurs de ses œuvres ont valeur de témoignage : elles représentent en effet les salons, cabinets de travail et autres pièces des palais impériaux, comme Saint-Cloud et le Tuileries détruits en 1870 et 1871 et Fontainebleau ; ces aquarelles, commandées par l'Empereur, restituent avec une parfaite et précieuse exactitude le dessin de chaque meuble, de chaque bibelot, le ton des boiseries, des rideaux et les tapis. Fournier, qui fit une partie de ses études à l'Ecole Polytechnique de Naples, laisse aussi des vues documentaires du Musée des Offices et des Palais de Florence .

Note: de Fournier was awarded the Légion d'Honneur in 1855 by the Emperor.

2) Roman d'Amat, *Dictionnaire de Biographie française* (1979) :
Jean Baptiste Fortuné de Fournier

Né à Ajaccio en 1798, on lui doit des aquarelles et des miniatures qu'il exposa aux salons de 1843 à 1864: 'Vue intérieure de la tribune de Florence, salle des Médicis, 1843 ; vue intérieure de la Grande salle de Niobé, galerie des Offices à Florence 1852; salon Louis XIV aux Tuileries, 1855 huit vues du Palais des Tuileries;

deux portraits de Napoléon III ; la salle des maréchaux aux Tuileries, aquarelle ; souvenir de l'Exposition Universelle des Beaux –Arts de 1855, 1857 ; des panneaux décoratifs 1863.'

En tant que graveur, on relève dans son œuvre: Vénus d'Ailes, 1824 ; des planches pour la Galerie Pitti, de Bardi ; le Comte L. de Bombelles d'après Ingres, 1830; Nicolas de Demidoff, lithographie, 1825 ; Danse au perroquet, 1831 ; Bartolini d'après Ingres; Isabella Bartolommei et la divina fanciulla, lithographie, 1848 ; Dr. Lazzarini ; Leblanc ; Mme Leblanc ; Portrait de femme, d'après Ingres.

Il est mort à Paris le 17 février 1864.

Note: I ordered through Mme de Cerval, 3 photographs of
1) Le cabinet de travail de Napoléon III aux Tuileries (aquarelle)
2) La salle du conseil des ministres aux Tuileries (aquarelle), and
3) Napoléon III. All the originals are at the Château de Compiègne.

LEGAL SEPARATION OF JOSÉPHINE AND FRANCESCO PALAMIDESSI

On August 17, 1886, the "Tribunale Civile e Correzionale di Lucca" granted the separation.

Palamidessi was ordered to pay Lire 200 monthly, as a "pensione alimentare" to Joséphine, for herself and the three children, who are to remain with their mother, under her care and responsibility for their education.

Palamidessi is also condemned to pay all legal expenses arising from the case.

The text mentions the deterioration of the marriage after a few years of happiness, which resulted in Joséphine applying for separation on April 4, 1882, complaining of "sevizie, percosse e minaccie". However, before the completion of the legal proceedings, she effected a reconciliation with her husband and dropped the case—much to the distress of her lawyers, A.P. points out.

However, on September 17, 1885, she applied again for separation, *denunziando nuovi eccessi per parte del Marito, posteriori alla avvenuta conciliazone.*

Palamidessi denied these, but the Tribunal found that notwithstanding the reconciliation of 1882, new facts had now been advanced *i quali per la loro natura ed essenza danno diritto a chiedere et ottenere la separazione personale.* According to the testimony, Palamidessi in 1883, 1884 and 1885

> *percosse più volte la di lui Moglie Giuseppina, producendo nel di lei corpo contusione e lividure, ciò alla presenza non tanto dei teneri loro figli, quanto delle persone di Servizio, come del pari e accertato che spesso fece contumelia alla medesina con parole degradanti la di lei morabilità, e la costrinse ad esequire i più bassi ed umili servizi domestici nonostante que la Casa loro fosse fornita di sufficiente personale di Servizio.*

The Tribunal notes that the majority of these facts had been attested by the plaintiff's mother. Her testimony was required by law
> pure il timore che l'affetto verso la figlia abbia potuto in qualche modo far velo al di lei intelletto, e eliminato affatto dai deposti di altri testimoni, i quali non tanto convalorarono l'assunto della Madre della attrice, ma deposero di altri fatti che come addetti al Servizio dei Conjugi Palamidessi presenziarono.

Under the final heading "Per Questi Motivi" the Tribunal's verdict is summarized under five counts.

Notes

The "Decree" (as it is called in the family correspondence) of the Lucca Tribunal has occasionally been invoked to justify one or both of the two following claims:
1. That after the final separation of Joséphine and her husband, she and her children had the right to continue to use the name de Castelvecchio, instead of Palamidessi.
2. That Joséphine and her children continued to have the right to use the title of Count or Countess de Castelvecchio.

In fact, the Tribunal does not address itself to either of these points.

As far as the first is concerned, there seems to be no reason, according to Italian usage, why Giuseppina and her children should not continue to use the family name.

With regard to the title, the Tribunal ignores the question of its use altogether.

My impression, from the text of the decision, is that the Tribunal was totally unconcerned with these matters, and that Joséphine felt free to attribute to it any position she felt it would or should have taken, had it done so.

GEORGE SLYTHE STREET

George Slythe Street was born in Wimbledon in 1867, the younger son of a businessman in the City of London. His father died when George was 7 and he was educated—at Temple Grove, Charterhouse, and Exeter College, Oxford—at the expense of his guardian, possibly with an eye to his entering the family business, a large advertising agency in Cornhill. George's education entirely unfitted him for this career—and, as it turned out, for any other. It is probable that this chubby pleasant young man, who had acquired a fastidious taste in clothes, books, friends and racehorses, was never out of debt for the rest of his life. He came down from Oxford in 1890, having already (it is said) mortgaged his small inheritance on a disastrous horse race, and determined to be a writer. Even in these early days he was master of a keen, precise and slightly affected English, and he became a signing contributor to the *National Observer* and the *New Review*—Tory papers run by W.E. Henley, the poet, with a taste as fastidious as Street's but more violent. He published Yeats, Conrad, James, Kipling, Barrie and Wells, and gave Street a showcase for his first essays and satires. In 1894 appeared *The Autobiography of a Boy*, a delicate and ironical portrait of the fat-headed aesthete of the period. It was followed in 1895 by *Episodes*, an ambitious collection of short stories in the Maupassant manner—cold, brief, and grimly elegant. It was at this point, when success seemed to lie at his feet, that George Street's life went wrong. In desperation for money, he bound himself unwisely to his publisher, John Lane, a hard bargainer who held Street to his bond without on his part making the effort to market Street's books—which were widely praised and very badly handled. Street was forced to leave London because he could no longer afford to live there; he took lodgings at seaside places and in farmhouses and struggled to pay off his creditors by writing in the newspapers and the monthly reviews. His social and literary criticism reveals a fineness of intellect and an exquisite balance of temperament, and it is hard to realize that it is so thoroughly forgotten. At about this time he seems to have suffered greatly from the failure of a serious love affair. It is not clear how he could have married on 2 guineas a week, but it seems certain that he would have married—if she would have had him—the beautiful and formidable Elisina de Castelvecchio (herself a remarkable critic), but she broke off the engagement and married the publisher Grant Richards. After years of hard work and poor payment Street scraped together enough money to return to London (early in 1905) to two dark tiny rooms in Curzon Street where he lived for the next 30 years. He published several more books of essays, which combine delicate and humorous statement with a Johnsonian breadth of common sense and a strong feeling for the recent past, especially the 18th century. He was in the best possible sense an exquisite writer. In 1913 it had become almost impossible for him to stave off bankruptcy and his friends persuaded him to apply for the post of Reader of Plays to the Lord Chamberlain. He was appointed in January 1914 and retained the post with its small salary until his death. He was trusted both by the conservatives and the radicals in the theatre; he had never been narrow in sympathy, and he presided over the liberalization of the Censorship in the months before the Great War. After 1918 he seems to have written almost nothing, too discouraged by ill-health and his official duties. His friends—including Max Beerbohm and H.G. Wells—prized him for the real warmth behind his apparent reserve and did their best to win his books an audience—without success. He went blind in one eye and was cut off wine, hitherto a great consolation. He died in October 1936 with most of his youthful ambitions laid to rest unmourned. He had wanted to reform the Tory party with a blend of young England and Fabianism. He had wanted to dazzle the English stage with the most stylish comedy since Congreve. He had longed to find and adore some ruthless passionate high-bred lady who possessed intellect and beauty—an unfettered full-blooded *femme d'esprit* of Charles II's court, such as he had read of in Grammont and dreamed of at school. And in this last ambition, who shall say that he was not successful?

Paul Chipchase

Note: I am most grateful to Mr. Chipehase for having written for me this delightful piece on George Street.

OBITUARY NOTICES ON JOSEPHINE

(1) *New York Herald Tribune* Dec. 20, 1932, p.14, column I

Countess dies penniless here; Napoleon's kin

Joséphine de Castelvecchio Frabasilis passes at 68 in City Ward, Blind, Crippled

---

Grandniece of Emperors

Glamorous Actress of 90s Played with Ellen Terry

Funeral services for Countess Joséphine de Castelvecchio Frabasilis, grandniece of Napoleon III and once a glamorous figure on the stage, will be held at 2 o'clock today at 307 West Fifty-first Street. Formerly a brilliant and popular figure, she had fallen on evil days and died Sunday of arthritis at the Metropolitan Hospital, Welfare Island.

As Elouina Oldcastle she played with Ellen Terry and appeared on the stage here in Daly's Company during the nineties. In her prosperous days she maintained a salon which was frequented by French and Italian celebrities, but in recent years she had been in and out of hospitals, her health failing, her funds gone. On October 31 she had a stroke at the house of a friend on Staten Island. There she was taken to French hospital. She had her third stroke on Saturday night and died in the early morning.

Gallant fighter to end

The Countess put up a gallant fight against ill-health, poverty and the encroaching years. She was gay and full of reminiscences, even during her last days in the hospital, so that the other patients would gather around to listen to her. Her life was a patchwork of excitement, distinction and obscurity. She was married twice, first to Francesco Palamidessi, her music instructor who wasted her fortune and left her destitute with four children at twenty-four, and the second time to Chevalier Antonio Frabasilis, who was a special translator in the New York courts up to the time of his death in April, 1927.

The Countess was born in Paris in 1864 in a palace across from the Emperor's office of state. When Napoleon Bonaparte turned the Republic of the Netherlands into the Kingdom of Holland he put his brother Louis on the throne. Louis was married to Hortense, a daughter of Joséphine, after which [sic] the Countess was named. Before taking the throne he contracted a morganatic marriage with an Italian noble-woman, and the son by this union was Count de Castelvecchio who married Baroness Pasteur d'Etreillis. The youngest of the four children of this union was the Countess. She was, therefore, the grand-daughter of a king, the grand-niece of a king and the grand-niece of two emperors of France.

Disappointed the Emperor

"The Emperor was full of hope that I would be a boy", the Countess related on one occasion. "He waited patiently in his office for five hours, gazing across to the balcony of my mother's home, where a signalling of blue and white flags was to indicate my sex. "Girls are of no importance to Emperors' he exclaimed upon my birth". Her father died when she was 10 years old, leaving a considerable fortune. Her music teacher was hailed as another Mozart, and by the time she was fifteen her mother had planned a match between them. The marriage turned out badly, and when she found herself destitute at twenty-four, she began to teach languages. This took her to England where she met Ellen Terry. She was tall and of superb figure. Her eyes and hair were dark and her voice musical. She spoke English with a slight accent, but when Ellen Terry showed an interest in her career, she strove to subdue her inflexions and find a place for herself on the English stage.

Brought to U.S. by Daly

The Countess appeared as Patience in "Henry VIII" during the long illness of Mrs Pauncefort. She took a number of minor roles, then was brought to this country by Augustine Daly thirty-five years ago. At different times she appeared in W.A. Brady's production of "Trilby" and with James K. Hackett in "Plot and Passion". She played also in "Romeo and Juliet" and "Quo Vadis". She had intended to stay in the United States for six months, but she made this country her home and became a citizen. In 1903 she was married to her second husband, who was a court interpreter in New York for sixteen years. He was a Marquis, son of the Duke of Castel-Saraceno, and for many years served as official translator to the Greek government. He spoke and read fifteen different languages.

The Countess was also a proficient linguist and served as interpreter for various women's congresses where different nationalities were represented. She was active in politics and in the suffrage movement. During the World War she founded and presided over the Club le Salon, and her activities in behalf of the Allied cause, and relief work brought her recognition from the French government in the form of a medal. After the war, she and her husband bought a small farm at Bridgeton, N.J., in a colony settled by the French, but a year and a half ago she found it necessary to advertise rooms for rent, while she continued to occupy one tiny corner of the house, which was known as "Mon Bon Plaisir". The handbill which she sent out on this occasion read "In quaint old farmhouse—every comfort and some luxuries. A widow lady offers to desirable tenants, family or group of people, four, five, six or seven rooms permanently or for summer months. Children not objected to if well behaved".

Blind and partly crippled
In 1923, she suffered a fractured leg in a fall at the farmhouse. She was taken to Bellevue, where the romantic story of her life became public knowledge. Her husband was still alive to look after her. But in recent years she had had several falls and had been in hospitals constantly. Cataracts had virtually made her blind, so that she could not get about without difficulty.

The Countess had many accomplishments. She taught piano, French, Italian, diction and painting. She had a collection of cans, paper bags and boxes containing cross-word puzzles and brain twisters in many languages. The friends who stood by her throughout her later years said that she was charming and full of entertaining anecdotes to the very end.

The only one of her children who ever lived with her was a son, Napoleon. One of her daughters is an instructor in Italian at an English university. A second daughter lives in England and a second son in South America.

(2) *New York Times* December 20, 1932

Josephine de Castelvecchio Frabasilis Granddaughter of Bonaparte King of Holland

---

Debut with Ellen Terry

At her suggestion took stage Name of Elouina Oldcastle – Brought here by Augustin Daly

---

Josephine de Castelvecchio Frabasilis, known here as the Countess de Castelvecchio, niece of Napoleon III and former actress of the American stage, died on Sunday of arthritis at the Metropolitan Hospital, a city institution. She had been ill for more than two years, spending most of the time in various hospitals for treatment. She passed the summer with friends at New Dorp, S.I., and at Thanksgiving time was removed to the French Hospital. She was recently taken to the Metropolitan. Her age was 68.

It was said yesterday that the Countess, who before her illness, had earned her living giving French and music lessons, had recently been dependent on friends for financial assistance.

She was the widow of Anthony Frabasilis, who was for many years a special interpreter in New York courts. According to friends here, her father, the Count de Castelvecchio, was a half-brother of Napoleon III and was treasurer-general of finances under his régime, and her mother, the Baroness Pasteur d'Etreillis, was a member of one of the oldest French families. Her grandfather was Louis Napoleon, King of Holland from 1806 to 1910, and brother of the first Napoleon. The Countess was born in Paris in 1864 in a palace facing the Emperor's office of state. An early marriage was contracted for the girl with Francisco Palamidessi, her music instructor, a musician of great promise, but he squandered her fortune and at 24, with four children in her care, she was destitute. The marriage was later annulled.

She then went to England to teach French and music. Her talent and beauty led Ellen Terry to offer her small parts in Shakespearean plays and for about three years she appeared in English productions with Miss Terry and Sir Henry Irving. She appeared on the stage as Elouina Oldcastle, the first name being selected by Miss Terry from the initials of her children—Elisina, Louis, Lina and Napoleon—and the last name being a translation of the Italian Castelvecchio. She was persuaded to come to the United States from England by Augustin Daly.

Her identity was not generally known until after 1900, after she had been appearing on the American stage for several years. For many years she played leading roles in "Quo Vadis", "Romeo and Juliet", "Macbeth" and "Trilby". She made several tours of the country. For the last thirty years she had been an American citizen.

She was married to Mr. Frabasilis in 1903. After her retirement from the stage she lived with her husband in an apartment in West Eleventh Street, where she resumed her tutoring. During the war she founded and presided over Le Salon, a club of writers, artists and actors which engaged in relief work for the allied cause. The club met every Thursday night for four years and aided many Belgian and French war sufferers.

The funeral will be held at 2 o'clock this afternoon at the Stafford Funeral Church, 307 West Fifty-first Street. Three of her children survive, a son living in South America and two daughters in England.

(3) *New York Herald Tribune* December 21, 1932

French Anthem sung at Service for Countess

'Marseillaise' in March Time asked by Mme Frabasilis, Grand-niece of Napoleon III,

The funeral of Countess Joséphine de Castelvecchio Frabasilis, grandniece of Napoleon III, who died Sunday at the Metropolitan Hospital on Welfare Island, was held yesterday afternoon at the Stafford Funeral Chapel, 307 West Fifty-First Street. Attending the services were many former members of the European nobility now living here, and theatrical people who knew the Countess when as Elouina Oldcastle, she had played with Ellen Terry and other noted actors from decades ago.

Above the bier where the Countess laid in state, surrounded by white roses, lilies and other floral offerings, were draped the Tricolor of her native France and the American flag. In accordance with a request she had made a month before her death, the service was closed with the singing of the 'Marseillaise'.

"Sing 'La Marseillaise' in quick time as I make my last step out" she had said and her wish was fulfilled. Ransom Castegnier Steele, a young baritone from Newark, sang two choruses of the air in March tempo. He was joined by most of the persons crowded into the little funeral chapel.

Following the services, which were conducted by the Rev. George F. Clover, superintendent of St. Luke's hospital, cremation took place at the Fresh Pond crematory in Queens. The ashes will be returned to France for burial in the ancestral plot of her family in a cemetery in Paris.

The pallbearers were Prince A.S. de Matta, Arthur L. Doremus, Vice-President of the Crocker-Wheeler Electric Manufacturing Company, 30 Church Street; Dr. Charles G. Pease, Bernhardt Niemeyer, an actor, and John Brophy and J.E. Levy, friends of the Countess. In contradiction of published reports that the Countess was in impoverished circumstances at the time of her death, Miss Marguerita P. Williams, of the Russell Sage Foundation, a close friend, pointed out that in recent years she had lived in a small home on Long Island and had received money once a month from a daughter Mrs R. D. Richardson, an instructor in Italian at an English University, and another daughter who lives in France. Miss Williams also said that, contrary to reports, the Countess had a son in South America. Another son, Leon Gower, now lives in New York City, while a third son died in South Africa several years ago. Miss Williams explained further that the reason the Countess was taken to the hospital on Welfare Island was that the series of three strokes which caused her death had come so unexpectedly that she had to be taken to the nearest institution. Once there, it was impossible to move her, Miss Williams said.

Among those at the funeral were Count and Countess Giacomo Quintano and their son Leonard Quintano; Countess L.A. de Murabito, Lucien de Vannoz, singer and voice instructor; Mme Carlo Polifème, of the Alliance Française de New York, and G. Aldo Randegger, composer, who played several piano selections.

Also Professor Maurice La Farge, voice and piano instructor; Mme Catherine de Felice, Dr. J. Jehin de Prume, who was associated with the Countess at the National Theatre in Montreal; Mme Ida Haggerty-Snell formerly of the Metropolitan Opera Company; Mme Francis M. von Ardyn and Mr and Mrs Leon Gower.

A delegation attended from the Five Arts Club of New York, with headquarters at the Astor, of which the countess was vice-president. Present were Mrs Kurt Gloeckner, the club President; Mrs Fadwa Kurbon, Mrs Joseph Rohr and Mrs Alice Meyer.

(4) *The New York American*
August 31, 1933

Grand Niece of Napoleon leaves relics

Will of Mme. Frabasilis, Widow of Court Interpreter, filed; Estate valued under $1000

Containing intimate glimpses of the Napoleonic regime in France, the will of Joséphine de Castelvecchio Frabasilis, grand-niece of Napoleon Bonaparte and grand-daughter of Louis Napoleon, King of Holland, was filed for probate yesterday, disposing of an estate of unknown value.

The attorney who filed the will said the estate probably consisted of several plots of real estate in Medford L.I. A petition filed with the will stated the assets are "less that $1000".

Princess gets shawl

The bequests of personal property recall many historic personages. A shawl which Empress Eugénie, wife of Napoleon III draped about the shoulders of the testator's mother in the gardens of St. Cloud is bequeathed to the Princess Marie Clotilde, address not given, and the leather embossed and painted card case carried by Napoleon I at the battle of Jena is willed to 'the little Prince Napoleon' brother of Princess Marie Clotilde.

General Henri Gouraud, military commandant of Paris, is to receive a photograph of 'our beloved departed Prince Imperial'. To Arthur Levy, Bonapartist historian of Paris, is left an oil portrait of the Emperor Napoleon astride a white war charger, a painting ascribed to Meissonier.

One paragraph of the will sets up a series of bequests based upon the hope that her shares of stock in Venezuela Speculations, Inc., would have reached a handsome total, not realised however.

Under the terms of this paragraph the Actor' Fund of America, the Church Alliance, the 'Orphans of France', St. Luke's Hospital, the Society for the Relief of the Aged and various individuals share in the bequests.

Mme de Castelvecchio Frabasilis was the widow of Chevalier Antonio Frabasilis, for years an interpreter in New York courts. She was the daughter of Count Louis de Castelvecchio, the son of Louis Napoleon, King of Holland. Louis Napoleon was the brother of the first Napoleon. He first served as Treasurer-General of Finances in the regime of Napoleon III.

Notes

These articles contain a number of inaccuracies, some probably due to inaccurate reporting but most of them due to Joséphine's stories about herself to her friends. So *caveat lector*! I will confine myself to a few major points:
1. Joséphine was born in 1857, not 1864, and was almost 76 when she died.
2. She was not born in a palace, but in her parent's apartment, 216 rue de Rivoli, which was visible but not "across from the Emperors office of state" in the Tuileries.
3. Louis Bonaparte did not contract a morganatic marriage with the mother of his son François Louis Gaspard Castelvecchio.
4. Joséphine was the third child. The fourth and youngest, Adrien, died probably in the 1860's.
5. Her father died when she was 12—not 10—years old.
6. Her mother did not plan her marriage to Palamidessi. On the contrary, she strongly opposed it.

ELISINA TYLER

During the years of their marriage, Elisina was a great asset and help to her first husband. She had a good head for business, whereas he had poor judgement, in contrast to his exceptional flair as a publisher. While she was charming, brilliant and socially attractive, and successful, Grant Richards had constant problems in his personal relations. He tended to alienate friends and make enemies.

Not long before she left him for Royall Tyler, Elisina helped to found, and was the Editor of a quarterly, *The Englishwoman*, of which we have the first four volumes. Somewhat surprisingly, it strongly supported women's rights. Among the contributors in our volumes we find: Laurence Alma-Tadema, Max Beerbohm, John Galsworthy, Elisina Grant Richards, Laurence Housman, Eric Maclagan, Juan Meragall, John Masefield, G. Bernard Shaw, G.S. Street, Royall Tyler, and Miguel de Unamuno.

Grant Richards went bankrupt for the first time in about 1906, and Elisina played a major part in putting the business back on its feet; but he went bankrupt again in 1909, just at the time Elisina left him. However she continued to try to help him and even managed to obtain some financial support for him from close friends of Royall Tyler, Mildred and Robert Bliss.

In 1910, Royall Tyler applied for, and obtained the position of Editor of the Calendar of State Papers (Spanish) as successor to Martin Hume, from the Public Record Office. Not long after I was born, Elisina and he went off to Spain, where Royall spent some time working in the National Archives at Simancas. Within a short time, Elisina had mastered Spanish sufficiently to transcribe original documents. They then went to Vienna to work at the Archives there before returning to Paris prior to the outbreak of World War I. During the war Elisina worked very closely with Edith Wharton, devoting her administrative and executive ability to the cause of relief for Belgian and French refugees. The founder and President of the Organisation was Edith Wharton, with whom she and Royall had become friends shortly before the war broke out. Edith Wharton asked Elisina to join her as Executive Director. Their work was recognized by the French Government. They were both awarded the Legion d'Honneur; and, in a report read by Raymond Poincaré on November 25, 1920, before the French Academy, were jointly awarded the Gold medal of *Le Prix de Vertu* pour leurs oeuvres de guerre". The text of the award, published by the Institut de France, as of the above date, is as follows:

"Another gold medal, likewise struck with the likeness of Richelieu, is awarded to the American houses of convalescence. France does not forget the magnificent contributions that came from overseas even before the United States abandoned neutrality. All of America then opened to us its money and its heart. From New York to San Francisco, all purses were open to relieve the misery of our refugees, and all souls flew to the battlefields where the soldiers of the Meuse and of Verdun were dying for the freedom of the world. Today when, after a victory won in common, each of the allied nations has returned home and feels tempted to close itself off somewhat, let us remember the spontaneous impulses that brought us together. We rediscover in these memories the purity of our feelings and the force of our enthusiasm. A re-reading of some of the fine pages that a superbly talented American, Mrs. Edith Wharton, wrote on France will remind us that France has never been better understood or better loved. But Mrs. Edith Wharton is not only a writer. She is also a woman of action and of worth. It is she who, with the invaluable assistance of Mrs. Royall Tyler, created the *Accueil franco-américain aux réfugiés belges et français*, the project of assistance to the children of Flanders, the project of assistance to those whom the war afflicted with tuberculosis, and these *Maisons américaines de convalescence* to which we now award one of our gold medals. For all their foundations together Mrs. Wharton and Mrs. Royall Tyler raised more than 9,250,000 francs, which they then employed to the most ingeniously worthy ends. In the dispensary that they opened at 12 rue Boissy d'Anglas, for Belgian and French refugees from the occupied regions, they experienced the pain of witnessing a long and terrible procession of pale women and malnourished children, in whom doctors had discerned all too easily the first signs of the affliction eating away at modern societies. Mrs. Royall Tyler and Mrs. Edith Wharton immediately sought ways to protect these poor fugitives from the progress of tuberculosis, and they had hardly conceived their plan before they put it into practice. Under the two pleasing names of Belle Alliance and Bon Acceuil, they installed in two neighboring parks, at Groslay, a fully-equipped sanatorium; and Mrs. Royall Tyler urged the dispensary administration to send to this establishment all the women and children whose health seemed to require plenty of fresh air. But these unfortunate women, who had had to flee the enemy and abandon their devastated homes, feared a new disruption, which seemed to them a new exile. They refused to leave Paris and declined the care offered them rather than continue their journey into the unknown. To overcome their resistance, Mrs. Royall Tyler had recourse to an innocent subterfuge. She had the poor patients at the dispensary offered a Sunday round-trip, free, from Paris to Groslay and back. This country excursion succeeded brilliantly. The women liked the place and no longer felt tempted to use their tickets back to Paris. Today, these American convalescent houses offer six hundred beds to those suffering from or threatened by tuberculosis. These beds are divided between Groslay,

Taverny in the department of Seine-et-Oise, and Arromanche in the Calvados region. There is also a rest house at Auteuil, a dispensary on the Boulevard de la Gare in Paris, and a re-education house [*maison de rééducation*] at Villejuif. All this is due to pass next July to the department of Seine-et-Oise. Let us hope that by then the last refugees will have been able to return to their ravaged homes and begin rebuilding the ruins. However, since consumption will still be working its ways in the Paris metropolitan area, the beds will still serve, and the patients who occupy them will bless the names of Mrs. Royall Tyler and Mrs. Wharton. Mrs Wharton wrote, "Eloquent expression of feeling not translated into action sinks to the level of mere rhetoric." And she added, "In France today, expression and act are continuous, and each reflects the other." Never has this fertile alliance of talent and will affirmed itself more powerfully than in this American woman who, after writing the fine work entitled *The House of Mirth*, turned her attention to the unfortunate in order to free them from poverty and sickness."

> *Une autre médaille d'or, à la même effigie de Richelieu, est attribuée aux maisons américaines de convalescence. La France n'oublie pas les magnifiques offrandes qui lui sont venues d'outre-mer, avant même que les Etats-Unis fussent sortis de la neutralité.*
>
> *L'Amérique entière nous donnait alors son argent et son cœur. De New-York à San Francisco, toutes les bourses s'ouvraient pour les misères de nos réfugiés et toutes les âmes s'envolaient vers les champs de bataille où les soldats de la Meuse et de Verdun mouraient pour la liberté du monde. Aujourd'hui qu'après la victoire remportée en commun, chacune des nations alliées est rentrée chez elle, avec la tentation de s'enfermer un peu, rappelons-nous les mouvements spontanés, qui nous ont rapprochés. Nous retrouverons dans ces souvenirs la pureté de nos sentiments et la force de nos enthousiasmes.*

Relisons quelques-unes des belles pages qu'une Américaine de grand talent Mrs Edith Wharton, a écrites sur la France, et nous nous dirons que jamais la France n'a été ni mieux comprise ni mieux aimée. Mais Mrs Edith Wharton n'est pas seulement un écrivain, elle est une femme d'action et une femme de bien. C'est elle qui, avec le précieux concours de Mrs Royall Tyler, a créé l'Accueil franco-américain aux réfugiés belges et français, l'œuvre des enfants des Flandres, l'œuvre des tuberculeux de la guerre, et ces Maison américaines de convalescence auxquelles nous avons réservé une de nos médailles d'or. Pour l'ensemble de ces fondations, Mrs Wharton et Mrs Royall Tyler ont recueilli plus de 9,250,000 francs, et elles les ont employés avec la plus ingénieuse bonté. Dans le dispensaire qu'elles avaient ouvert, au numéro 12 de la rue Boissy-d'Anglas, pour les réfugiés des régions envahies, Belges et Françaises, elles avaient eu la douloureuse émotion de voir défiler un long et lamentable cortège de femmes blêmes et d'enfants chétifs, chez beaucoup desquels les médecins avaient trop aisément aperçu les premières menaces du mal qui ronge les sociétés modernes. Mrs Royall Tyler et Mrs Edith Wharton avaient aussitôt cherché les moyens de protéger ces pauvres fugitifs contre les progrès de la tuberculose et, à peine avaient-elles conçu leur dessein, qu'elles le réalisaient.

Sous les deux jolis noms de Belle Alliance et de Bon Accueil, elles installaient dans deux parc voisins, sur le territoire de Groslay, un sanatorium complet et Mrs Royall Tyler recommandait aussitôt à l'administration du dispensaire d'envoyer à cet établissement toutes les femmes et tous les enfants dont la santé paraissait exiger le séjour au grand air. Mais ces malheureuses, qui avaient dû fuir devant l'ennemi et abandonner leur pays dévasté, s'effrayaient d'un nouvel éloignement qui leur semblait un nouvel exil ; elles refusaient de quitter Paris et renonçaient aux soins qu'on leur offrait plutôt que de continuer leur chemin vers l'inconnu. Pour vaincre leur résistance, Mrs Royall Tyler dut recourir à un innocent subterfuge. Aux pauvres clientes du dispensaire, elle fit offrir une promenade dominicale, avec un billet gratuit, aller et retour, de Paris à Groslay et de Groslay à Paris. Cette partie de campagne eut le plus grand succès. Les voyageuses trouvèrent le logis à leur gout et ne furent plus tentées d'utiliser les coupons de retour. Aujourd'hui, l'œuvre des maisons américaines de convalescence comprend six cents lits pour tuberculeux et prétuberculeux. Ces lits sont répartis entre Groslay et Taverny en Seine-et-Oise et Arromanche dans le Calvados. Il y a, entre outre, une maison de repos à Auteuil, un dispensaire boulevard de la Gare à Paris et une maison de rééducation à Villejuif. Le tout doit passer au département de la Seine en juillet prochain. Espérons qu'à cette date, les derniers réfugiés auront pu regagner enfin leur commune détruite et commencer à relever leurs ruines. Mais, comme la phtisie n'aura pas terminé ses ravages dans l'agglomération parisienne, les lits serviront encore, et les malades qui les occuperont béniront les noms de Mrs Royall Tyler et de Mrs Wharton. 'Quand l'éloquente expression d'un sentiment ne se traduit pas en action, a écrit un jour Mrs Wharton, elle tombe au niveau de la rhétorique.' Et elle ajoutait : 'En France, aujourd'hui, l'expression et l'acte se continuent et se reflètent l'une l'autre.' Jamais cette féconde alliance du talent et de la volonté ne s'est affirmée avec plus de force qu'en cette Américaine qui, après avoir composé ce beau livre intitulé Chez les Heureux du Monde, s'est penchée sur les malheureux pour les arracher à la misère et à la maladie.

Shortly after the war ended, Elisina went to Austria to see some old friends she and my father had made during their stays in Vienna in 1911 + 1912. She was so shocked by the appalling conditions of poverty and undernourishment that she decided to raise money to help the population of Vienna. She told me that she could not forget attending a performance of *Der Rosenkavalier* given in her honor by the Austrian government, and seeing the wretchedly clad and weak-looking women and children standing at the entrance of the Opera House watching people go in. She went to the United States where she raised a large sum of money for civilian relief—about $250,000, I believe it was. She was made an Honorary Officer of the Austrian Red Cross.

In 1922 my parents were finally able to buy Antigny, the property in Burgundy which they had coveted since they first saw it during a trip in 1912.

In 1924 my father had been appointed the Deputy Commissioner General of The League of Nations in Hungary. Elisina spent part of each year in Budapest, but most of her time was devoted to repairing Antigny and making it habitable, a task she accomplished entirely on her own.

In June 1940, when the fall of France was imminent, she left Geneva (where my father was an Official of the Economic and Financial section of the League of Nations) by one of the very last trains permitted to enter France, and arrived at Antigny only a few days before the Germans.

There can be no doubt that her presence there, and the measures she took to obtain such official documents as the Embassy in Paris was able to provide certifying that Antigny was U.S. property saved the place from looting and devastation. As citizen of a neutral country, she authorized two or three German Officers and their orderlies to quarter themselves at Antigny. For herself she reserved her "apartment" consisting of what is now our bedroom, a bathroom and a small writing-room. On the outside of the door giving access to these rooms, she hung a framed notice: Ms Royall Tyler, *Privat Wohnung, 1940*. I found it there still when I arrived at Antigny in a VIIth U.S. army jeep, from Chalon-sur-Saône, early on a rainy morning, in September 1944.

Elisina issued detailed written instructions, which she had herself drafted, (we still have the drafts) to the German Officers. Among the other things they were told on which day of the week each might take a bath, and how much wine she would allow each man to drink *per diem* under her roof (one litre—and of course not our wine). The Officers and men behaved very correctly, clicking to attention and saluting her when she left and entered the house. She ate by herself upstairs in her room, served by the faithful Vincenzo and Carla, through whom the Germans were instructed to communicate with her, should they wish to do, by a written note. Also in attendance, one might say, on her, was Henry Clarke Smith, Edith Wharton's chauffeur—and Englishman from the Isle of Jersey, who had first come to France as a young man several years before World War I, had served with the British forces in the war, and had stayed on in France thereafter, as a mechanic and chauffeur, finally, in the service of Edith Wharton. When she died, he told Elisina that he had nothing and no one to go back to in England, and that he would be very happy if he could work for her. So Smith became, as it were, a member of the Antigny household, which he only left with his death in 1978, at the age of 94. He lived in a little house at Antigny-le-Château, and was nicknamed "Churchill" by the local inhabitants. More formally, he was addressed as "Monsieur Henri". While my mother was there he lived upstairs under the roof in a room we still refer to as "Smith's room". At one point, fortunately while my mother was there, a car arrived with a German Officer and an orderly to remove Mr Smith and take him, as an enemy alien, to a concentration camp. My mother describes the scene in her Journal: "and the car left again, without Mr. Smith!" He is now buried, in accordance with his wishes, in that part of the Foissy churchyard which is nearest to the château.

Elisina rented a house at Arnay-le-Duc after the Germans left Antigny permanently for Dijon, and spent the winter of 1940-41; returning to Antigny in the spring in order to pursue her efforts to obtain an *Ausweiss*, or permit, to enable her to cross over into then unoccupied France, and join Royall in Switzerland. She describes her repeated visits to the *Kommandantur* in Dijon. Finally, the permission was granted in July 1941, less than six months before Pearl Harbor and America's entry into the war—which would have meant internment for her, at the age of 66.

She wrote a long account of the year 1940-41 in the form of a letter to me, which we call her Journal, and gave it to me when we saw each other again in 1944. It is at Antigny.[4]

After the war, she continued to administer the *Edith Wharton Foundation* which was created by friends of Edith Wharton after her death, in her memory. With the assistance of a Committee, she developed a program of mobile x-ray equipment for use in the poorer regions of France for the benefit of the underprivileged elements in the population. In 1953, after Royall Tyler's death, Elisina arranged for the equipment to be taken over by the Ministry of Public Health, which awarded her its highest decoration.

---

[4] This typescript diary, bound in two volumes, exists now also in .pdf format.

Linetta at 60

LINETTA RICHARDSON

University Of Birmingham Gazette (1977)

The following has been written by Professor Philip McNair.

The University has lost its first woman Professor and its last living link with the Napoleonic age in Linetta de Castelvecchio Richardson, who occupied the Serena Chair of Italian from 1921 to 1946, and who died on 4 June 1975 in her ninety-fifth year at her home in Corton Parva, near Warminster, Wiltshire.

Linetta de Castelvecchio Palamidessi was born on 13 October 1880 in her parents' country house at Pescia, near Lucca, in Tuscany. Her father was Francesco Palamidessi, a Professor of

Music at Florence. Her mother was the Comtesse Joséphine, third daughter of the Comte François Louis de Castelvecchio, half-brother of Napoleon III (who ennobled him in 1860) and natural son of Louis Bonaparte, ex-King of Holland and brother of Napoleon I, by a lady of Rome. After her father's early death, her family exchanged his surname with the more prestigious distaff title, and she became known as the Contessa Linetta Palamidessi de Castelvecchio.

Linetta was educated at the Regio Conservatorio di Sant'Anna in Pisa, where she was awarded the school's bronze medal (the last ever coined) for general excellence in 1895. The following year she came to England armed with a Diploma equivalent to the *Patente Normale Superiore*, and in April 1897—mstill only 16½—she succeeded her elder sister as Italian mistress at Cheltenham Ladies' College. In July 1903 she moved to London, where she made both a living and a reputation as a public lecturer and private teacher of Italian, and began to be invited far and near to speak in schools, societies and lecture-halls on the literature of her native country—particularly *The Divine Comedy* for English interest in Dante reached its zenith in the reign of Edward VII.

Her active concern with the social problems at this time brought her into touch with Herbert Hensley Henson (1863-1947), then Rector of St Margaret's, Westminster, and later Bishop of Durham—one of the most forceful Anglican prelates of this century. As their acquaintance ripened into friendship, she was led by his influence not only from the Roman to the Anglican Communion but also into the *avant-garde* circle of Modern Churchmen, where she met another Christian scholar who was to exert a long and incalculable spiritual influence on her life: William Ralph Inge (1860 – 1954), who became Dean of St Paul's in 1911.

It was probably through the Gloomy Dean that Linetta began her association with Cambridge. Although never a lecturer at the University, or a member of either women's college, she did in fact teach undergraduates from both colleges in 1912-13, and numbered a future Mistress of Girton and a future Principal of Newnham among her pupils.

In 1915 she was appointed Lecturer and Head of the Italian Department at King's College, London, and took up her appointment in January 1916 with a course of lectures on Dante's *Purgatorio*. While tutoring external, undergraduate and graduate students of London University (and one of her pupils was later the first woman Vice-Chancellor of any University in Britain), she found time to commute to Cambridge in 1916-17, and again in 1918-19 when she added men from Caius to her undergraduates from the women's colleges. She taught in the 'Waiting rooms' over Hawkins the baker, and was (recalls Miss Lois Simpson, O.B.E), 'the most brilliant and stimulating teacher of my experience in Cambridge'.

When Linetta was granted leave of absence from London to study abroad from May 1919 to July 1920 she was at the height of her promise. Henson noted in his journal on 27 September 1919: 'I wrote to L. who has now made up her mind to stay on in Italy for another year, to take a degree at the Roman University, and to publish her essay on *Ossian in Italian Literature*. She is a most courageous person as well as very brilliant, and, if her health does not give way, she will yet astonish the world. Her description of Italian feeling with respect to d'Annunzio's raid on Fiume is illuminating: "The universal feeling here shows that we are in a mood to accept even the military dictatorship of a theatrical maniac rather than submit to Wilson's dictatorship".' (*Retrospect*, vol. I, p. 314) She took the *Diploma di Abilitazione* in Rome before returning to London in the summer of 1920 to live with the Inge family in the Deanery of St Paul's.

It was at this time that four new Chairs of Italian were established in England with generous benefactions from Mr Arthur Serena. In 1918 he endowed one at Cambridge (which curiously does not bear his name) and those at Oxford and Manchester (which do). Now he turned his attention to Birmingham. Italian had been taught at Mason Science College since 1891 by the Professor of French, Clovis Bévenot, and at the University from 1904 by the Lecturer in Spanish, don Fernando de Arteaga y Pereira, who retired in 1921. In that year the Birmingham Chamber of Commerce, acting with the University, provided funds to supplement Serena's endowment, and on 3 March the Serena Chair of Italian at Birmingham was advertised at £600 *per annum*.

Linetta applied, with strong testimonials from twelve referees who included Henson, Inge and G.M.Trevelyan. Her runner-up was Dr Angelo Crespi, Lecturer in Italian at Birkbeck College, London, and at the interview on 10 May they ran neck-and-neck. To decide the issue, the committee gave them both a topic, and half-an-hour to prepare a lecture on it, before they were each in turn summoned to give voice. On 1 June 1921 the Council of the University met and elected Signorina Linetta P. de Castelvecchio to the Serena Chair.

The new Professor—only the second woman to bear the title in Britain—gave her inaugural lecture in the Birmingham Reference Library at 8 p.m. on Tuesday, 4 October 1921, when the University's then Principal, C. Grant Robertson, took the chair. The subject was Dante, since the year was the sexcentenary of his death, and he was her major professional interest. Curiosity about her appointment and the attraction of her theme combined to make the evening a personal triumph: within fifteen minutes of the opening of the doors, 'Standing room only' notices were displayed, and when the speaker arrived she was at first refused admission.

Her reputation as a lecturer crossed the Atlantic, and she was invited by the American Federation of University Women to tour the United States in 1922, when she is said to have given 200 talks in one month. But such strenuous successes were short-lived: in the long run her occupation of the Serena Chair proved a disappointment to her. There came to her ears hurtful slanders that she owed her election to favouritism; friction followed with the Chamber of Commerce about the terms and duties of her post; and there was a long-standing disagreement with the University, who gave her the degree of M.A. in 1922 but insisted that her appointment was part-time, a notion which she resolutely resisted to the end. (In her twenty-fifth and final year in the Chair, when her stipend was at last raised from £650 to £800, she was teaching for a minimum of 13 hours a week.) She began to feel that, without supporting staff of at least one language assistant who would teach Italian from scratch, the title of Professor was an empty one, and that she was denied the opportunities for literary research which she would have enjoyed if she had remained in London.

In 1929 she married—from the Deanery of St Paul's, London—the Rev. Dr Robert Douglas Richardson, Vicar of Four Oaks and Harborne, Canon of Birmingham Cathedral, a distinguished scholar and a Modern Churchman. Two years after her retirement from the Serena Chair in 1946, he was appointed Principal of Ripon Hall, Oxford and they went to live on Boar's Hill. Here Linetta began to hold Dante readings in October 1948 (attended by among others Professor Gilbert Murray, O.M.), and was invited to speak at the Oxford Summer School of the Society for Italian Studies in 1949. Three years later, Canon Richardson retired to the Rectory of Boyton, near Warminster, and Linetta lived the rest of her long and active life in rural Wiltshire.

Professor Richardson won her considerable reputation as an eloquent speaker and infectious teacher: her scholarly publications were comparatively few. They include the reports she wrote on Italy for the Anglican and Foreign Church Society for every year from 1908 to 1915 (except 1910, when the reporter was John Wordsworth, Bishop of Salisbury). Later she sprang to the defence of the controversial Bishop of Birmingham in 'Bishop Barnes on Science and Superstition: A Reply to'.

Dr. Edwyn Bevan' (*Hibbert Journal*, vol. XXXI, No. 3 (April 1933), pp. 358-71. But her projected books on Giordano Bruno and Ossian in Italy remain embryonic notes in her meticulous and scholarly hand.

Birmingham's first woman Professor, who enjoyed a wide circle of friends and was greatly beloved by all who knew her, is survived by her husband, to whom the University extends its sincere sympathy in his loss.

LETTER FROM JOSEPHINE TO LINETTA RICHARDSON

Breathless tone and unpredictable punctuation sometimes make this typed letter (in French) hard to follow. I have not consistently capitalized the words capitalized by Joséphine. These include, among others, personal pronouns and adjectives like "You," "Your," "He," "His," etc. The letter sheds further light, whether reliable or not, on several matters touched on by my father. I have omitted the original.

105 West 11th Street
New York, January 14
1 9 2 5

My adored Daughter,

I sent You this morning a so-called "letter2," which I had to write in haste because I had made a mistake and thought I had plenty of time to write to Louis, then I noticed at the last minute that I only had time to answer his good letter, which I enclose for you here, so that you should read it and send it back to me immediately, If You Please!

The letter is so interesting that I know you will be glad to read it, and, as you see, *I* don't hide any little secrets! I am sending You Your Brother's letter, after giving You His address, and if I am not sending you the photos that He gave me, that is only for fear of losing them in the post and because, as You see, He says that He will have others made, and because, now that You are back in touch, He will certainly send them to You, too.

At present, You undoubtedly know that the five dollars You kindly sent me for Christmas, my Darling, reached me safe and sound, and did not molder in my coffers! I of course wrote to You immediately to thank You, and I assure You that they came at the right moment, because—this is already some time ago—I mean, several days—I had invited Miss Williams to come and "dine" with us, and I found myself in a considerable spot of trouble, because the Professor had absolutely nothing to give me, and two of the little girls I teach (I currently have three), being ill, had not come for their lesson, and I was consequently "done." But even with that little contribution, I didn't have enough for dinner. Anyway, as "Billy" says, "All's well that ends well," and the Manna that You sent me, my Darling, saved the day!

I have already told You, my dearest Darling, that the ever-so-nice Miss Oliver came immediately, but that, thanks to Christian Science, to which I turned toward the end of the last hour, even though doing so went against the Professor's wishes as well as Your own, as You know, she found me, if not wholly recovered, then at least so much better that she must have believed I had been exaggerating; but I swear to You, my Darling, that I had been doing nothing of the kind. When Miss Clemsen came to see me, more than ten days before I decided to turn to Christian Science, she and Miss Jackson, the friend she had with her, left me in tears because "I smelled of death," and there was certainly no doubt about it! I had no illusions, because I felt that it was only too true; otherwise, I would never have thought of asking You to have me cremated. You will understand that one does not make such a request in jest!

I am DELIGHTED, my sweet Love, that my idea regarding Grandfather's [François Louis, Pitzy's grandfather] seal pleases you. I racked my brains for something I could send You that You did not already have, something useful without being too down-to-earth... Then the great light dawned! I still had Grandfather's other seal, the one without our coat of arms, but with just His monogram and a Count's crown on the other side; so I sent that one to Louis, for Christmas, and had the one with our coat of arms on it copied for You. You can get Grandfather's monogram easily enough, whenever You like, because it is the one on my silver and on the crystal that Elise and Grant "bought" (despite my never having received a penny of the price, and even though Miss Genevieve Ward put in 50 pounds sterling, in a kind effort to save it for me). It consists of two crossed "L"s, with a "C" in the middle, *over* the "L"s; and as for the little crown, everyone knows that it is the crown of a Countess! I do hope that Louis will use this seal, so that You can see it soon.

As for Francesco, it seems to me that You must have put Your finger on the problem, my blessed Love; it seems quite impossible to me that the situation should be otherwise, but what can we do? Besides, there is such an uproar going on in Italy at present that one cannot possibly foresee, so it seems to me, just how long this régime will last. This "Peppino" Garibaldi…(can one allow oneself to parody such a name?) is committing all sorts of outrages, …and he is not the only one! but the last part of his name gives him more weight than all the others together. Che Dio ce la mandi buona! I fear for the Italian Royal family an end like the poor Czar's, if Mussolini continues with his "prepotenze." *How* I would love to have Francesco and his whole family here!

But now, my Darling, You ask me some rather difficult questions. Should You track down Grandfather's birth certificate, I would be very, very grateful if you were to let me see it. Grandmother [Elise] always said that he had been born in Rome. Grandmother felt certain that Grandfather's Mother was one Princess Borghese; then, in her last years, she sometimes spoke of "Colonna." This lady came to see her Son when Grandfather, still very small, was living in his Father's Ristori Palace on the Lung'Arno, in Florence. Immediately after her visit Grandfather, not yet five years old, was sent to the Collège Cigogni, at Prato. From there, the Comte de Saint Leu sent him on to the Silligs, at Vevey. Then He recalled Grandfather to Him, in Florence, not long before His death, if I am not mistaken. Or was Grandfather called back *after* the death of *my* Grandfather? There is a gap in my memory here, because

Grandmother herself was unsure. It is then that Grandfather first met Grandmother, who was in Florence because *my* Grandmother had left the Baron d'Etreillis, her husband, in order to follow Mr. de Bruges Dumesnil Decamps (they had decamped, you see—sorry!). This the same Mr. de Bruges Dumesnil Decamps who made that generous donation to the Musée de Cluny. She had left her son, Baron Sainte Aure d'Etreillis, then still a child, with his father, and had taken off to Italy, which in those days was the end of the world. Soon after that my Aunt Suzette was born. Mr. Decamps was very rich, and they passed for husband and wife, frequenting the best society, etc. Grandmother (Maman-Bonne, because she did not want us to call her either Bonne Maman or Grand'Mère) had completely forsaken her son, without even pretending to look after him in any way. I know nothing about the family of Maman-Bonne, but I know that she had lived on a farm, where she made jam, not far from Paris, and that it was there that Baron d'Etreillis discovered her. Maman-Bonne was of course not noble, but she was *very* pretty, nicely put together, with a charming foot, pretty hands, and a perfect waist. She was still a coquette and capricious during my childhood; she preferred one or the other of us, turn by turn, and "the current favorite could do whatever she wanted (with Maman-Bonne)," as long as her reign lasted; but beware of thunder when it ended!! She was vivacious, a coquette, took excellent care of herself, and hated losing at any game. She had worn out the whole family's patience and had lost 260 pairs of gloves with my governess (I still remember that enormous number very clearly) when, as a last resort, and despite my being only six years old, I was set to playing bezique with her. A lost cause! I won every time, which only made her more impossible than ever! I remember that there were 6000 "points" in the game, and a *heap* of cards…and that is all I remember. Grandfather had first, of course, to live at Nice, where the Emperor sent him immediately after the annexation, saying, "You know, Castelvecchio, you must inspire the people to love France and 'our' family!" My Father undertook to do so, and he did indeed inspire devotion wherever he went, thus influencing the people to favor France and the Bonaparte family. However, he always preferred to live incognito. Unfortunately, Grandmother did not behave as she should have done. She claimed that the climate in Nice did not suit her, or me, either, and went to spent her winters with me in Paris, leaving my own Grandmother to manage the house. Her real reason, however, was *not* our health, but rather a certain Mr. Bosino, half Austrian and half Greek, who died some time (about two years) after Grandfather, leaving us 10,000 francs each. I never knew what he had left my mother. We traveled in Germany every summer, always with this Mr. Bosino. One summer, when we were at Baden-Baden, Louison became extremely ill (I forget what the matter was), and Grandfather came to see her, and brought her a beautiful music box (the forerunner of the modern Victrola). Grandfather *never* came without announcing his arrival by telegram. Once, at Nice, there were quarrels that were not even hidden from us, and the next morning Grandfather took us to the flower market and bought a big, beautiful bouquet, and then we hurried home (he had taken us without asking Grandmother's permission), felt around for a while in the buffet drawer, where the visiting cards were kept, and sent us—Aunt Louison and me—with his bouquet to Grandmother, after having inserted into it one of the cards that he had found in the drawer. I thought it was very funny at the time, but I now see in it a heartbreaking tragedy.

Grandfather was transferred to Rennes, in Brittany, We did not go there until he had moved in completely. Mr. Bosino came with us. But there, too, "the climate" did not suit Grandmother's health. Nice was too dry; Rennes was too damp. Father rented a nice apartment in Paris, 50 Boulevard Malesherbes (right behind the Saint Augustin church), and it is from this time that I have the clearest memories. In 1869, May 29th, we were at Ems (again and always with Mr. Bosino) when we received a telegram in the hotel drawing room, where we did our lessons with our governess. Delighted, we took it to Grandmother, her Mother, Aunt Linette...and Mr. Bosino, out in the garden. We assumed that the telegram announced Grandfather's arrival....It announced his death *"by accident"*...suffocated in his bath. It was a new bath, with hot water heated by a fire-box attached to the bath itself. Apparently the butler [*intendant*], having run out of the special coal required for this new invention, had filled the fire-box with ordinary coal, and the gases suffocated Grandfather. Whatever actually happened, when the doctor was summoned, it was too late! The doctor said there was only one slender hope of saving him: an infusion of warm, living blood. Instantly, the arms of *every* member of the household staff were bared, and all vied to give their blood in order to save Grandfather's precious life. The Doctor chose a certain Mr. Longjarret, the Chargé de pouvoir [not sure what this means]; but the procedure was in vain. Grandfather was dead. We returned to Paris. The shock of Grandfather's death stopped Aunt Linette's [Marceline's] periods. In spite of every effort, even a trip from Paris to Nice in a special train, with a doctor in attendance in the train itself, nothing helped, and my poor sister died after a year, a month, and a day of indescribable suffering, in Paris, on June 30, 1870. Then came the war, then the Commune. Uncle d'Etreillis behaved with his natural heroism, but he always had a distinct aversion for "Mon ami Bosino," as I called him. We left Paris and took refuge in Switzerland. The Silligs lent Grandmother enough to provide for the family, since it was now impossible to obtain funds from France. That was when I learned to knit. I made a pair of socks each day for our soldiers passing in rags through Switzerland. Poor Aunt Louison never managed to rise that high in her mastery of the art of knitting....she knitted scarves! Bosino was still and always with us. In the end, he had to go to Germany, I don't know why, and there he became so ill that Grandmother left us and went to see him in Munich. He died while she was with him, looking after him. She took this chance to go and see the Emperor, who was in prison, but he refused to see her. After that we were in "disgrace" at Court.

At Lucerne, where we went two years later, we came to know Mr. Baese, to whom Grandmother desperately wanted to marry Louison, despite the fact that she had no wish to accept him. We went to Berlin, if you please! and the marriage was performed there. We went back to Paris, to pack up all our things, and we went to Italy, supposedly in order to visit Aunt Suzette. Marquis Garzoni came to meet us at the station. Maman-Bonne had stayed in Paris, and my governess was on a month's holiday. The succession of shocks that I had received since my father's death culminated in a brain fever that resulted in 17 days of delirium, days that my overheated imagination very sensibly spent learning Italian; and when I returned to myself it took more than ten minutes for my Mother to notice how my way of expressing myself had changed. I could make no sense of it either, and I have never been able to understand what happened. Grandmother took an apartment in the house of the Engineer Poggi, 5 Via Guelfa, and had all our furniture come there from Paris. Marquis Garzoni had a key to this apartment and came there whenever he felt like it, day or night. Then, I wanted to go on studying the piano, but I already knew more than anyone else in Florence. That was when the lawyer [Avvocato] Lorini conceived the evil idea of introducing a young genius to my mother, as the only person able to teach me anything further about the piano. He brought Professor Palamidessi to our home. The key quickly moved to another pocket: from that of Marquis Garzoni to this newcomer's…and you know the rest! My governess left as soon as I was engaged; Aunt Louison and Aunt Suzette refused to see me; my Grandmother and my uncle d'Etreillis no longer wrote to me; and, without having the slightest idea why all this was happening, I found myself completely isolated, until I formed other friendships, such as with Tata Sofia, Del Rosso, and so on, who all favored Palamidessi, or at least dared not betray their thoughts on the subject. But, to go back a little, I must tell you, my Darling, that Aunt Louison is right to tell you that she was born at 16 Via de' Benci. Mr. Decamps had bought the palace, and his daughter, Aunt Suzette, had inherited it, or so I imagine; either that, or they [*elles*] had reached an arrangement with Maman-Bonne after Mr. Decamps died. The fact is that Aunt Suzette had married Uncle Adrien de Larderel, whose death left her still young and exceedingly beautiful. She had had only two children, Elise de Larderel [punctuation confusing hereafter], (for she married her first cousin, the son of Frédéric de Larderel, (Florestan) brother of Adrien, and Adrienne Franzoni. She met Marquis Cesare Mastiani Sciamanna, and....Bang! She had Louise Monti, a very ill-brought-up girl who caused all sorts of trouble even before her marriage with Mr. Monti, and who continued to get drunk, and get her children drunk, "for laughs." Louisina wore velvet gowns with a train on the Lung'Arno, at Pisa, without even picking them up, got herself courted by the students and the Officers and anyone else who felt like it, and it was such a scandal that when they found someone willing to marry her they didn't look too carefully into who the Monti were.

Aunt Linette [Marceline] was born long before Aunt Louison in this same palace, and so too my little brother Adrien, who died in infancy a good while before I was born. As for myself, I was born, as you know, at 216 Rue de Rivoli, Paris, across from the Emperor's office, so that, when I was expected, the Emperor had given Grandfather a little flag, or rather two little flags, one sky blue and the other white, asking him to put the blue one in the drawing room window if I was a boy, and the white one if I was a girl! He wanted to know even before anyone had had time to inform him of the great event!

When we returned from Paris, after my marriage, we went on living at 5 Via Guelfa, and it is there that Elisina was born. Your Father led me immediately to become better acquainted, at Pescia, with your uncle Charles and your Palamidessi Grandmother, better than I had been able to become earlier on the occasion of two or three visits. He left me with the Palamidessis as soon as I arrived in Pescia and did not take me home again until after midnight, when he found me asleep on the drawing room table. Grandmother, who had taken a different route from Pistoia and returned to 5 Via de' Benci, while my husband and I set out toward Pescia, joined us the following day. We were then at the hotel (so to speak) "Tedesco," at Pescia. During that summer Palamidessi and Grandmother (because I myself never counted, not in the least) rented the Villa Norfini, and bought Le Cave, which belonged at the time to the Allegretti family. No, my Darling, neither Le Cave nor anything else ever belonged to the Palamidessi family, which was in extreme poverty, having nothing but a tiny, village chemist's shop to support the whole family. However, I have to say that Julie Galeffi Palamidessi, Your Father's mother, had been decent enough, as had been her eldest son Charles, to tell Grandmother several episodes of Your Father's life, and to tell her also that one could expect nothing very good from such a marriage. The brother of my mother-in-law, a "Pretore," was then appointed Judge at Barga, thanks to the efforts made by his wife, who was far more energetic than he and thoroughly fed up with the endless poverty in which they had always lived.

You ask me also for our addresses in Paris, Nice, and Rennes, my Darling. As for Paris, I have already given them to you: 216 Rue de Rivoli, then a good many hotels during the winters that I spent with Grandmother. Among them, I particularly remember the Hotel Windsor, Rue de Rivoli. There we had a pretty apartment on the first landing, and my maid was named Julie. It is there that I cut the hair of my favorite doll, to make it grow longer. You can see how grown-up I must have been! Another time, we lived at 14 Rue St. Florentin, then 50 Boulevard Malesherbes. In Nice, Grandfather's office was located to the right of a big staircase, and to the left, on the same floor, was the door of our fine apartment, in a big palace—a marble palace, if I am not mistaken, and in any case built of beautiful stone, 15 Place St. Dominique. In Rennes, I don't remember the address but it was the General Taxation Office [la Recette Générale], right next to the Prefectural Administration [la Préfecture]. At the Prefectural Administration there were three children, Armand, Marthe, and "Rikiki" (Henri) Lefebvre. I had, or rather we had, our own gardens, Aunt Louison and I, under a beautiful magnolia tree. The coachman gave us oats to mark the line that separated "our gardens," and we planted so much that the oats crowded themselves out even before they grew! Spitz was our dog, which Grandfather had bought in order to save him from a cruel carter, and who saved the Taxation Office twice, in Nice, by barking his head off when thieves tried to get in.

I'm afraid that there's nothing much to be proud of in everything that I've told you about our family, my sweet Darling; but, for Grandmother, one must put it down to the period and the morality [*moeurs*, twice misspelled] then prevailing—or missing; to the way she was Brought Up, in a simulacrum of a family, kept in the greatest luxury by a simulacrum of a father, who was very good to her and adored her and spoiled her in every way. Then, her engagement and her marriage to Your angel of a Grandfather, who went on treating her in a way no human deserves to be treated [meaning that he treated her well, surely—a strange way to put it]; then her [what?] deep studies, which prevented her from participating as she should have done in her family, her children, her house [what on earth is Joséphine talking about?]; the idleness almost forced on her by her habits, the human passions given free reign, the almost irresistible charm that everyone felt in her presence, and which very often redoubled the difficulty of resistance, and, finally, the unlimited luxury by which she had always been surrounded. I don't defend her, because there are some things that are impossible to defend but that can be explained in certain circumstances by human weakness. However, I have felt that I was doing the right thing by not hiding too much from you. There are other things, of which I spoke to you frankly long ago, but I could not tell you all that much as long as you were a baby. However, thanks be to God, I have NEVER claimed the right to judge my Mother, even when her behavior concerned me all too closely; and I maintained her in comfort, if not luxury, until her last breath, at the cost of any sacrifice, even while poor Aunt Louison kept telling me that I was mad not to put her in a charity home for old people! I do not envy Aunt Louison that.

You can't imagine how happy I would be, my sweet, lovely Darling, if I could give Aunt Louison a "cure" of Christian Science! Will you not speak to her on the subject? That is the only thing, you know, that could ever heal her; but her character is so distant that I am very much afraid... Well, it would be worth trying, wouldn't it? It's like for your own dear little *crocs!* [what does this word mean?] But I don't want to be preachy. Do as You wish, of course, but as far as I am concerned, I know very well what cured me!

I am sending you Louis's letter, my adored Sweetie; please do not lose it, and send it back as soon as you have read it! But my letter is almost as long as the one the lady once wrote to a gentleman who complained that her letters were too short. She took one of those paper bands that you put under ribbons and replied on it in enormously stretched-out writing. He could no longer complain that her letters were too short!

Good-by, my sweet, beautiful, dear Child. If there is anything else that you want to know, ask me, and it will be my pleasure to satisfy you as well as I can.

How I would love to be rich and to be able to buy 16 Via de' Benci and give it to Aunt Louison… But that will be for a little later. If Louis could provide us with enough to live on for a year or a year and a half, so that the Professor did not have to work at the Court, he could finish his great work on numbers, and soon we would all be millionaires… but there seems to be little chance of that. At any rate, as long as they are well, Louis and the Professor, I care about nothing else—or close to it, although if the Professor were to fall ill again without finishing his great work…. May God keep us all, that is my prayer!

Please excuse the errors that must so abound in this letter, because I was interrupted so often that I no longer know whether you will be able to get any simple sense out of it. For one as learned as my Daughter, though, surely nothing like that could be too difficult!

You did not tell me whether you know if Miss de Bassompierre is still Prince Napoleon's secretary? Do you know the London address of Queen Olga of Greece? Tell me, my Darling, what became of Miss Ames? And all her brothers? I saw in the newspapers that the King of England honored Miss Ellen Terry with a medal. Very good! Excellent! Bravo!

The Professor sends you a kiss, and it is with joy that I undertake to transmit it. Ah, if only I could do it "by mouth"! As for myself, my sweet, beautiful Daughter, I send You everything that is best in me and clasp You against my heart with my whole love!

> Your Dear Little Mummy [Ta Mémère Mérette]
> who is very well indeed!

P.S. My letter being "too short," I have reopened it in order to urge you not to forget to send the Professor a nice little word for his saint's day, the 28th of this month. You will surely have time to do that after receiving this volume…as long as you do not wait to have actually finished reading it all!

LETTER FROM MARGUERITA P. WILLIAMS TO LINETTA RICHARDSON

> This letter conveys, better than the ones my father knew, the way Joséphine's New York friends saw her during her last years. Miss Williams makes it clear that many people (including herself) were sincerely devoted to Joséphine, but she also acknowledges frankly that Joséphine could be very trying.

130 East 22nd Street, New York
May 27, 1932

Dear Mrs. Richardson,

I have your letter and am glad to answer promptly, both to reply to questions which you raise and to give you the latest news of your Mother. I had been intending to write about this time, to tell you about the operation. When Dr. Crigler, the eye surgeon, examined your Mother's eyes the day she went to the hospital for the operation (May 18th), he decided that there would be more assurance of success if, instead of the single operation which your Mother wished, for rather obvious reasons, he performed a preliminary and a secondary operation. This he did, without telling her until afterward. Her eye has healed remarkably, he considers, and the final operation is set for about June 8th. Of course your Mother is dreading it, as they cannot give ether for this operation, and the local anesthetic does not overcome all the pain and the mental distress. They are operating on one eye only, as the other cataract is not "ripe" yet. They seem to ripen very slowly in her case. With the readiness with which all wounds heal in your Mother's case, it would seem as though we might hope for a successful outcome, if that is one of the main factors (on which point I am not informed). As soon after the final operation as the result can be determined, it was your

Mother's thought to have me send a cablegram to you. I note you wish this sent to the University.

Your letter for your Mother came yesterday and I took it to her last evening, with other mail. As she is not using her eyes for reading or writing at present, she asked me to read her letters, including yours. When I reached the second part of your note she grew greatly excited. I had to repeat the word "manoeuvering" several times before she seemed to comprehend it. When I finished, she said very forcefully that "that ended everything." I asked what it was that made you feel so strongly, as I "knew that you had always been so devoted a daughter." She asked "*how* I knew that," and said, "We will not discuss the matter. You always think that I am the one to blame." She was evidently so wrought up that I at once turned the conversation to other matters I knew she wished to have attended to—some letter-writing, etc. No further reference was made to you or your letter, though I was there for some time afterward. If there were any opportunity for me to learn how she has found out the school which your nephew attends I would take advantage of it, but she has mentioned these matters very little to me. Possibly she may think we keep more or less in touch by correspondence—anyway, she knows that when she has of late months referred to the present unhappy situation between you, she has found that I have been more ready than she liked to emphasize the fact that you have been a loving daughter, from all she had told me in the past and I had myself gathered, and that you must have some reason for your present feeling!

Your Mother and Mrs. Rothwell had a falling out months ago, which greatly hurt Mrs. Rothwell, as she had been a good friend. I very seldom see her, but when I next do and there seems any opportunity, perhaps I can learn if there was any information your Mother learned from her regarding her grandson. Do you suppose his Mother could have dropped any information in writing to your Mother? I know that sometime in the winter she had a letter from her, or earlier, rather, as she referred to it while at St. Luke's Hospital.

Your mother does not like the boy being called "Billy." She has a horror of the name William, I have just learned in another connection, because she at once joins it up with Kaiser Wilhelm! Hardy Bradshaw, now living at "Mon bon plaisir," has a little child named Edward William, whom they were calling by his second name, but your Mother so disapproved of this on the above ground, that they now call him Eddie!

Through my recent office of reading her letters to your Mother, when addressed in my care, I learned that she had written to Dean Inge's secretary asking how names could be legally changed in England. To her surprise, Dean Inge himself replied, in a brief note, giving the desired information—that the Christian name given in the Registry of Births and Deaths, rather than the baptismal name, was the legally recognized one, and to change it public notice only was required, or for a minor, action by parent or guardians. Your Mother evidently had Gerard in mind, as she remarked his name after I read the note, and didn't see why he had been so named, instead of Louis, I think.

If you feel at any time that the Inges have been mystified by your Mother's letters, might it not be possible to let them know that you have had word from close friends of your Mother here that owing to age and physical infirmities and natural temperament, with strong imagination and a leaning to the dramatic, she impresses them as being often quite irrational in her viewpoints and in her attitudes toward those who are really friends, and concerned for her welfare. The least little thing that displeases her will cause her to break with good friends, and then she has nothing but the most unkind and unjust criticisms to make of them. When she left the Fifth Avenue Hospital, it was due to an obsession that all they were expecting and planning for—the doctors and nurses—was her death, and the privilege of dissecting her body. She has some painful little growths that can be felt in the abdomen, and they took many X-ray pictures to try to determine the nature of them, but the pictures would not come out well enough, because of excess fat. So they gave her medicine to reduce this. Her explanation of this was that they wanted "a nice lean corpse to dissect." She also complained to us all of the neglect of the nurses, and that once she rang the bell (or rather, pressed a button which lit a summoning light outside her door) 263 times. This she told to all her visitors, and they all said it indicated that her mind was not working right, for how could she ever count to that figure! She became so afraid of remaining at this hospital (one of the newest and finest in the city, and Dr. Bancroft who arranged for her entrance there a real friend of hers) that she became so weak she expected to die momentarily, and scrawled a will, leaving the Dividing Creek home to Hardy Bradshaw, and telling poor Leon of this act when he called. Two or three days later she hurriedly arranged with friends and the Mrs. Richter in Staten Island to whose home she went years ago from Bellevue Hospital, that she go there until she got strong enough for the eye operation. The hospital doctors thought she was not strong enough for the trip, but she took the responsibility upon herself. After a few days at Mrs. Richter's she was wonderfully improved. Then a week later she had a falling out with poor Mrs. Richter, and left the next day, coming back to a rooming house where she had been before going to the Fifth Avenue Hospital. The close friends of your Mother whom I know, all feel that in some ways she is not quite responsible. One, Mrs. Martin, says she is living back in the early part of the nineteenth century, and expects everyone to bend to her wishes as a matter of course.

 Now I have written what you asked to know regarding the Fifth Avenue Hospital matter. You also refer to her plan to write her memoirs. As far as I know, she has written nothing as yet, but is waiting until she has her eyesight again, if the operation results successfully. But during the winter she was gathering old portraits, of herself and relatives when she was a child and young girl, some of these having come into my care from a nephew (I think) in Italy. When her benefit concert was held, she gave reminiscences of her early life, beginning with baby recollections, and continuing down to her stage career. They included nothing that seemed unkindly meant toward anyone, and we all thought them interesting. Mrs. Martin's daughter, Joan Grayson, is the person to whom your Mother looks, thus far, to make contact for her with a publisher, when the time comes. If the book is really ever written, and it contains derogatory references to family, I think it would not be difficult to persuade her advisers to insist that such matter be omitted, lest it lead to legal trouble. Even if she thought no one would take legal action, they might persuade her that they would themselves not take any chances of this, and so lead her to exclude such references. I would not let this matter worry me, if I were you, from such light as I have upon it. If this writing is ever done, and I can be helpful later, I am willing to do whatever I can to prevent anything unpleasant. I can't see what object she thinks would be gained by making hurtful references to her own flesh and blood.

It is too bad to have to write at such length in this way, but it is evident from your letter that the fragments of facts which you have are only cause of much pain and worriment, and your mind will be more at ease knowing the situation in more detail. So I hope this letter will bring a little comfort. One thing is certain, that your Mother is in the hands of an eye surgeon of high reputation, and he is doing this as a friend (and wholly without charge), and as he said to Mr. Doremus, "as he would wish it done if he were the patient." And her friends keep in close touch with her, doing many little things that add to her comfort. At this time of year, many are leaving town, to her great distress of mind, but some of us will remain for some time yet. I do not go away until August, by which time I hope she will be in quite a different state.

Do not worry about what people here may think. Those who really know your Mother understand her idiosyncracies, and don't judge others by what she says of them, when she is peeved at them.

With sympathetic greetings, and greetings also to your Husband, I remain,
      Faithfully yours,
      Marguerita P. Williams

LOUIS DE CASTLE AND HIS VOYAGE TO CALCUTTA

More material on Louis has come to light since WRT discussed him, but most of it will have to await another hand and another day. Briefly, on June 10, 1890, at thirteen, Louis sailed for Calcutta as a deck hand on the *Falls of Clyde*. Why he went to sea so young remains unknown. In the first half of 1893 he sent his grandmother, in French, two letters (translated below) that describe his outward and homeward voyages.

He ended up in the state of Washington, where he identified himself on the 1900 U.S. Federal Census form as a "mechanical engineer" and reported that he had immigrated to the States in 1894. On May 20, 1901, in the mining town of Republic, he married Catherine Mary Downey. The marriage certificate names him as Lewis [sic] Percy de Castle (he clearly made up Percy to account for the P in his name); his father as Frank de Castle (Frank was his father-in-law's first name); and his mother's as Josie Gower. He gave his occupation as "miner."

On April 15, 1902, Catherine gave birth to Lewis H. de Castle. There is no further record of her. Lewis H. was brought up first by his grandmother in Umatilla, Oregon, then by an aunt and uncle, Julie and Charles Larsen, in Spokane. He married in 1935 and died in 1970, in Sonoma, California.

Soon after Louis's first marriage (they may not have known about it), Elisina and Grant Richards brought him back to England and then for some reason sent him to South Africa. He continued there in mining and in 1917 married Frances Wahl.

Louis was the manager of the Roodeport United Main Reef gold mine when, on March 27, 1918, the Rand Mutual Assurance Company wrote from Johannesburg to announce that the company had awarded his mine a prize. The letter praises the "very excellent result shown by your Mine" and notes that "the improved accident rate on your Mine is largely due to your own individual efforts." However, the measures that Louis took to achieve this success apparently alienated his colleagues and the mine workers. He soon resigned, never again held a stable position, and died penniless (apart from his wife's salary as a nurse), slowly overwhelmed by rheumatoid arthritis.

Louis (front, center) among a group of mine workers in South Africa

The *Falls of Clyde*, now a U.S. Historical Landmark, awaits restoration in Honolulu Harbor. Built in 1878, she is the only four-masted, full-rigged, iron-hulled sailing cargo ship left. Photographs of her in her present state are available on the Internet, and Wikipedia has an article on her.

Photo: Stan Shebs

3/2/93.

Ma chère Grand'mère

Je crois que dans ma dernière lettre je t'ai promis de te raconter mes deux voyages de mer, et j'espère que tu me pardonneras pour t'avoir fait attendre si longtemps.

Puisque tu veux le récit de mes deux voyages il faudra que je commence par le jour où j'ai mis pour la première fois le pied sur un navire à voiles; ce jour mémorable pour moi fut le 10 Juin 1890. Comme tu le sais, j'avais à ce temps la seize ans et comme je n'avais jamais encore vu un navire qui fût vraiment grand jusqu'à ce jour, je fut vraiment fort étonné en voyant le "Falls-of-Clyde" qui était un navire à quatre mâts et de 1746 tonnes registrées c'est-à-dire qu'il pouvait porter à peu près 3000 tonnes de cargaison. Premièrement il m'a

First letter

                    10 Wellington Square
                    King's Road
                    Chelsea
                    S.W.

                    3/2/93 (3 Feb or 2 March 1893?)

My dear Grandmother,

I believe that in my last letter I promised you an account of my two sea voyages, and I hope that you will forgive my having made you wait for it so long.

Since you want an account of my two voyages, I shall have to begin with the day when I set foot on a sailing ship for the very first time. That day, so memorable for me, was 10 June 1890. As you know, I was then thirteen years old, and until then I had never even seen a genuinely large ship, so the sight of the *Falls of Clyde* astonished me: a four-master of 1746 tons, that is to say, capable of carrying about 3000 tons of cargo. My first impression was simply of a mass of ropes, masts, and spars in a state of utter disorder. However, it took me less than three weeks on board to discover my error, for not only did each of those ropes have its proper function, but hardly two of them ever even touched!

The *Falls of Clyde* had luck with her when she sailed from Liverpool, because we had two days of splendid weather. We had no bad weather until we were off Holyhead in Wales, but that third day the weather was bad indeed, and the horrible rolling immediately made me seasick. Toward evening we lost sight of land. The captain sent two of my companions to tell me to come out, even though I was still sick. I had no sooner set foot on deck than I felt sick again, and I ran as fast as I could to the side of the ship. Knowing nothing yet of the rules of seafaring, and not having had time even to think, I had unfortunately rushed to windward, so that everything blew straight back on me as soon as it came out! Ugh! It was awful! As soon as it was over, the first mate came to me and told me to try to walk. Easily said, but not easily done, because the ship's movements were so irregular, and my legs were still so weak, that at every step I took—or, rather, tried to take—I staggered like a drunkard!

However, my seasickness and inability to walk lasted only a few days. Then at last I began to work like the others.

At first the work struck me as pretty hard, because, of course, at home I had never performed any manual labor, but I soon became accustomed to it, as I did to all the other difficulties. The officers give me two weeks to learn to climb to the top of the main mast (about 150 feet high), and in a week I managed very well to reach 120 feet, because rope ladders went up that far. For the last thirty feet, though, you had to go up a rope. Every day I enthusiastically climbed my 120 feet, then stopped dead, gazing up at the top of the mast! Remember, dear Grandmother, that the further you go up a mast, the more you feel the continual pitching and rolling of a ship at, sea and it was this continual rocking that made me a little nervous. When my fifteen days were up, and the First Officer ordered me to climb, I reached my usual station but dared not climb higher. At last the officer saw that shouting at me to go higher would achieve nothing. He summoned one of the sailors and sent him to help me go further, providing him, to encourage my efforts, with a length of rope about two feet long, with a knot at the end. I knew all too well what that bit of rope was for, and I told myself that I would rather break my neck than have that sailor beat me! When the sailor got up there, grinning with pleasure at the thought of all the fun he was about to have with that bit of knotted rope, he was amazed to see me already at the very top. As for me, I was delighted to see him disappointed, although at that height I was trembling all over. I could see the whole ship from there, and leagues and leagues of sea in all directions! Once I had climbed up there once, I had no trouble doing so again, although at first I was always somewhat nervous.

When we were first out of Liverpool we discovered two stowaways. In other words, two boys too poor to pay for their apprenticeship had hidden themselves on board and revealed their presence only when the steamer [tugboat?] had left us. Liverpool is the port from which stowaways are most likely to come, because the people of the city are generally poor and low-class, and the boys there, unable to find work on land, are forced to go aboard ships in the way I have just explained. Before a ship leaves Liverpool, the crew searches it thoroughly for any such boys, and it is fortunate for the company that owned the *Falls of Clyde* that we did so, because we put ten of them back on land before we sailed, and if we had forgotten to take this precaution, the company would have had twelve boys to feed instead of two!

The hideouts that these boys find are sometimes remarkable. You know that the bowsprit of a modern ship is always made of iron, but not solid iron. Four of them had stuffed themselves into it, the smallest all the way in and the biggest near the "entrance." We would never have found them, were it not that the smallest became frightened after spending more than a day in there and had begun to cry out. Naturally the sailors heard him. They had no idea what the sound was, but they soon found out, and they dragged the poor little devils out one by one! One of those whom we discovered when we were out at sea had hidden in a roll of rope. When one of my companions went below, he was astonished to see a head as ugly as a monkey's, with a snub nose and a mouth that seemed to split the head from one side to the other, suddenly protrude from the roll. He seized it by the hair and, little by little, out came a boy about of about twelve! He told the boy to go up on deck. After taking a look at him, one of the officers sent him to the captain, who told the boy he would feed him of he worked well. Two or three hours later we discovered another of about eighteen, and the same thing happened to him. He had rolled himself up in a sail.

The *Falls of Clyde* had only 18 sailors; four apprentices, of whom I had the honor to be one; four officers; plus the captain, one carpenter, one cook, two sailmakers, and one servant, who was in general service to the captain and the officers. The men—the sailors—were divided into two teams of nine each, one team working while the other slept. One came under the orders of the 1st and 4th officers, the other under those of the 2nd and 3rd. The captain always does as he pleases. He sleeps, eats, or works when he likes, and for leading this indolent life, burdened nonetheless with weighty responsibility, he receives 240 pounds stirling per year, or roughly 6000 francs. The First Officer receives £96, or about 2,400 per year; the Second £72, about 1800 francs per year; the Third £60, or about 1500 francs per year; and the cook and carpenter, the two sailmakers, and the captain's servants receive £48, or 1200 francs. The sailors generally get £36, or 900 francs, but their salary depends to a great extent on the port and the country from which they sail, since in Australia or America they get from £36 to £180 (4500 francs) per year! I do not mean to say that the general rule in Australia or America is to pay a sailor 4500 francs, but it does happen sometimes in summer, when almost all the sailors currently on land go home to shear sheep. Merely by shearing sheep they can sometimes earn 25 francs per day, since they get 1.25 francs per sheep!

But none of this has anything to do with my voyages, so I will get back to the main subject of my letter.

After five or six weeks on board I began to find life somewhat monotonous, even though every day brought something new.

First of all, we can across some porpoises or "sea swine," so called for several reasons. Their head closely resembles a pig's, although it is perhaps a little rounder; in the water they make a noise very like a pig's grunting; and, when eaten, their meat is pale like a pig's; in fact, it also tastes quite like pork. Two or three hundred leagues further south we encountered flying fish. Those who have never seen them generally believe that they are two or three feet long and that they fly on wings. They are completely wrong about that, because flying fish are hardly ever more than seven or eight inches long, and it is extremely rare to find one eleven inches or a foot long. They by no means fly with their wings, which they use only to keep themselves out of the water. They propel themselves with their tails, which they flip back and forth with astonishing speed. Flying fish live in fear of bonitos, which eat almost nothing else. These bonitos rot alive, because when you catch one and open it, you find its intestines, and even its flesh, filled with worms. If you eat a lot of it, you get horrible headaches, and your face swells up as though you had stuck it into a beehive. Catching one is very simple: you just tie a bit of white cloth, with a big hook hidden in it, to the end of a line, and then you jerk the cloth about it the water. The bonito takes it for a flying fish and discovers only too late that, instead of catching it, it is caught itself. Sometimes, when cleaning one to eat it, I have found two or three flying fish in its stomach, and it was still greedy enough to want a fourth!

Now we come to the sailor's mortal enemy, the shark. You have probably heard so much about the shark that I have no need to explain it, so I will not bore you by describing this horrible creature. We were past the equator when we caught one that was eighteen feet long. It was a Sunday. There was no breath of wind, and the heat was enough to give me an idea of what the poor devils must suffer in Hell! When we were woken at 4 a.m. and called up on deck, it was already light enough that one of the sailors saw the dorsal fin of a shark circling the ship. He immediately told the carpenter, who got out a steel hook specially made to catch sharks. The carpenter got about two pounds of salt meat from the cook, put it on the hook, and threw the hook into the sea. It was past noon when at last the shark was foolish enough to bite; but finally, after having held back for four hours or so, the shark took it. The carpenter, who was holding the other end of the rope, jerked it back, and hook sank into the shark's mouth. Fortunately the rope was tied to the ship; otherwise we could have said good-by to the shark, the rope, and the hook, because the shark began to struggle the instant it felt the hook, and it nearly broke the rope. Once we were sure that it was securely hooked, and that the rope was knotted so well that it would not come undone, we left the shark in the water to tire itself out. Then we began to pull on the rope, gently at first so that the hook should not hurt the shark too much and start it struggling again fiercely enough perhaps to drag one or two men into the water. Finally, after pulling on the rope and relaxing it again for a hour or an hour and a half, we finally managed to get the shark up onto the deck. Two or three sailors had armed themselves with long, sharpened poles, in order to attempt to kill it; because if man gets too close to a shark, the shark could break his legs with a slap of its tail.

After we had thoroughly amused ourselves with the shark and properly tormented it, it became so weak that the carpenter finished it off with a blow from his ax.

In these hot latitudes there are, I believe, far more fish species than elsewhere. That might possibly be because the continual calms (Doldrums) give one more time to observe them, but I know that it is between 15 degrees north and south latitude that I noticed the most intriguing fish. There occurs in these latitudes a phenomenon extremely difficult for ships: it is what in English is called "squalls," that is to say, small storms that last about twenty minutes or a quarter of an hour. They do not last long, but nonetheless, many ships are lost in these "squalls." Fortunately, one can always see them coming, but sometimes they come so quickly that one has hardly any time to lower the sails! Torrents of rain usually fall while the wind blows. I have seen it rain so hard that you could hardly see more than fifteen or twenty feet ahead! When it rains that hard you can hardly breathe, and you feel just as though you had stuck your head out the window of a railroad train going thirty-five leagues an hour! [1 *lieue* = ca. 4 km.]

Another rather curious fish found in these latitudes is the dolphin. It has a rather square muzzle, and when you catch one, it changes while dying from red to pink to blue to green—all the colors of the rainbow; and when dead it is a beautiful pearl grey.

When you travel on a sailing ship, you pass through all four seasons of the year within a few weeks. Within two or three weeks we passed from the boiling heat of the equator—you hardly dare touch anything for fear of burning your hands, and melted tar flows along the deck—to the almost glacial cold of the Cape of Good Hope. Since were traveling from west to east, we had to go ten or twelve degrees further south than the cape itself, because if you get closer than that to land, there are currents that carry you endlessly westward.

Many other things in these latitudes caught my interest, too.

The first birds we came across were "cape pigeons," so called because you always see them close to the two capes, the Cape of Good Hope and Cape Horn. Unfortunately, these birds are too fat and greasy to be really fit to eat.

There are two ways to catch these birds. Both are very simple. In a strong wind you usually catch them with a pin bent into a hook and baited with a bit of meat or bread. You catch them then so quickly that you get tired of pulling them out of the water. The other, almost simpler method requires a rope and a man. These birds see a ship so seldom that that they have no fear of it, and they come so near that in fine weather a sailor has only to slide down the rope to the water, stretch out his hands, and take as many as he pleases. A remarkable thing about all the sea birds I have encountered is that as soon as they touch the deck of a ship they become seasick!

Before coming across the "cape pigeon" we came across they "boobey," another very amusing bird. Almost as soon as it touches anything solid, it goes to sleep. Once asleep, it wakes up again only with great difficulty. You may see one at the top of a mast, and even during a storm it just stays there, balanced on one leg; and despite the noise of the storm and the movement of the ship, you can go up there and just take it, without its ever waking up. If you catch it with your hand, you have to be careful to seize it by the beak so that it cannot bite you. Otherwise, it might take the end of your finger off.

After the cape pigeon and the boobey, there is the albatross. This bird is the eagle of the ocean. The body is only two or three feet long, but from wingtip to wingtip it measures twelve or fourteen feet. It is therefore very strong and can easily lift a man out of the water. That happened once, several years ago. On a British man o' war a sailor was being flogged when, almost mad with pain, he threw himself into the sea. An albatross immediately attacked him, because the albatross always tries to snatch the eyes out of a man that it sees in the water. The man struggled with the albatross for several minutes and managed to seize it by the legs. The albatross tried to take off, but with the sailor holding onto its legs, it had to take the sailor with it. It took the sailor to a rock, the breeding ground on which it was born. There the sailor survived by drinking the eggs of the birds that had made their nests there, until at last a passing ship saw him and took him aboard.

At this point in our voyage we encountered whales. They say in England that a whale is more like a cow than a fish, and it is true. It is only in shape that a whale resembles a fish, and even then, the shape is not really the same, because a whale's tail is horizontal, whereas a fish's is vertical. The whale gives birth like a land animal. Many books say when a whale surfaces it shoots water into the air like a double fountain, but this is wrong, because a whale sends up very little water, and almost all of that is vapor.

Nothing really noteworthy happened to us for over a month, that is to say, until two weeks before we reached Calcutta. Then, one day, I was on my way aft (I forget why), and I had almost reached the mainmast when I heard a great Crack! Crack! against it. At first I thought that one of the sails had torn, and I stepped back little to see what was going on when something fell almost at my feet. Upon stepping closer, I saw with horror that it was a man! I shouted out as loudly as I could what had happened, and every man then on deck rushed up. It was one of the stowaways, the older one. He had been up the mast and slipped. They picked him up immediately and carried him into the shade. He was unconscious, of course, since he had fallen eighty feet. He died the next day, Saturday, at six o'clock in the evening. Never have I spent three more miserable days than that Friday, Saturday, and Sunday. No one even opened his mouth except to eat or to speak of the deceased. Almost perfect silence reigned. You never heard anyone laugh, or rarely even speak.

The evening he died, I had a very unpleasant task to perform. This is it. When someone aboard a ship dies, the practice is to wrap the body in canvas after attaching coal or some other heavy weight to the feet, so that the body should not float. Since the poor by had died on a Saturday, the captain decided to keep his body overnight so that he could be buried on a Sunday. The body had been placed on one of the hatches [hatch cover?], wrapped in canvas and covered with the British flag. About 10 that evening the wind rose, causing the body to roll from one side of the ship to the other. I was sitting in the cabin when the First Officer summoned me. I went out, and he told me to find out what was rolling around on the deck. I went, and I reported that it was the body, which the movement of the ship had caused to fall off the hatch. He replied, "Well, why the devil don't you tie it down to keep it from rolling?" I did not dare answer that I didn't want to touch a dead body. Instead I raced forward to ask a sailor to help me, but to no avail. No one would come. The night was as black as the inside of an ink pot, and small flashes of heat lightning constantly lit up a portion of the sky; which only made the darkness seem darker, while at the same time adding a sort of mystery to the silence around me. None of this did anything for my courage, but in the end the voice of the officer, demanding to know "what the devil I was doing," brought my back to myself. I took the body in my arms, and at every step I heard the dull crack of stiff bones, and I imagined that the body was moving! At last I managed to tie it down securely. I must have been pale, or something, when I returned to the cabin, because my fellows asked what was the matter with me. I told them what I ha had to do, and they all made fun of me, but I am sure that they would have been just as pale as I was if they had had to do the same thing.

Two weeks later we reached Calcutta, and I will keep the story of my adventures there for another time. If this letter bores you, dear Grandmother, please feel free to let me know, and I will bore you no longer with my foolish little adventures, if they even deserve that name.

Good-by, dear Grandmother. Kiss Linette for me, and Aunt Louison, and Aunt Sophie, and everyone for me, the next time they come to see you.

Your devoted grandson,

Louis

Second letter

10 Wellington Square Chelsea
Kings Road

Dear Grandmother,

Here, finally, is the rest of the letter that I began so long ago.

I ended my last letter by saying simply that we reached Calcutta. I doubt that that will be enough, because I do not want to leave anything out of my story. We reached Calcutta on September 17, 1890, after a 99 day voyage from Liverpool to the mouth the Hooghly River. Sailing up the river afforded us a beautiful, constantly changing view. Both sides were magnificently green, with palm trees, banana trees, and all kinds of other tropical trees mixed together in picturesque groves. Now and again you could see an Indian hut half hidden in the greenery, and in truth it was a pity that the greenery did not hide them completely, because the Indians usually make little effort to keep the area around their dwellings tidy. Four bamboo poles, a few very long and wide banana leaves, and cow dung or, sometimes, mud are sufficient for them to build what they call a house.

The first Indians I saw did not much please me. We were just at the mouth of the river when we saw an Indian boat in front of us, or nearly in front. It was waiting for us to come nearer, so that it could throw us a rope and tie up to our ship. At first the Indian boats struck me as rather strange. They have the shape of a quarter moon, with the stern point rising much high than the bow one. There is a cabin aft; the back of its roof leans or, rather, balances, on the boat's tall, pointed stern. This roof also provides a seat for the man who directs the course of the boat, while the one who propels it by means of oars [or an oar?] is always forward. When we got close enough they threw us a rope—one that hardly deserved the name—and climbed up it onto our deck. The first to touch the deck was a man of about fifty, most indecently undressed, with a bit of string around his waist and, hanging from it, a rag that must have been white in its youth but was now an indescribable color, one that God must have forgotten to create when he created the rainbow!

The first thing this interesting gentleman did when he reached the deck was to apply the palm of his right hand to his forehead, bow his head, and say, "Salaam, sahib!" This is their way of greeting someone, and "salaam" is a word very useful to them. It is always "Salaam sahib" when they want to thank you, and also "Salaam sahib" when they greet you. When they say "Salaam, sahib," you can be sure that it conveys respect or thanks. Another thing about this old Indian that struck me, is that his lower belly (to be polite) was covered with horizontal scars about three inches long. I found out later that they signified a special "caste." These "castes," or religious subdivisions, are very curious in India, and one sometimes sees an Indian lord, or "baboo" as people call them there, carefully kiss the feet of a beggar—feet by no means as clean as one might wish—simply because this beggar is of a higher caste! This is just one example of the folly of their religion, which offers notions madder still. For example, a Hindu [? *mahomide*] never eats meat, because, they say, when they are young cows feed them with their milk, and to eat the meat of a cow would therefore be almost as great a crime as eating one's mother! What an idea! Nonetheless, these people detest women, and when an Indian woman comes across an Indian man, she stays as far away from him as possible, for fear of being kicked! I will tell you an anecdote on this subject. A British traveler was out walking one day with an Indian gentleman when they say an old Indian woman coming toward them. As soon as she got closes enough, the Indian gave her great kick—where, you may well guess. The British man turned to him and said, "How can you be such a coward as to kick a woman?" "What does it matter?" the Indian calmly replied. "It was only my mother"!

If Indian woman dressed in the European manner they would be less persecuted by their men, because the horsehair cushion that almost every lady ears inside her dress would protect them against the often stiff kicks administered by their men. What do you think, dear Grandmother?

But none of this has anything to do with my story, so with your permission I will continue.

All the Indians (there were four of them) were dressed like the first, except for a boy whose only garment consisted of a necklace made of two threads of red wool. You can imagine the figure he cut. Three of them came up on the deck and left the boy in their boat, which was full of bananas, pineapples, guavas, mangos, and a lot of other excellent fruit that unfortunately does not grow in Europe.

They had brought all this to exchange for old clothes of every kind. For an old waistcoat they gave me two big clusters of bananas, a bottle of goat's milk, half a dozen eggs, a pineapple, and two pomelos (a kind of great big orange peculiar to the tropics), and I might have got twice as much if I had not feared be unable to get rid of it before it all went bad—something that happens very quickly in the Indies because of the extreme heat of the sun.

I forgot to tell you at the beginning of this letter that as soon as we saw land we took down all the sails and dropped anchor. It was only the next morning that the steamboat began towing us toward Calcutta.

Since to reach Calcutta you have to go about eighty miles up the Hooghly River, and since we were roughly 150 miles from the mouth of the river when the steamboat took us in tow, we had to anchor again in the evening, because the river is so dangerous to navigate that even the pilots do not dare do so at night. This was the first time since we left Liverpool that I had slept through the night. As you know, when we are at sea, we rest only for hours, then work four hours, day and night.

We were woken up at sunup, that is to say at 5:30 a.m. When I reached the deck, I was astonished by the beauty of the Indian sunrise. The water was mirror-calm and reflected all the magnificent colors of the sky. The rays of the sun, which had just risen, made the tropical greenery along the banks even more beautiful and made the dewdrops on the trees sparkle like millions of diamonds. The calm surface of the water was broken from time to time by a little Indian boat, with the man in it singing; and his strange song only added charm to the peaceful silence that surrounded us. While I contemplated this view, which I fear I have conveyed very poorly, my mind had wandered off Heaven knows where, but certainly far from the ship that had carried me so well all these thousands of leagues; and it is the rough voice of one of the officers that recalled me rather disagreeably to myself.

It was 6 o'clock in the morning, hence time to get back to work. We began to raise the anchor, which took us nearly two hours, because it had sunk into the soft mud of the riverbed and so become enormously heavier than it already was—two and a half tons, or 4536 British pounds. At last we got it up out of the water and the steamboat resumed towing us toward our long-awaited destination.

The Indian boats became more numerous as we approached Calcutta, but of course we had to let many go by, since otherwise the ship would have become so crowded with Indian merchants that we could not have obeyed our officers' orders as promptly as necessary on a ship coming into port.

It is astonishing how cheap goods and services are in India. While we were going up the river, an Indian told me that for a piece of soap seven inches long he would take me around and show me everything worth seeing in Calcutta. Unfortunately I was unable to take him up on this tempting offer because the next day he had to leave with his master, the pilot. In Calcutta, you can have for 80 centimes a carriage and two horses, carriage driver included, for a day!

It was past 7 in the evening when we reached Calcutta and the berth assigned to the *Falls of Clyde*. (A ship may not stop at any port or in any river unless its owners have rented a space for it before it arrives.)

Now, a few words about the port of Calcutta.

In truth, it is hardly a port at all, since all the ships that shop there remain in the river, across from the city—which, as I believe I mentioned earlier, is 80 miles from the sea, hence not at all near it, as one might first assume. The Hooghly River is very dangerous for several reasons. First, it flows very fast, sometimes up to 15 English miles per hour. It therefore carries a great deal of soil and sand, with the result that a ship going up it can suddenly find itself caught on a sandbank that was not there ten minutes earlier and probably will no longer be there ten minutes later! Of course this is extremely bothersome, not to say dangerous for passing ships, but the river is also a great threat to human life. Anyone foolish to swim in it takes a terrible risk, because it is full of fresh water sharks—water tigers, the sailors call them—and of poisonous snakes. There are even crocodiles and alligators, and many other aquatic carnivores. Underwater currents are another imminent threat to the swimmer; they can drag down even one of the Indian boats. You can imagine what would happen to a man caught by such a current. However, these currents are not the only danger that one might encounter, if one were rash enough to wish to cool off a little in this land where heaven and hell touch. There is another, if possible even worse. Imagine a man falling from a ship into the river and having the good luck to escape the dangers that I have described. He could still be so caught in the soft mud of the bottom that he could not escape from it. Naturally—or, rather, unnaturally—his fate would then be to be drowned or smothered in this disgusting mud.

This last characteristic of the river had provided the Indians with an opportunity to create a new religion. Its member are called "Juggernauts." These Juggernauts worship the mud of the river. When a man falls in and never comes up again, they say that the devil got into his body, and the god took him in order to purify him. Now, how could it be possible for as filthy a god as that to purify anything, even when that thing is a devil? This reminds me of another ridiculous aspect of their religion. When the Indians see a man drowning, it never occurs to them to try to save him. Oh no! On the contrary, they look on even with pleasure. That is because they believe that there is a ladder up to heaven, one that all must climb if they have been good enough to do so; but that this ladder is always laden with souls climbing heavenward, so that, of course, when someone newly dead turns up, he must take the place of whoever is closest to the earth. As a result, everyone on the ladder must climb one rung higher in order to make room, and the one at the very top finally enters heaven! There is another fine idea! I hope that you have understood it, dear Grandmother. Good God! It does not take much to arouse the faith of these savages!

But I have digressed again.

It was only on the following day, at 6 p.m., that the captain gave us shore leave, and it was with great pleasure that we exchanged our dirty clothes for our uniforms. Sunday is of course the only day when we wear our uniforms, except when we are in port. Then we wear them to go ashore in the evening. You may not be familiar with this uniform that we wear in tropical countries, so I will explain it to you, and I hope that my explanation will not bore you.

The shoes are of course the same ones that we always wear. The trousers are made of cotton, and they protect one very well from the cold, of which there is none in Bengal. No waistcoat or *camisole*, either, but the shirt and collar must be perfectly clean and white. The trousers (white) are held up by a shiny black leather belt with a gilded brass buckle and ornamented by an anchor surrounded by a laurel wreath. The jacket is navy blue and decorated by gilded buttons on each side, with three more on each sleeve. These buttons have anchors on them, too, but they are purely ornamental. It is too hot to make any use of them. On your head you wear a white cap an embroidered black band around it, and with a gold cord that holds in place an anchor and the company flag, crossed, surrounded by a laurel wreath. Of course, this costume is very different from the one we wear aboard, at sea. That one usually consists only of a pair of trousers and a shirt. The trousers are rolled up to the knees and the shirt sleeves up to the elbows, and the chest and neck are bare. Sometimes, during a storm in the tropical latitudes, we even do without the shirt!

As soon as we were ready to disembark, we summoned a "dingy," one of those little Indian boats, which took all four of us to terra firma for the colossal sum of two annas (ten centimes). Once on land we took a carriage to the most beautiful park in Calcutta. It is called the Garden of Eden, and it certainly deserves the name, because the garden in which Adam and Eve gave in to temptation could hardly have been more beautiful.

After taking a walk in the garden we returned to out carriage, which was waiting for us at the gate, and we continued on our way toward the center of the city.

Twenty minutes later the carriage stopped at a market, and here another strange spectacle met our gaze. Indians, half naked as usual, were running about hither and yon, bawling like madmen in a language that I naturally did not understand. The crowd was a mixture of soldiers, sailors, bourgeois, aristocrats, Indians, and Chinese, rushing about in every direction. Heaps of toys and trinkets, tobacco, lace, fish, pipes, mirrors, matches butter, and all sorts of other things too numerous to name where spread out pell-mell on every side. Horribly deformed beggars came to ask for alms, while other Indians stuck perfumes, cigars at 40 centimes for a hundred, and all kinds of other, equally cheap articles under our noses. That is the scene we saw upon alighting from our carriage, but what a difference after having taken a few steps! Everything changed. The trinkets, etc., were all nicely arranged in little stalls, and suddenly the market looked like a European bazar. You could buy anything in this market, from a needle to an anchor.

After looking around the market we had to return to the ship, because we were not allowed to remain ashore past 11 p.m. Later on the officers changed this rule, having noted that after the first week it was impossible to enforce.

The scene changed again in the area around the market. Little Indian huts, made of straw and bamboo, were ranged in parallel lines. They had no doors, only three "walls" and a "roof." These were the Indian restaurants where all the sailors and soldiers go to eat, and where 40 centimes gets you quite a good meal. Each of these restaurants has its special patrons, and my companions and I patronized one know by the thoroughly plebeian name of Jimmy's Tuck Shop."

You generally find in each of these restaurants an Indian boy known as the "punkah wallah." He moves the "punkah," a fan hung from the ceiling, with a bit of string. This is, naturally, very refreshing after a long walk under a blazing sun! However, this is only one of the things that make a punkah wallah. Even before being good at his job, he must be able to endure the curses and sometimes the kicks that he receives in order to make him fan a little faster, and my impression is that the curses and the kicks are about the only remuneration that he gets.

Sunday is the day when Calcutta offers the most curiosities of all, because no one on the ship works then, and many magicians and jugglers come aboard to earn some money. They perform tricks that are truly amazing since, being all but naked, they cannot possibly hide anything in their clothes. There are also many poor, deformed devils who come to beg for alms. One woman who came aboard had a normal left leg and right one, shaped like an elephant's foot, that came down no further than her left knee. Some men come on board with dancing bears or goat tightrope walkers, and by evening you have a whole circus for just a few pennies.

After two weeks at Calcutta I went to see the Port Inspector, for whom I had a letter of introduction. A lady had given it to me before my departures. The Inspector was very nice to me and a companion of mine, whom I took the liberty of introducing. When he had us to dinner at home he always sent his carriage for us, and sometimes he sent his little steam launch instead.

I could not help laughing sometimes when he sent a conveyance for us, because twenty minutes earlier the two of us had been working on board in our filthy, salty clothes, our hair a mess and sticky with half-melted salt, our faces dirty, our feet bare and dirty, our clothing stiff with salt that had melted and then dried, covered with splashes of red, yellow, and all the colors of the rainbow; and yet there we were, suddenly transformed into gentlemen in uniform, riding in a carriage with a pair of horses, driven by a liveried coachman with one lackey in uniform at his side and two more in the rear; and every time we turned a corner they got down and ran forward, shouting for people to get out of the way!

Now and again people in other carriages recognized Mr. Bushby's and turned to see who we were, and every time someone came aboard to see the captain we hid for fear that the person might have seen us in Mr. Bushby's carriage.

The Indians' resistance to heat is remarkable. I have seen whites faint and collapse unconscious because of the heat, but the Indians seem happier the hotter it gets. As far as I can see, that is because such heat gets them accustomed in good time to the heat to which they will be subjected after death. They never wear a hat and only rarely any kind of head covering. Some even shave their heads. How fine they look, without hair!

We remained in Calcutta until December 10, 1890. Then we sailed for Boulogne-sur-mer, loaded with 13,400 bales of jute; and since each bale weighed 448 British pounds, you can imagine that our ship was no small one. Our return to Boulogne took until April 21, 1891, and I will tell you what happened in my next letter.

I hope that you will forgive me for having made you wait so long for this letter, but I was able to write a few lines now and again, as Aunt Sophie will gather easily enough from the difference in the writing from page to page.

With a big hug from me, my dear grandmother, and hoping that this letter will interest you, I remain your devoted grandson,

Louis

Many greetings from me to Aunt Sophie, Aunt Louison, and Linette, when you see them again.

FINIS

10 Wellington Square
King's Road
Chelsea

Monday, 29 May 1893

E.H.M. GOWER

According to Matteo Giunti, a genealogical researcher in Livorno, Gower's full name was Erasmus Henry Mauritius Gower. He was born in Livorno in 1830 and died from a heart attack in 1903. He married his third wife in December 1890, in a church in Westminster. The online Births, Marriages, and Deaths Index of England does not give her name, but it records that a Joséphine Marie de Castelvecchio was also married in the same month, in a church in Westminster. He was 60, she 33.

Still according to Giunti, Gower returned to England from Japan in 1890, then went from there to Chioma, a village south of Livorno where there are still a Villa Gower and a Gower Street. It is there that he died.

The following document was retrieved from http://d-arch.ide.go.jp/je_archive/society/wp_je_unu48.html

Transfer and development of coal-mine technology in Hokkaido
Author: Kasuga, Yutaka

Instead of Shiranuka, the Hakodate Magistrate's Office came to concentrate on the development of the Kayanuma coal mine, which was discovered by a fisherman in 1856. The reasons for the switch were that Kayanuma was close to Hakodate and the quality of its coal was good. The year after the discovery, the Hakodate Magistrate's Office sent officials to begin extraction. It is said that subsequently this coal mine had an annual output of about one hundred straw bags full of coal. But after the cave-in of an adit in 1860, when coal extraction was stopped temporarily, the mine functioned only sporadically. This situation lasted until the Meiji Restoration, when it became clear that the mine was unprofitable due to expensive costs entailed in such items as coal transport. In the interim, however, attempts were made to develop this mine into the first Western-style coal mine in Japan with the successive introduction of government-employed foreign engineers. First of all, R. Pumpelly, an American geologist and mine engineer, and W.P. Blake, a mining scientist and mine engineer, undertook a geological survey of the Kayanuma coal mine in 1862, at a time when operations had been suspended. In July of the same year, they established a miners' school in Hakodate and taught mining science to the Japanese. Among the students were such people as Takato Oshima, Yozo Yamao and Hisaburo Takeda, who became the pioneers of the modernization of mining in Japan. In 1867, E.H.M. GOWER, a government-employed British engineer, was sent to the Kayanuma coalmine and made an attempt to restore its operation. (In view of the fact that the geological survey conducted by Blake had revealed that the quality of Kayanuma coal was good, full-scale extraction had been started in 1864 under the leadership of Takato Oshima, who employed eight miners and fifteen labourers transferred from the Shiranuka coal mine. Nevertheless the operation proved to be unprofitable as Kayanuma coal was 50 per cent more expensive than the average market price of coal in Nagasaki. Thus extraction had been again discontinued.) In order to restore the mine, GOWER first of all built a road from the mine to the coast (for horse-cart transport) and increased the number of pitmen. (Initially five pitmen and later seven pitmen were added from the Shiwatari mine.) At this stage, however, mechanization both inside and outside the mine remained untouched, and the output for that year was again no more than 100 tons.

LEON GOWER

The British Register of Births for April-June 1889 shows that Leon Gower was born in Croydon, Surrey on 21 March 1889. (His parents were married only in December 1890.) His name was registered at birth as Napoleon Louis A. G. de Castelvecchio. The G must stand for Gower, but the A is unknown. He died in June 1964.

U.S. World War I Draft Registration Card
dated 5 June 1917

Age: 28
Address: Towaco, Morris County, New Jersey
Occupation: Farmer
Employed by: John McNaughton, Towaco
Color of eyes: gray
Color of hair: dark brown

US-Canada border crossing records

Entered Canada at Bridgeburg, Ontario on 23 Dec 1917
Entered US at Niagara Falls, NY on 11 Dec 1918

Particulars of Recruit
Drafted Under Military Service Act, 1917 (Canada)
Date: 19 Dec 1917

Address: Edrans (?), Manitoba, Canada
Place of Birth: London, England
Marital status: Single
Religion: Christian Scientist
Trade or calling: Farm laborer
Name of next-of-kin: Countess de Castelvecchio
Relationship: Mother
Address: 101 West 93rd Street, New York, NY
Place of medical examination: Portage La Prairie, 20 Nov 1917

Height: 5 feet 5 ½ inches
Hair color: brown

US Federal Census, 1940

Leon described himself as a "guard" for "Interborough": Interborough Rapid Transit, the IRT subway. He was then 51. In the same census his wife, Minette, gave her place of birth as New York, her year of birth as 1890, and her occupation as "maid" in a "private house." She indicated that the highest school grade she had completed was grade 8. Their address was 3004 Heath Avenue, Bronx. This is the same address as the one given as Josephine's "last residence" on her Certificate of Cremation, dated December 20, 1932. This document names her next of kin as "Leon Gauer."

U.S. Draft Registration Card, 1942

Name: Leon N. Gower
Address: 3004 Heath Avenue, Apt. 29, Bronx, NY
Telephone: None
Age: 53
Place of Birth: London, England
Date of Birth: March 21, 1889
Employer's Name and Address: I.R.T. Division, Board of Transportation, 250 Hudson Street
Place of Employment: 242 St., Bronx, NY

Leon died only a few months before I (RT) arrived in New York to begin graduate study at Columbia University. I first rented an apartment in the Bronx, not far from Heath Avenue. I well remember the 242nd st. Van Cortlandt Park station.

REGISTRATION CARD—(Men born on or after April 28, 1877 and on or before February 16, 1897)

SERIAL NUMBER	1. NAME (Print)	ORDER NUMBER
U 2354	Leon N. Gower	

2. PLACE OF RESIDENCE (Print): 3004 Heath Ave Apt 29 Bronx NY
(Number and street) (Town, township, village, or city) (County) (State)

[THE PLACE OF RESIDENCE GIVEN ON THE LINE ABOVE WILL DETERMINE LOCAL BOARD JURISDICTION; LINE 2 OF REGISTRATION CERTIFICATE WILL BE IDENTICAL]

3. MAILING ADDRESS: Same

4. TELEPHONE: None

5. AGE IN YEARS: 53
DATE OF BIRTH: Mar 21 1889

6. PLACE OF BIRTH: London, England

7. NAME AND ADDRESS OF PERSON WHO WILL ALWAYS KNOW YOUR ADDRESS: Same

8. EMPLOYER'S NAME AND ADDRESS: I.R.T. Div. Bd of Transportation 250 Hudson St

9. PLACE OF EMPLOYMENT OR BUSINESS: 242 St. Bx NY

I AFFIRM THAT I HAVE VERIFIED ABOVE ANSWERS AND THAT THEY ARE TRUE.

Leon N. Gower
(Registrant's signature)

D. S. S. Form 1
(Revised 4-1-42) (over) 16—21930-2

REGISTER OF FAMILY MEMBERS IN PÈRE LACHAISE CEMETERY, PARIS

(S. G. N° 3900.)   (Y. N° 187.)

EMPLACEMENT DE LA SÉPULTURE

60° Division   12° Ligne   Neuve B° Avenue   20 de la 59

75. — Typ. Ch. de Mourgues Frères. — 4985.

DATE DES INHUMATIONS OU RÉINHUMATIONS, Numéros des plaques.	NOMS des DÉCÉDÉS.	ACQUIT DE LA TAXE de 2° INHUMATION.	OBSERVATIONS (Réunions de restes, exhumations, transports, etc.)
1. 3 Août 8° Arrondt. N° 7130 Année 1887	Lise Pasteur B^{on} d'Treilles Charles Jules Pindioux	N° d'ordre de la quittance 7406 délivrée le 3 Août 1887 à M. Racinet 4/	Reste Atersee à gauche et 1 desse
2. 118 - 26 Janvier 16° Arrondt. N° 462 Année 1954	Tyler Royall	N° d'ordre de la quittance 3793 délivrée le 26-1-54 à M. Lane 5/	Reste 2 Cases
3. 824 - 18 Juillet 1957 Ext. Arrondt. N° Année 1957	Vve de Royall Tyler née Palamidessi de Castelvecchio	N° d'ordre de la quittance 1684 délivrée le 19 Juillet 1957 à M. Lecoeur Frères 6/ Elesina	V^t de Hyères (Var) + 7 Juillet 1957 Une place dans le vide sanitaire en réunion avec 1 tinsoir à gauche et 1 descente
4. 14 Février Ext. Arrondt. N° Année 1870	de Castelvecchio François Louis Jaspard	N° d'ordre de la quittance délivrée le à M. 1/	329604 + 23/5/1863 à Rennes (35) Neveu de Napoléon Ier
5. 2 Juillet 8° Arrondt. N° 1159 Année 1870	de Castelvecchio Cassilde Marie	N° d'ordre de la quittance délivrée le à M. 2/	334724
6. 22 Novembre 8° Arrondt. N° 1822 Année 1849	Longuet Ve Pasteur. d'Estrebilis Suzanne Sophie.	N° d'ordre de la quittance délivrée le à M. 3/	1223
° Arrondt. N°		N° d'ordre de la quittance délivrée le	

(Marie Cassilde de Castelvecchio is Marceline.)

GENEALOGICAL CHART A

Louis Bonaparte (1778-1846) and an unknown Roman lady, possibly Countess Carolina Negroni

François Louis Gaspard Castelvecchio (1826-69) m. 1847, Elise Caroline Pasteur d'Etreillis (1826-94)

- Marceline (1848-70)
- Louise (1854-1929) m. 1872 Wilhelm Baese (?-?)
- Joséphine (1857-1932)
  - (1) m. 1874, Francesco Palamidessi (1849-91)
  - (2) m. 1890, Erasmus Henry Maurirus Gower (1830-1903)
  - (3) m. 1903, Antonio Frabasilis (1854-1927)
- Adrien (1860-62?)

Napoleon, known as Leon (1889-1964), m. "Minette" (1890-?)

- Louis (1876-1929)
  - m. 1917, Frances Wahl
- Giuseppino (1878-80)
- Linetta (1880-1975) m. 1929, Rev. Robert Douglas Richardson (1893-?)
- Giuseppina (b./d. 1883)

(1) m. 1901, Catherine Downey (1876-?)
 — Lewis H. de Castle (1902-70)
(2) m. 1917, Frances Wahl

Gerard Blanckenberg de Castle (1918-?) m. 1955, Gillian Dalrymple (1931-)
- Elisina (b. 1956)
- Linetta (b. 1957)
- Monica (b. 1961)

Francisca ("Paquita," b. 1954) m. 1984, John Wheeler Marrin (b. 1951)

Elisina (1875-1957)
 (1) m. 1898, Grant Richards (1873-1948)
- Gioia (1900-69)
- Gerard (1901-16)
- Charles (1902-59)
- Geoffrey (1906-83) m. 1925 Thomas Cary Owtram (1893-1992)

- Helen Gillian (b. 1926) m. 1946 Julián de Zulueta (b. 1918)

- Felicity (b. 1948) m. 1977, Sedat Kahya (b. 1942)
- Cayetana (b. 1951) m. 1980, Marco Laganà (b. 1946)

(2) m. 1914, Royall Tyler (1884-1953)
- William Royall (1910-2003) m. 1934, Bettine Mary Fisher-Rowe (1910-1987)
  - Royall (b. 1936)
  - Matilda Eve (b. 1939)

GENEALOGICAL CHART B

Charles Thomas Pasteur d'Etreillis (d. 1865)
m. 1825, Suzanne Sophie Longuet de Breuil (1797-1879).........Marcel Duménil de Bruges de Camps (d. 1854)

- Charles Jules Ferdinand Saint-Aure (1820-85)
- Elise Caroline (1826-94)
  m. 1846, François Louis de Castelvecchio
- Suzette (1831-86)*
  m. Adriano de Larderel (?-?)
  - Elise (1850-1902)
    m. Florestano de Larderel (?-?)
  - Federiga (d. 1948)
    m. Pompeo Aloisi (1875-1949)
  - Folco (1907-?)
    m. Maria Guicciardini

- Adriana (1872-1925)
  m. Piero Ginori Conti (1865-1939)
  - Giovanni (1898-1972)
    m. Lucia dei Principi Colonna
  - Fiammetta
    m. Guliano Gondi (1893-1962)
  - Federigo (1909-76)

Additional first names for figures in Genealogical Chart A

Marceline — Marie Cassilda
Louise — Marie Hortense Eugénie
Wilhelm — Christopher Emil
Joséphine — Marie Suzanne Juliette
Francesco — Alberto Giovanni Vito
Louis — David Marcello
Linetta — Adolfina Giuseppina
Gioia — Vivienne Mary Elisina
Julián — Andrés Luis
Felicity — Inés Soledad
Cayetana — Francisca Ampero
Francisca — Carmen Bulán

NOTE 1: There is a discrepancy between the date (1825) of the marriage of C. T. Pasteur d'Etreillis and Suzanne Longuet be Breuil is, as his death certificate states, he was 65 when he died. 1825 suits Elise's date of birth, but this is inconclusive, particularly in view of Suzanne and Marcel's relations.
NOTE 2: After Adriano's death, Suzette went to live in Pisa with Cesare Mastiani-Sciamanna. He married her on her death bed and died in 1906.

Made in the USA
Las Vegas, NV
07 January 2022